PRACTICAL CELTIC MAGIC

A working guide to the
magical traditions of the Celts

PRACTICAL CELTIC MAGIC

A working guide to the magical heritage
of the Celtic Races

MURRY HOPE

THE AQUARIAN PRESS

First published 1987

© MURRY HOPE 1987

Hope, Murry
Practical Celtic magic.
1. Magic, Celtic
I. Title
133.4'3'09361   BF1622.C/

ISBN 0-85030-624-8

*The Aquarian Press is part of the
Thorsons Publishing Group,
Wellingborough, Northamptonshire,
NN8 2RQ, England.*

Printed and bound in Great Britain by
Biddles Ltd, Guildford and King's Lynn

3   5   7   9   10   8   6   4

CONTENTS

ACKNOWLEDGEMENTS

My sincere thanks to Dolores Ashcroft-Nowicki, Maureen Ballard, Paul Greenslade, Roy Claridge and David Furlong for trusting me with the loan of rare and valuable reference books.

Acknowledgements and thanks are also due to authors and publishers who have kindly granted permission to quote from the following books: Harrap Limited; *Myths and Legends of the Celtic Race*, by T.W. Rolleston. Century Hutchinson Limited; *The Mysteries of Britain*, by Lewis Spence. A.P. Watt Limited (Literary Agents); Faber & Faber; *The White Goddess*, by Robert Graves. Shire Publications Limited; *Discovering Hill Figures*, by Kate Bergamar. Celtic expert Michael Howard for permission to quote from a review.

DEDICATION

To Win Beacon,
who was a true servant of the Old Ones.

INTRODUCTION

The interpretation of the One Truth by any culture is undoubtedly influenced by many factors, such as physical locale, ethnic conditioning, dominant racial personality traits, and modes of collective expression, with their accompanying compensatory factors. The religious and magical requirements of the ancient Egyptians, for example, were eminently practical being an integral part of their material as well as their spiritual economy, as may be evidenced in the natures and deeds of their god-forms. African magic and its offshoots veered towards the instinctive, while the Greeks of old adopted a more logical, analytical approach. Eastern ethical and esoteric codes differed yet again, with their tendency towards philosophic eschewal of material values in the pursuit of abstract spiritual achievement.

In contrast, the strongly artistic, musical, romantic and matrist accents of Celtic mysticism almost belie the general, historically rendered picture of a physically strong, fearless, vainglorious, volatile, and often warlike people. The aura of intangible, fairytale-like surrealism surrounding their tenets tended to evoke a sense of wonderment and childlike response in the human psyche, which was encouraging of a closer relationship with nature and the more hidden life forms with which we share this planet.

A general subconscious resurgence of these old Celtic leanings may be observed in the popularity of the Tolkien literature and the film industry's preoccupation with those evergreen and ever popular fabulous themes of Robin Hood, Merlin, King Arthur and other heroes and heroines of myth and legend.

In order to understand the psychology behind this kind of heroic, romantic mysticism, we must take a trip into the past and examine the history and origins of the race that made these magical imprints upon the sands of history, art, philosophy, and fable.

Murry Hope

PART ONE

HISTORICAL, ORAL AND MYTHOLOGICAL SOURCES

A numerous race, and fierce, as fame reports them,
Were thy first colonists, Britain, chief of Isles:
Natives of a country in Asia, and of the region of the Grafis,
A people said to have been skilful; but the district is unknown,
That was mother to this progeny, these warlike adventurers on
    the sea.
Clad in the long dress, who could equal them?
Celebrated is their skill; they were the
Dread of Europe.

The Pacification of Llud

1. ORIGINS, DRESS AND APPEARANCE

The chronicles of the classical nations in the five hundred years preceding the commencement of the Christian era abound with accounts of the nature and deeds of a people known as the Hyperboreans or Celts. The name 'Celt', which is said to be derived from a root word meaning 'hero', makes its first historical appearance in the writings of the geographer Hecateaus, around 500 BC. In fact, Celtic allusions in classical history are more numerous than can be recounted in a work which sets out primarily to deal with the magical and metaphysical emphasis in Celtic beliefs and traditions. I am therefore obliged to keep historical references to the required minimum, confining them to Part 1 of this work, while supplying a detailed bibliography for those with the inclination to afford this aspect of the study the time and attention it demands.

Although past records have supplied us with a wealth of information regarding the nature, travels and conquests of this highly versatile race, their origins are, like their philosophy and magic, shrouded in mystery. So while archaeology may view the Hallstatt period as representing the earliest concrete evidence of the Celtic racial identity, researchers from other disciplines have derived their conjectures from those ancient literary and oral sources which lend credence to the idea that the Celts constituted a distinct cultural group as early as 2000 BC.

The Celts were a southern European people of Indo-Aryan origin who first surfaced in Bohemia and travelled west in search of the home of the sun. Science has recently established their basic blood group as 'O', in keeping with their modern descendants, which designates them as a separate race from the aboriginals of the southern Indian subcontinent, where the 'B' blood group predominates.

History tells us that there were two main Celtic groups, one of which is referred to as the 'lowland Celts' who hailed from the region of the Danube. These people left their native pastures around 1200 BC and slowly made their way across Europe, founding the lake dwellings in Switzerland, the Danube valley and Ireland. They were skilled in the use of metals and worked in gold, tin and bronze. Unlike the more familiar Celtic strain these people were an agriculturally orientated race, being herdsmen, tillers and artificers who burned rather than buried their dead. They blended peacefully with the megalithic people among whom they settled, contributing powerfully to the religion, art and customs they encountered as they slowly spread westwards. Their religious beliefs also differed from the next group, being predominantly matriarchal.

The second group, often referred to as the 'true' Celts, followed closely behind their lowland cousins, making their first appearance on the left bank of the Rhine at the commencement of the sixth century BC. These people, who came from the mountainous regions of the Balkans and Carpathians, were a military aristocracy. Reputed to love fighting for the sake of it they were frequently to be found among the mercenaries of the great armies of those early times. They had a distinct class system, the observance of which constituted one of their major racial features. These were the warlike Celts of ancient history who sacked Rome and Delphi, eventually marching victoriously across much of Europe and the British Isles.

But in spite of their martial inclinations they were also known for their qualities of chivalry, courage and dauntless bravery, their more aggressive tendencies being balanced out by a great sensitivity to music, poetry and philosophy. Unlike the lowland Celts these people buried their dead, and their elaborate religious rituals held in honour of Lugh are well recounted in the pages of the recorded past.

Dr Anne Ross, in her book *Everyday Life of the Pagan Celts* informs us that the word 'Celt' has different meanings for different scholastic approaches. To the linguist, for example, it signifies those who spoke and still speak Indo-European languages of great antiquity. Two speech groups emerged from the original Celtic tongue; one being known to philologists as 'Q' Celtic or Goidelic, so called because it retained the original Indo-European 'q^v' as 'q', later becoming 'k' in sound, but written as 'c'. This branch of the Celtic language was spoken and written in Ireland and the Isle of Man and introduced into Scotland in the late fifth century AD. The second group, known as 'P' Celtic, Brythonic or Brittonic, turned the Indo-European 'q' sound into 'p', e.g. *cenn* 'head' in the Goidelic and *penn* 'head' in the Brittonic. The latter was the branch of Celtic spoken widely in Europe and known as Gaulish or Gallo-Brittonic, and also the language spoken in Britain during the Roman period, which later became divided into Cornish, Welsh and Breton.[1]

Archaeologists see the Celts as those recognizable by their distinctive culture. They apparently possessed a great talent for improving upon the ideas of other nations, as may be evidenced in the La Tène relics. But no matter whose art, inventions, designs or concepts they borrowed, these were eventually endowed with such a strong Celtic flavour as to render them totally unrecognizable to their originators, so distinct was the Celtic influence.

The Celtic historical tradition being an oral one we are left with little to identify their origins and the early days of their race. Archaeological finds are therefore considered by many scholars to constitute the most reliable sources of information regarding Celtic life and custom. But although these are the mainstay of established Celtic history there is also a wealth of conjectural literature on the subject, derived mainly from Greek, Roman and Irish sources.

The Hallstatt culture, which is dated around 700 BC, provided archaeologists with the sort of tangible information that their discipline demands in the form of the first identifiable traces of Celtic culture. During this period, which encompassed the years from 700 BC to 500 BC, changes of great technological importance took place in Europe, with iron replacing bronze. Although the latter was much favoured by Celtic craftsmen it was iron that proved to be the Celts best military ally.

The Hallstatt site lies in the moutainous country above the western shore of the lake of that name, near Saltzburg in Austria, in the Saltzkammergut. Although it is realized that Celtic culture by no means originated in this area, certain artefacts that came to light there in the nineteenth century gave name to that entire period of Celtic history. Salt mines were situated nearby, this commodity being a major factor in the wealth of the Celtic economy. The Hallstatt site afforded archaeologists a wealth of information regarding the ordinary everyday lives of the Celtic people, their eating habits, clothing, artefacts, ornamentation, metalwork, living accommodation and general pattern of existence. The evidence betokens a high standard of civilization and considerable commerce; amber from the Baltic, Phoenician glass and gold leaf of ancient workmanship, iron swords with hilts and sheaths richly decorated with gold, ivory and amber. The National Museum in Dublin contains many superb examples of Celtic Irish decorative art in gold, bronze and enamels of the type to be seem among the relics of Hallstatt and La Tène. Evidence reveals that strong trade connections had been effected between the Celts, Etruscans, Greeks and Romans as early as the third century BC. The graves of the Celts, Dr Ross tells us, were singular, having been derived in part from Etruscan funerary traditions, while A. Mahr speaks of the Celtic civilization of that period as being far superior to that of the Bronze Age generally.

The second phase of Celtic evolution is characterized by the discoveries at La Tène in Switzerland. These had a strong religious flavour, and accorded with the Irish and Welsh beliefs concerning the after-life and the Celtic god-forms that were currently worshipped. It must be borne in mind, however, that these finds are highly local and, as Mahr emphasizes, both La Tène and Hallstatt are not clear-cut chronological units which commenced and terminated simultaneously in all the provinces.[2]

What we do know is that during the period referred to by Rolleston as 'The Golden Age of Celtdom', the fifth and fourth centuries BC, the Celts waged three highly successful wars which greatly influenced the course of south European history. Around 500 BC they took Spain from the

Carthaginians, while a century later they were engaged with the Etruscans in the conquest of northern Italy. They settled in large numbers in Cisalpine Gaul where they left a legacy of place-names to testify to their occupation. The Latin poet Virgil was, in fact, of Celtic stock, his name meaning 'very bright' or 'illustrious'. His love of nature, mysticism, and the decorative use of language and rhythm being markedly Celtic qualities.

Both classical and native sources furnish us with some first class descriptions of the early Celts whom, it would seem, were highly distinctive in both appearance and demeanour. It is generally agreed that they were tall and powerfully built, with blue eyes and blond or reddish hair. Diodorus Siculus describes the men as favouring moustaches to beards, while both sexes were highly conscious of their appearance and anxious to make the most of their natural good looks, Celtic women vying with their menfolk in size and comeliness.

Strabo makes special mention of their hair which, he tells us; 'Is not only naturally blonde, but they also use artificial means to increase this natural quality of colour. For they continually wash their hair with lime wash and draw it back from the forehead to the crown and to the nape of the neck, with the result that their appearance resembles that of the Satyrs or Pans, for their hair is so thickened by this treatment that it differs in no way from a horse's mane'.[3]

Irish sources described the Celtic aristocracy as being fair of hair, with light skin and oval faces, while Strabo stresses the 'very moist and white flesh' of the Gauls as contrasted with the dark skins of other Mediterranean peoples, and also comments on their tall stature.

Apparently the Celts placed strong emphasis on the colour and quality of the hair, the epic tales making special mention of 'flowing hair, fair yellow-golden streaming manes'. But according to other authorities their fairness was more of a reddish kind rather than the ash blonde usually associated with the Germanic or Anglo-Saxon peoples, this auburn emphasis also appearing in those among them with darker tresses, with the Celtic skin tending towards freckles. The Roman writer Dio Cassius describes the Icenian Queen Boudïcca in some detail: 'She was huge of frame and terrifying of aspect with a harsh voice. A great mass of bright red hair fell to her knees.'[4]

Overall we may safely say that the general impression from all sources of evidence designates the Celtic aristocratic society as being tall, physically powerful men and women with fair or reddish hair, grey-blue eyes, light skins, oval faces, and fresh complexions. Diodorus Siculus makes one odd remark concerning their children whom, he tells us, 'Are born for the most part with grey hair but as they advance in age they are assimilated to the hair colour of their parents.'[5]

Like the Teutons, the Celts were dolichocephalic, meaning that they had heads which were long in proportion to their breadth, as evidenced from remains found in the heavily Celtic-populated Marne basin. One skeleton of a tall Gallic warrior, complete with his tools of war, is now housed in the Musée de St Germain. The inhabitants of the British Isles are generally long-headed, the brachycephalic, round-headed or Alpine-type, occurring very rarely, while those of modern France are round-headed.[6] (Those interested in this study are recommended to a monograph entitled *The Distribution of the Human Blood Groups and Other Polymorphisms* published in the 1970s by Oxford University Press. Only library editions are available to order, however).

The Celts are mentioned in history as being so highly fastidious in their appearance and apparel as to suggest vanity. They were also very figure conscious, and it was considered a disgrace to become corpulent. Strabo tells us: 'The following is a further peculiar trait, they try not to become stout and fat-bellied, and any young man who exceeds the standard length of the girdle is fined.'[7] Perhaps a little of that medicine might be good for a lot of us today!

The generous Celtic use of jewellery and colour may be evidenced in relics and designs that have filtered through to modern times. Their style of clothing did not, however, meet with the approval of their contemporaries. J. J. Tierney remarks, 'To the frankness and high spiritedness of their temperament must be added the traits of childish boastfulness and love of decoration. They wear ornaments of gold, torques on their necks and bracelets on their arms and wrists, while people of high rank wear dyed garments besprinkled with gold. It is this vanity that makes them unbearable in victory and so completely downcast in defeat.'[8] They would certainly appear to differ considerably in temperament from the recognizably stoic traits of the more northern peoples, and according to Spence, the older school of anthropology labelled them Sanguine/Bilious (Fire/Air to the occultist).

That the Celts loved display there is little doubt, their sense of drama and intensely emotional natures being emphasized in rich ornamentations and horse trappings in bronze and enamel as skilfully wrought as anything in Cretan or Mycenaean art. Their love of gold was a special feature in their artefacts and apparel; even their cuirasses were made of it while their temples and sacred places, according to both Posidonius and Diodorus Siculus, were full of unguarded offerings of gold that no one ever touched!

When Vercingetorix conceded to Caesar at Alesia, after conferring with his assembled chiefs, he armed himself with his most splendid weapons, decked his horse with its richest trappings and, after riding three times around the Roman camp, surrendered his sword to Caesar. This scene of the Vercingetorix' surrender is not actually recounted by Caesar himself, but rests mainly on the authority of Plutarch and the historian Florus, and is generally accepted by scholars as an historic fact.

Polybius records an historic scene from the battle of Clastidium (222 BC) where the Gaesati (a tribe who took their name from the gaesum, a kind of Celtic javelin, which constituted their principle weapon) were in the forefront of the Celtic army, stripped naked for the fight, and the sight of these warriors with their great stature and fair skins, on which glittered the collars and bracelets of gold so loved as an adornment by all Celts, filled the Roman legionaries with awe. But sadly, at the end of the day, the golden ornaments went in cartloads to deck the capitol of Rome and Polybius's final comment was: 'I say not usually, but always, in everything they attempt, they are driven headlong by their passions, and never submit to the laws of reason.'[9] It was further commented, apparently, that the chastity for which the Germans of the time were noted was never a Celtic characteristic, which leads us to believe that in spite of their kindly, deeply emotional, generous, extroverted and highly artistic natures they were basically hedonistic. Only in the realms of religion and magic did they respond to the stern finger of obedience and personal discipline.

It is a pity that we are not afforded some tangible evidence of the early growth stages of the Celtic peoples, their migrations from northern India, and from whence they derived some of the advanced metaphysical concepts that are concealed within the 'mysteries' of their most secret cults. But then, this intangibility is surely akin to the very natures of the Celts themselves, who have ever been travelling in search of some divine Avalon. There must be something of the gypsy in the Celtic character, for even today many of us who have the old Celtic blood coursing through our veins feel the need to up roots from time to time, broaden our horizons and move on, if not in body, then in our never-ending search for the answers to the enigmas of life and death.

Endnotes
1. Ross, Dr Anne. *Everyday Life of the Pagan Celts,* p. 18.
2. Ibid. Ross, p. 29.
3. Ibid. Ross, p. 51.
4. Ibid. Ross, p. 56.
5. Ibid. Ross, p. 57.
6. Rolleston, T. W. *Myths and Legends of the Celtic Race*, p. 44.
7. Op. cit. Ross, p. 61.
8. Op. cit. Ross, p. 61.
9. Op. cit. Rolleston, p. 41.

2. HISTORICAL OBSERVATIONS AND COMMENTS

The Celts were by no means the only peoples inhabiting the prominent European territories of those times. There were also the Germans and the Teuto-Gothic tribes who eventually replaced the Celts as the great northern menace to classical civilization. Although these are mentioned by Pytheas, the eminent Greek traveller and geographer about 300 BC, they do not appear to have exerted a particularly strong influence upon history until, as the Cimbri and Teutones, they marched on Italy and were vanquished by Marius at the close of the second century. The ancient Greek geographers prior to Pytheas assigned all the territories later referred to as Germanic to various Celtic tribes.

Some scholars therefore assume that the Germans of those times, in keeping with certain Gaulish and Irish tribes, were a subject people living under Celtic dominion with no independent political existence. Evidence of the Celtic influence on the subsequent development of the Germanic races is to be found in words connected with law, government and war that are common to both Celtic and Teutonic languages, being borrowed by the latter from the former. The following list is submitted by Rolleston, according to Jubainville:

reich — empire; *amt* — office; *reiks* — a king (Gothic); *bann* — an order; *frie* — free; *geisel* — a hostage; *erbe* —

an inheritance; *werthe* — value: *weig* — sacred; *wini* — a wife (Old High German); *skalks, schalk* — a slave (Gothic); *hathu* — battle (Old German); *helith, held* — a hero, from the same root as the word Celt; *heer* — an army; *sieg* — victory; *beaute* — booty; *burg* — a castle, and many others.[1]

The etymological history of these words and others shows distinct root links between many modern European words and the primitive Indo-European tongue from which they were obviously derived. The associations between the early Celtic peoples and the Germanic tribes therefore calls for deeper investigation when considering the occult significances of relevant folk mythology, such as the Edda, in a later chapter.

While on the subject of root connections between the Celtic tongue and languages currently spoken in northern India, I am reminded of a firsthand story told to me by a former Indian Army officer during my five years working at the Officers Association in London. He recounted an instance in which some Welsh speaking recruits had been posted to his unit near the northern frontier. Their English, however, left much to be desired and there was some concern regarding their ability to make themselves understood by the natives. One day when they were chatting together in Welsh, one of the local Indian boys joined in the conversation, claiming that he was able to understand more of their words than the brusque English accents of the officers. It appeared that the two languages had too much in common for this to be an isolated coincidence.

To return to our ancient Celts who failed, it seems, to impose either their religion or language in its entirety on the subjugated German tribes. It was, no doubt, this inward or concealed festering of racial pride which led to the ultimate German uprising that overthrew Celtic supremacy. German and Celtic deities are on the whole named differently, although they represent similar principles. People have always reserved the right to call God by whichever name they choose and any interference with this freedom is viewed as being oppressive. Funerary rites also differed between the two peoples.

As Ireland was neither visited nor subjugated by the Roman legionaries and therefore maintained its independence against intrusive cultures until the close of the twelfth century, the Celtic influence there was unbroken for the longest period. Celtic institutions, art, literature and the oldest surviving form of the Celtic language are to be found in Ireland, and many scholars opine that the Irish tongue constitutes a more ancient form of the Celtic language than Welsh. The Goidelic or Gaelic Celts, said to have been the first of their race to colonize these isles and who were later forced to the extreme west of Ireland, used the earlier pronunciation of the 'p' which was more in keeping with the old Indo-European particle 'pare', whereas this was subsequently changed, in about the sixth century BC. So, from a study of Irish and Welsh words it is possible to divide the earlier invasions from the later Celtic arrivals. The two well-known and established facts regarding the Celts, which goes for their race over the whole period of their ascendancy, are undoubtedly their predilection for the art of war and the subtlety of speech *'rem militarem et argute loqui'*.[2]

Most of the knowledge contained in current history books concerning the nature and religion of the Celts can be attributed to Roman sources, notably Caesar, who renders a careful and highly critical account of the Celtic character, customs and beliefs as he encountered them in Gaul. He describes them as eager for battle, but easily dashed by reverses. Being extremely superstitious, they submitted to their Druids in all public and private affairs, regarding excommunication from their religious practices as the worst possible punishment;

They who are thus interdicted (for refusing to obey a Druidical sentence) are reckoned in the number of the vile and wicked; all persons avoid and fly their company and discourse, lest they should receive any infection by contagion; they are not permitted to commence a suit; neither is any post entrusted to them.... The Druids are generally freed from military service, nor do they pay taxes with the rest.... Encouraged by such rewards, many of their own accord come to their schools, and are sent by their friends and relations. They are said there to get by heart a great number of verses; some continue twenty years in their education; neither is it held lawful to commit these things (the Druidic doctrines) to writing, though in almost all public transactions and private accounts they use the Greek characters.[3]

Some modern writers, notably Isabel Hill Elder, strongly refute the Roman view of the Celts, judging much of it as destructive propaganda designed to belittle the Celtic peoples in the eyes of the then civilized world. Of course, this is true of opposing nations in any age, and no doubt Caesar's slanted accounts are no different in kind from those rendered both by the British and their allies on the one side, and the Germans and Japanese on the other in World War II.

Celtic Gauls were spoken of as being ever eager for news of any kind, besieging merchants and travellers for gossip, easily influenced and sanguine. This observation is later confirmed by Edmund Spenser who writes of the Irish 'that they use commonlye to send up and down to know newes and yf any meet with another, his second woorde is, What Newes?'[4] Here we have a distinct racial characteristic that has been carried down the centuries.

Although the Romans were obviously disdainful of many aspects of the Celtic character and beliefs, they most certainly respected their strength, courage, ingenuity and fortitude in battle. While winning, none was so bold as the Celtic warrior, but morale would appear to have been one of their main energy sources and once defeat reared its ugly head the tears rolled.

The geographer and traveller Strabo, who died in AD24, left a great deal of information concerning the Celts. He observed that their country, in this case Gaul, was thickly inhabited and well tilled with no waste of natural resources. Their womenfolk were prolific, and excellent mothers. The men he describes as warlike, passionate, disputatious, easily provoked, but generous and unsuspicious, and easily vanquished by stratagem. They showed themselves eager for culture and established centres of education in their towns. Being natural horsemen they fought better when mounted than on foot, and later formed the flower of the Roman cavalry. Their houses were large and constructed of arched timbers, with walls of wickerwork plastered with clay and lime and thickly thatched. Caesar noted the strength of the walls surrounding their towns, these being built of stone and timber, while both Caesar and Strabo marked the very strict class system that was observed among Celtic peoples everywhere. This social discrimination, it was felt, corresponded roughly to the racial distinction between the true Celts and the indigenous or aboriginal populations they subdued. One interesting point that is very relevant to the later chapters in this book: Caesar mentions the Druidic belief in the immortality of the soul, to which Strabo adds the concept of indestructability or the divine infinity of the material universe. Advanced thinking for what the Romans otherwise thought of as a barbarous race!

The reports of Polybius and Diodorus Siculus we have already considered in an earlier chapter, but Ammianus Marcellinus also has some comments to add. While confirming the statements of the other writers concerning the blue-eyed fairness, bearing and stature of the Celts he makes special mention of the physical strength of their womenfolk who were also the equal of their men in courage, valour and independence. Shades of the fiery-hearted Maeve, Grania, Findabair and Deidre of the legends, and our own Boadicea (Boudicca).

In spite of the fine organization within Celtic society, its attention to the arts, to music, poetry and to clean, organized living, the question must arise as to why a people so able to create a civilized society and defend itself in war should have fallen to its less cultured adversaries who later rent its peoples apart. The Romans themselves supply the answer to this one, the root of the problem, they felt, lying in the Celtic religion. Most civilizations that have conquered, risen and stayed in a position of power for any period have relied to a great extent on loyalty to the state or patriotism, doubtless engendered by the concept of ego-racial supremacy. While the Celts did not dismiss this idea there was a force in their society that dominated the civic-cum-political inspiration that was the unifying power behind most of the classical nations; this was their sacerdotalism. The Druids were the sovereign power in Celtica, a fact confirmed from both Roman and Irish sources. All affairs of state were subject to their office and they ruled with a rod of iron. Their priests drew their authority from supernatural sanctions which, in the eyes of the more materially inclined Romans, constituted Celtica's undoing. Whether, in fact, temporal rulership by a priestly caste does constitute a disaster area in the power of national politics must surely be re-evaluated in the light of modern events. The Romans certainly thought this way but we today are faced with a situation where the balance of world power is, to an extent, in the hands of religious and ideological fanatics, and one wonders what Caesar would make of that!

Endnotes
1. Rolleston, T.W. *Myths and Legends of the Celtic Race,* pp. 31 & 32.
2. Ibid. Rolleston, p. 37.
3. Ibid. Rolleston, p. 37.
4. Ibid. From Rolleston. 'View of the Present State of Ireland', p. 37.

3.   IRISH MYTHOLOGICAL SOURCES

It was the policy of the early Druids never to commit their most sacred truths to writing so, unlike other earlier races whose creation myths have been well documented and analysed, much of what is considered to comprise Celtic beliefs is purely conjectural, unless a few scraps of helpful information can be gleaned from the legends of those lands in which their influence was strongest.

In the old Irish records, the tellers of tales and weavers of romances transplanted the old, oral, secret cosmogony into an Irish setting, and in so doing provided one of the most comprehensive Celtic and pre-Celtic mythological references available. I am obliged to abridge these tales, however, as they are meant to constitute only a part of this work.

Irish mythical and legendary literature in its most ancient form falls into four main divisions:

The Mythological Cycle or Cycle of Invasions.
The Ultonian or Conorian Cycle.
The Ossianic or Fenian Cycle.
A collection of miscellaneous tales and legends that could apply
    to any period of history or system of religious belief.

It is the mythological cycle, however, that concerns us in this narrative as it affords the occultist the chance, reading between the lines, to arrive at some very definite conclusions regarding the 'hidden' truths of Celtic Druidism. While we will deal with the deeper metaphysical aspects later, the initial sources provide a good starting point for both analysis and conjecture.

The Mythological Cycle comprises the following sections:

The coming of Partholan into Ireland.
The arrival of Nemed.
The Firbolgs entry into Ireland.
The coming of the Tuatha de Danaans or People of Dana.
The Milesian invasion and subsequent dismissal of the Danaans.

From the Milesians onwards, the pages of orthodox history are open for us to consult, the sons of Miled representing the more familiar Celtic line from which the ruling families of Ireland are purportedly descended. The Danaans are seen as gods or supernaturals, while the earlier arrivals are of insufficient substance to afford anything other than a phantasmic identity.

Caesar tells us that the Celts believed themselves to be descended from the God of the Underworld. Partholan, Ireland's first visitor, is said to have come from the 'Land of the Happy Dead' in the west, where the Irish believed fairyland to be located. Partholan's Queen was named Dealgnaid (pronounced Dalny), and the couple were accompanied by a band of companions of both sexes. However, the legend is careful to inform us that Ireland was, in those days, a different country physically from what it is now, there being but three lakes, nine rivers and one plain. During the reign of the Partholanians the land changed contour, one new lake was named Rury, as it was said to have burst out as a grave was being dug for Partholan's son of that name.

However, the Partholanians did not arrive on totally uninhabited shores, Ireland being already peopled by a strange and forbidding race known as the Formorians. These were a huge, misshapen, violent and cruel lot believed by many to be personifications of the powers of evil. One of them was named Cenchos, meaning 'The Footless', shades of the Vedantic Vritra (or Vitra) who had neither hands nor feet. Partholan fought the Formorians for the rulership of Ireland and eventually drove them out towards the northern seas, from which position they continued to harass later settlers from time to time. The Partholanians were eventually wiped out by a pestilence, which was possibly caused by the release of certain bacteria during seismic upheavals.

Since there are no Partholanian or Formorian records (either oral or otherwise), how, then, did the Irish come to know this story? The tale was told in a series of legendary narratives one of which is called *The Book of the Dun Cow*. The earliest manuscript, which can be dated back to AD 1199 is entitled 'The Legend of Tuan macCarell' and the story runs thus:

St Finnen, an Irish Abbot of the sixth century, apparently sought hospitality from a chief by the name of Tuan macCarell, who lived near to the Saint's monastery at Moville in County Donegal. Tuan refused to admit him, however, which troubled the good man to the extent that he elected to fast for a whole day on the chief's doorstep. Now according to the Irish custom of those times, a magical power was attributed to this action the effect of which could only be averted if the other person also fasted. The surly warrior finally opened his door and good relations were established between the two of them. Tuan later returned the Saint's visit during which occasion the monks enquired of Tuan's name and lineage. His reply astounded them. 'I am a man of Ulster', he told them. 'My name is Tuan, son of Carell, but once I was called Tuan, son of Starn son of Sera, and my father, Starn, was the brother of Partholan.'

'Tell us the history of Ireland, then', said Finnen, and so the tale began.

After the great pestilence related earlier, Tuan alone had survived 'for there is never a slaughter that one man does not come out of it to tell the tale.' For twenty-two years he wandered across the barren territory from one deserted fort and homestead to another until old age eventually overtook him.

Then Nemed, son of Agnoman, took possession of Ireland. He was my father's brother. I saw him from the cliffs and kept avoiding him. I was long-haired, clawed, decrepid, grey, naked, wretched and miserable. Then one evening I fell asleep and when I awoke on the morrow I was changed into a stag. I was young again and glad of heart. Then I sang of the coming of Nemed and his race, and of my own transformation... I have put on a new form, a skin rough and grey. Victory and joy are easy to me, a little while ago I was weak and defenceless.[1]

The story continues with Tuan then becoming king of all the deer in Ireland and remaining so all the days of the Nemedians.

Nemed and his people had sailed for Ireland in a fleet of thirty-two barks, each of which contained thirty persons. But bad weather had blown them off course and they were lost in strange waters for a year-and-a-half during which time most of them perished from hunger, thirst or exposure. Nine only escaped, Nemed himself and four men and four women. These landed in Ireland and in the fullness of time their numbers were increased to 8060 men and women. Then they, too, died mysteriously.

Once more old age fell upon Tuan but yet another transformation awaited him. 'Once I was standing at the mouth of my cave — I still remember it — and I knew that my body changed into another form. I was a wild boar.' Tuan continued his narrative with further rejoicing in his new found youth before proceeding with his history of Ireland. Semion, son of Stariat, settled in Ireland, from whom descended the Firbolgs and two other tribes which persisted into historic times. Yet once more old age overcame Tuan, and this time he is transformed into 'a great eagle of the sea' in which guise he again rejoices in his youth and strength.

His next story concerns the arrival of the fabled Tuatha de Danaans, 'From whom all Irishmen of learning are sprung', and these were, in turn, followed by the Milesians, or sons of Miled, equated by scholars with the Goidelic Celts. During the latter period Tuan stayed as a sea eagle until one day he felt another transformation coming on. He fasted nine days, then 'sleep fell upon me and I was changed into a salmon.' Again he rejoiced in his new life escaping the snares of fishermen, but eventually he was caught and brought to the house of Carell, chief of the country. Carell's wife was apparently quite partial to salmon and, as Tuan explained, '... she ate me by herself, whole, so that I passed into her womb.' And so Tuan, son of Carell was once again born into human form.

Here we have shades of the Welsh Taliesin story, in which

much form changing also took place. But in the realms of magic such things are quite common as we shall soon see. What we can glean from all this, however, magic aside, is the Celtic belief in reincarnation or the transmigration of souls and that this concept was not, in the Celts' eyes, limited to the human species.

So endeth Tuan's tale. But some analysis is called for. According to Tuan, the Nemedians and Partholanians were of the same race, one group simply representing a slightly earlier migration. Later, Irish Christians endeavoured to equate the Nemedians with scriptural patriarchs from Spain or Scythia, but it is more likely that they were a band of refugees fleeing the same lands as the Partholanians, which had suffered, or were suffering, the ravages of seismic turbulence. As for the Formorians, there being no actual legends regarding their arrival in Ireland, we must assume that : (a) they were the original indigenous peoples of that land; or (b) they represented the militant forces of nature which ran rampant prior to and following the Biblical Flood. The former seems more likely, however.

The Firbolgs are somewhat easier to identify. Their name appears to mean 'men of the bags' and there are various speculations as to how they acquired this appellation. Nennius opined that they, like their predecessors, came from the area of Spain, but another school of thought designates them early Goidelic Celts from southern Europe who strayed north and took to the seas, probably to avoid unfriendly tribes they encountered there.

Undoubtedly the most interesting of all the arrivals on the shores of Ireland were the Tuatha de Danaans, or 'folk of the god whose mother is Dana', Brigid being the most popular personality among them. So dear was this deity to the hearts of the Irish people that she was later incorporated into the Christian Church as St Brigid. Her name is also found in Gaulish inscriptions as 'Brigindo' and in Britian as 'Brigantia'. She was the daughter of the supreme head of the people of Dana — Dagda, the Good. According to some sources, Brigid had three sons, who appear to be three aspects of one Being known as Ecne — 'Knowledge' or 'Poetry', although other authorities more accurately assign these children to Dana. It is interesting to observe that although Tuan macCarell referred to the people of Dana as 'gods', they do not appear as immortals in the Irish legends. Christians later reduced them to pantheistic status or identified them with the Biblical Fallen Angels. And yet, even the later legends appear to invest them with certain supernatural or 'fairy' powers, as well as the virtues of Light, Wisdom and Knowledge.

Different people saw the Danaans as different things. To the Druidic caste they represented the deities of science and poetry, while to the ordinary megalithic element they were the spirits of fertility that dwelt in hills, streams, stones and similar elemental habitats. Although according to the good Tuan's tale the Danaans came from 'heaven', later tradition embroidered their land of origin as one of four great cities whose very names are evocative of mystery and romance: Falias, Gorias, Finias and Murias. In these places they had been schooled in science and craftsmanship by the great Sages that ruled those domains and from each city they brought a magical treasure.

From Falias came the *Lia Fail* or Stone of Destiny on which the High Kings of Ireland were crowned. Legend had it that a roaring sound was emitted if the rightful monarch was receiving the kingship. A stone conforming to this description did actually exist in Tara, but was supposedly sent to Scotland at the commencement of the sixth century for the coronation of Fergus the Great. According to an ancient prophecy, wherever this stone was, the King of the Irish-Milesian race would reign. We are told that this is now the famous Stone of Scone which was never returned to Ireland, but was removed to England by Edward I in 1297 and is now the Coronation Stone at Westminster Abbey. It would appear that the prophecy has stayed true, as the British Royal Family can be traced from the historic kings of the Milesians or Celts.

That the Coronation Stone is the actual original stone from Tara, let alone the legendary Danaan gift, strains the credulity somewhat! For years rumours have circulated in the occult world to the effect that the old magical stone was long since appropriated by some high initiate whose duty it was to guard it against violation by less scrupulous elements in the king-making scene, a suitable substitute having been provided. I have spoken personally with more than one Scottish occultist who has assured me that the genuine old Stone has never travelled south of the border, while Irish antiquaries insist that it never left Tara in the first place. We will leave that for our readers to decide for themselves, however, but it makes you think!

The second Danaan treasure, which came from the city of Gorias was the invincible Sword of Lugh of the Long Arm. From Finias came the Magic Spear and from Murias the Cauldron of Dagda, a cornucopia-type vessel that could feed an army and still remain full to the brim.

Armed with these gifts, the people of Dana arrived in Ireland, and under rather extraordinary circumstances to boot, being 'wafted into the land on a magic cloud' and making their first appearance in western Connaught. When the cloud cleared, the Firbolgs beheld a fully fortified and established camp, and promptly despatched a warrior named Streng to interview the mysterious newcomers while the Danaans replied with their representative who was called Bres. Both sides compared notes, examining each other's weapons with care and interest. The Danaan armoury was light and refined compared with that of the Firbolgs. Perhaps the originator of the legend was contrasting the power of science with that of brute force.

In spite of the superior Danaan technology, however, the Firbolgs were not convinced of their prowess when it came to an actual battle, so they challenged the newcomers to meet them at arms on the Plain of Moytura in the south of County Mayo. The Firbolgs were led by their King mac Erc and the Danaans by Nuada of the Silver Hand, who received his name following an incident in this very battle. His hand was severed during the affray, and one of the many skilled artificer/ healers of the Danaans made a silver replacement which worked just like a normal hand. In fact the description that has come down to us suggests the first record of a bionic limb! Because of their superior magical and healing skills the Danaans took the day, the Firbolg King was slain and his people allotted the province of Connaught for their territory with the Danaans appropriating the remainder of Ireland. As late as the seventeenth century, Irish scholars discovered that many of the inhabitants of Connaught knew of oral traditions which designated them the descendants of the Firbolgs, and described the aforementioned events as historical facts and not simply fairy-tales.

One cannot proceed with the Danaan story without

considering just who these people were and whence they came. Certainly not from Europe, it would appear, as the descriptions of their weaponry and general characteristics are dissimilar from those of earlier and later invaders. There would appear to be two schools of thought regarding this issue: (1) That the name 'Danaans' is suggestive of the Danube, and that these people therefore represented an early Celtic migration which consisted of a highly advanced priestly caste, probably of Lemurian or Mu-an origin who had brought their knowledge down the centuries from the region of northern India; or (2) That they were Atlanteans who had survived the Flood or were in the process of escaping from same. Since we have no actual dates to juggle with, it is anyone's guess.

To continue the Danaan saga, as no blemished man might be King of Ireland, Nuada was obliged to stand down to Bres, a man of suspect ancestry who was half Danaan and half native Irish. But Bres was not made of kingly material and his overthrow is an interesting story from a magical viewpoint. One day a poet named Corpry paid him a visit, but found himself housed in a small, dark chamber without heat or comfort. After a long wait he was eventually served with three dry cakes and no ale. Lack of generosity and hospitality being reckoned the worst of vices in Ireland in those days, Corpry took his revenge by composing a satirical magical quatrain which ran as follows:

Without food quickly served,
Without cow's milk whereon a calf can grow,
Without a dwelling fit for a man under the gloomy night,
Without means to entertain a bardic company, —
Let such be the condition of Bres.[2]

This type of poetic satire was believed to carry a highly potent magical spell. Kings dreaded it, and even an insect or humble rat could be exterminated by it. People throughout the land repeated Corpry's rhyme with delight and Bres was eventually forced to abdicate. By then Nuada's hand had been miraculously restored by the physician Diancecht or, according to some, the son of this great healer who was also called Diancecht which suggests a title rather than the name of an individual. One source mentions the actual regrowth of a new hand from the old stub but the more credible version is that by then Nuada had learned to manipulate his bionic limb and was therefore able to stand his ground in battle.

Bres, however, in the misery of his rejection, went to his mother, Eri, and asked her to reveal who his father really was. She finally confided in him that it had been Elatha, King of the Formorians, who had visited her secretly from across the sea and from which union Bres had been born. The details of the story from here on are too lengthy to recount, but suffice it to say that following the return of Bres to his natural father a further Formorian uprising took place and Nuada was no longer able to hold out against the brutal oppression exerted by these primitive and barbarous people.

Enter a newcomer in the form of Lugh, son of Kian (or Cian) later designated the Chief Sun God of all Celtica. The name of Lugh is by no means limited to Ireland and Irish myth as we shall see; in fact he was recognized as the Supreme Solar Force throughout Celtic Europe as well as other parts of the British Isles. With Lugh came a whole tribe of recognizable Celtic deities including Ogma, and Goban the Smith who was the great artificer and armourer of Irish myth, equating with the Teutonic Wayland, Greek Hephaestus and Egyptian Ptah.

Lugh eventually replaced Nuada as leader of the Danaans, indicating a change in religious polarity that was to influence the esoteric and exoteric beliefs and attitudes of the Irish for the ensuing decades.

One interesting observation concerning the Danaans which we may glean from *The Book of Invasions* is the power they were able to exert through music or sonics. On one occasion the Formorians carried off and imprisoned the harpist of the Dagda. Lugh, the Dagda and Ogma followed them, secretly entering the Formorian banqueting hall where the harp had been hung upon the wall as a trophy. The Dagda called to it magically whereupon it immediately flew into his hands, killing nine Formorians *en route*. The Dagda's invocation is a strange one, the meaning of which has been debated by scholars and occultists for centuries. It does, however, provide some definite clues as to the Danaans origins.

Come, apple-sweet murmurer, he cries, come, four-angled frame of harmony, come, Summer, come, Winter, from the mouths of harps and bags and pipes.[3]

The summer/winter allusion is suggestive of the Indian practice of allotting certain musical modes to different seasons of the year or even different times of the day, and ancient Egyptian records also refer to the three-stringed lyre as representing spring, summer and winter. The old Irish division of the year apparently also contained only three divisions, summer and autumn being lumped together.

Upon gaining possession of the harp the Dagda played 'three noble strains', the secrets of which were known to every genuine magical harpist: The Strain of Lament, The Strain of Laughter and the Strain of Slumber, which would appear to indicate the magical power of music to manipulate the emotions and therefore effect a degree of control over people. This is confirmed in the findings of modern psychology where different musical strains or modes are observed to produce mood changes, being evocative of certain chakric reactions on the one hand, or mass abreaction or hypnosis on the other.

The Dagda's harp is also reminiscent of the Egyptian sistrum which originally had four crossbars, each of which was 'tuned' to the note of one of the four elemental kingdoms (Air, Fire, Water and Earth). We are given to understand that in Atlantean times these were originally struck and not shaken. Later versions of the sistrum which appeared towards the end of Dynastic Egypt often had only three strings or bars representing, no doubt, the three seasons, the old meaning having been long since forgotten.

I shall be dealing with the magical aspects of the Danaan deities later in this book, but as far as the *Book of Invasions* contributes to legendary Celtic history we can stop at the point at which the Milesians arrived (significantly on 1 May) on the shores of Ireland. These people are conceived in Irish legends as being the first fully human race of conquerors, and yet their ancestry can also be traced back to 'Celtic' divine origins.

The Milesians were the sons of Miled, whose name occurs as a god in a Celtic inscription from Hungary. Miled was the son of Bilé, which was one of the names of the God of the Underworld. Their supposed arrival from Spain was the later historians' way of rationalizing the fabled 'Land of the Dead'. Graves' account of their having originated in Greece early in the second millenium BC and taken many generations to reach Ireland after wandering the Mediterranean sounds more feasible. The Milesians of Greek legend claimed descent from Miletos, a son of Apollo, who emigrated from Crete to Caria in early times where he built the city of his name after the similarly-named city in Crete.

According to an unknown writer cited by Plutarch (c. AD 46–120) and Procopius, who wrote in the sixth century AD, the 'Land of the Dead' is the western extremity of Britain, separated from the eastern by an impassable wall. On the northern coast of Gaul is a populace of mariners whose business it is to carry the dead across from the continent to their last abode in the British Isles. No doubt these and similar legends, which are also to be found in most other early mythologies, originated in the old Atlantean concept, Britain in those times representing the 'Western Islands' that were originally the 'Isles of the Blest' or last remnants of the Old Country.

Shortly after the Milesians arrival in Ireland, they defeated the Danaans in a fierce battle that was conducted just south of Tralee, where their warrior queen Scota was killed and buried. However, according to another story, Scota, who was purportedly of Egyptian descent, survived and travelled to Scotland where she conquered the Picts and gave the country its present name. The Danaans did not, however, withdraw from Ireland following this defeat but employed their magical arts to effect a veil of invisibility which, legend has it, they can use to this day as they deem fit. From then onwards there became two Irelands, the spiritual and the earthly. The Danaans dwell in the spiritual realms which are apportioned to them by the Dagda. These are the Fairy Kingdoms, visible only to the eyes of the initiated, the wise or the pure of heart. Those that dwell therein sustain undying youth and beauty and sometimes come to mortal men and women in times of love and strife. They are conceived of in the ancient mythical literature as heroic and beautiful to behold. In later Christian times when their memory was reduced to fairy romances, they became the people of the Sidhe (pronouned Shee). Where are they now, you may well ask? Where they have ever been and always will be, the belief or disbelief in any condition being no prerequisite for its actuality.

The Danaan/Formorian myth is said by some scholars to represent the eternal dualistic struggle between good and evil, darkness and light, with the Danaan reverence for poetry, music and artisitic skill standing for the Druidic concept of beauty and world order. The Formorian dullness, insensitivity and barbarism can therefore be summarized as the darkness of ignorance, and the inevitable clash between these two factions is indicative of the last fight and death throes of a more gentle and non-aggressive rulership.

It is the author's belief that this whole tale is not entirely allegorical, although it has doubtless been embroidered heavily over the centuries. There *were* actual landings, colonizations or whatever during the unwritten early history of Ireland, and both the Atlanteans and early Celts contributed in some way to the secret magical traditions that have been handed down to the initiated by the magic hand of time.

Endnotes
1.   Rolleston, T.W. *Myths and Legends of the Celtic Race,* p. 99.
2.   Ibid. Rolleston, p. 108.
3.   Ibid. Rolleston, p. 118.

4. THE WELSH TRADITION

A recent scientific publication[1] throws considerable light on the ancestry of the Welsh people and their genetic inheritance in particular. In addition to anthropometric, polymorphic and linguistic data, it includes a detailed survey of the blood groups and genetics of the indigenous population, which greatly aids the identification of the Celtic influence in the Principality.

Ancestral origins can be ascertained from the information provided by the genetic frequencies in blood groups. In Wales there are three main genetic groupings, the oldest of which is to be found in the moors and moorland fringes of western Wales, and in areas of megalithic significance associated with prehistoric settlement. It carries the *B* gene frequency, but without certain of the genetic identities usually found in the B blood group in the Far East. This genetic feature was not, therefore, imported from eastern Europe or adjacent Asia in historical times as was generally suspected, but probably formed part of the original indigenous frequency.

Those carrying this gene are few in number, however, when compared to the carriers of the *O* gene frequency, which occurs in much of central and northern Wales, and is generally associated with the Goidelic Celts. It is interesting to note that the genetic code of this frequency can be traced to tribes in the western Caucasus and Transcaucasia, the Mediterranean Islands, and parts of northern Africa, all

places from which the ancient Celts are reputed to have come.
Physical anthropology, linguistics and archaeology all offer
support for human migration from the eastern Mediterranean
to Britain in Neolithic times and our reference informs us that
the fundamental physical type in most of Wales is the long-
headed brunette, universally belonging to the fair skinned
Berbers or Mediterranean race of Sergi!

Finally, we come to the *A* genetic frequency which occurs
mainly in southern Wales and that Southern half of
Pembrokeshire which is known as 'Little England'. As this
gene was believed to be mainly confined to the Scandinavian
races, science suggests that this area of Wales was strongly
colonized not by marauding Viking invaders, but by peaceful
settlers who brought their wives, children and thralls with
them, thus keeping the genetic strain pure for · many
generations. High incidences of this same genetic frequency
also occur in Cornwall and Brittany and would appear to go
hand in hand with the Brythonic language. The Viking
consideration aside, the aforementioned information would
appear to confirm the two main Celtic migrations described in
Chapter 1, the former possibly relating to the darker haired or
Goidelic Celts, and the latter to the fairer or Brythonic group.

Having thus established our genetic links between Wales
and the ancient Celts, let us now turn our attention to more
traditional sources of Celtic information.

The mystical and magical literature of British Celtdom
which constitutes another main source of ancient Celtic
history and mythology is derived mainly from the Welsh
Triads and the *Mabinogion*, although the latter work is itself
something of a mystery both as to origin and content.

One of the characteristics of the Celtic race was a love of
story-telling. As with other races whose history is built upon
an oral tradition, the Celtic Bards possessed an extensive
repertoire, and although their story-tellers kept to the main
theme or essence of the tale, they were granted licence to
extemporize as they thought fit. The Iliad and Odyssey were
also relayed in this way, which accounts for their fluidity and ·
the slight variations that occurred over the pages of pre-
history, the very freedom that characterizes oral transmission
naturally lending itself to inconsistencies in coherence and the
obfuscation of original truths.

The Celtic story-tellers gleaned their information from two

main sources, mystery/folklore and history/pseudo-history. The Celts having been described as viewing history as what ought to have happened rather than what actually did, the demarcation line between fact and fiction in the *Mabinogion* is somewhat difficult to define. As with the myths and legends of most other early civilizations the sources are so obscure and the evidence so fragmentary as to make accurate interpretation or reliable restoration difficult to say the least. The Celts were decentralized from the time of their earliest migrations westwards; their pantheons, therefore, tended to collect local overlays wherever they settled which naturally gave rise to there being many names for one deity or principle. Add pantheistic, Roman, Gaulish, Greek and Christian influences to this admixture, plus a few centuries of wear and oral distortion, and the original Celtic god concepts are all but completely obscured.

The earliest written fragments of the *Mabinogion* date as recently as the thirteenth century AD, and there is ample evidence that the material had been greatly altered by then to accommodate the prevailing climate of opinion; what were previously immortal or god figures, for example, assumed the characters of historical personages with human properties. Names change from story to story and yet there is a basic continuity in the constancy of the principles they obviously represent.

But even allowing for the absence of a coherent paradigm, the *Mabinogion* still has a great deal to offer in its confirmation of the Irish myths, its profound insight into the Celtic psychology and its hints of a deeper, more esoteric and fundamentally enlightened understanding of cosmic principles.

Scholars are of the opinion that the *Mabinogion* stories were rounded into their present form somewhere between AD 1000 and 1200, but it is generally agreed that there must have been different oral interpretations in times previous. The earliest preserved manuscript fragments can be dated to AD 1225.

In spite of its many inconsistencies, the *Mabinogion* is considered to be a literary masterpiece, its virtues far outweighting its flaws. Its later tales, like the Irish sagas and the Greek heroic themes, tend to wander and in so doing lose focus. Other than where absolutely necessary I shall refrain from describing the heroic exploits when dealing with all these mythological sources as they tend to be over-humanized for one thing, while many of them are totally irrelevant to deeper archetypal and magical themes.

The earliest complete copy of the *Mabinogion* is to be found in the *Red Book of Hergest* (c. AD 1400). An earlier manuscript, *The White Book of Rhydderch* (c. 1325), is apparently incomplete although originally it probably contained all eleven tales. In fact, the *Mabinogion* was not well known, even in Welsh literature, until Lady Charlotte Guest brought out the English version in 1849. It was Lady Charlotte who also provided the title 'Mabinogion', which she arrived at in the following manner: each of the Four Branches ends with a specific phrase 'So ends this Branch of the Mabinogi'. As the Welsh word 'mab' means 'boy', Lady Charlotte concluded that 'mabinogi' was a noun meaning a story for children, with 'mabinogion' therefore being the plural for that word. 'Mabinogion' does not apparently exist in the Welsh language, although it appears once, in error, in the Pwyll, but 'mabinogi' is a genuine Welsh word, designating an account of earlier times or, in the case of an individual, one's childhood years. However the term 'mabinogion' is generally accepted and obviously here to stay.

The four Branches of which it consists are: Pwyll, King of Dyfed; Bran and Branwen; Māth, Son of Māthonwy, and Manawyddan, Son of Llyr. Also included in Jeffrey Gantz's translation are: 'The Dream of Maxen', 'Llud and Llevelys', 'How Culhwch Won Olwen', 'The Dream of Rhonabwy', 'Owein, *or* The Countess of the Fountain', 'Peredur son of Evrawg', and 'Gereint and Enid'.[2]

The Welsh material is neither as comprehensive nor as early as the Irish/Gaelic. The Taliesin saga, for example, which appears in Lady Charlotte Guest's work, is not included in *The Red Book of Hergest* but taken from a manuscript of the late sixteenth or early seventeenth century. The conception and birth adventures of the Bard Taliesin are immensely popular, with much obscure but truly magical poetry being ascribed to the authorship of this mythical personality. That Taliesin represents a profound occult truth there is little doubt, and the power and significance of the poetry that carries his name will be discussed and analysed later in this book (see Chapters 18 and 26).

Inconclusive though the Welsh texts may be there are many elements common to both these and the Irish stories which suggest a single origin, the ethnic overlays becoming apparent when exposed to the light of academic or occult scholarship.

Mythological figures common to all Celtica include the sky god Nudd or Lludd, who surfaces in many recognizable guises. One temple discovered at Lydney in Gloucestershire gave up a bronze plaque in which a representation of this deity is shown encircled by a halo and accompanied by flying spirits and Tritons. Here we have both a Danaan emphasis and a strong nautical connection, with threads stretching back into the distant pre-flood days of Poseidonian placation. An epithet in Welsh legend which means 'Of the Silver Hand' is also to be found in reference to Nudd, although there is apparently no explanation for this in the legend itself. It would seem obvious, therefore, that the Welsh Nudd and the Irish Danaan Nuada are one and the same. We are told that this deity, under the name of Lludd, had a temple on the site of St Paul's in London, the entrance to which, according to Geoffrey of Monmouth, was referred to as *Parth Lludd*, later translated by the Saxons as *Ludes Geat* and now known as Ludgate.[3]

The Welsh Llyr and his son Manawyddan cannot surely be other than the Irish Lir and his son Mananan, marine divinities, all of them. It is interesting to note that Llyd-cester, now Leicester, was once a centre of the worship of Llyr alongside that of the Triple Goddess.

In the third Branch of the *Mabinogion*, which concerns the legends of Māth son of Māthonwy, we encounter the name Llew Llaw Gyffes, interpreted therein as 'The Lion of the Sure Hand' or, according to Robert Graves, who is in no doubt as to the Llew/Lugh connection, 'The Lion with the Steady Hand'. Llew's rapid growth from childhood to adulthood is reminiscent of the Greek Hercules or the young Apollo, while his Leonine appellation suggests Egypto/Atlantean undertones. In his masterpiece, *The White Goddess*, Graves lists a number of towns that owe their names to Llew/Lugh, including Laon, Leyden, Lyons and Carlisle (Caer Lugubalion). His account of Lugh's parentage differs from the generally accepted myth. Instead of seeing him the son of Balor's daughter, Ethlinn (or Ethne) by Cian (Kian), his mother becomes Clothru, a single form of the Triple

Goddesses Eire, Fodhla and Banbha, giving a clear indication of the solar cult rising from the old matriarchal religion and eventually usurping it.[4]

Another Welsh interpretation refers to *Llugh Lamh Fada*, meaning 'of the Long Arm'. Either way, the two deities are undoubtedly one and the same, so one is left wondering if the whole story has no basis in fact and, like similar Egyptian, Greek and Babylonian epics, is purely representative of a cosmological or evolutionary drama in which the participating forces have become personalized into recognizable terms of human reference for communicatory purposes.

The two great families or houses of Welsh and Irish mythology are easily reconcilable. Dôn, the Mother Goddess, and Beli, whose descendants are the Children of Light, equate with the Gaelic Dana and her husband Bilé, the Irish god of Death. Likewise, the Welsh Llyr and the Gaelic Lir also represent the same principle. According to some authorities the gods of the House of Llyr were not so much immortals as an admixture, probably the progeny of those enigmatic couplings involving those whom the Bible describe as the 'Sons of God and the Daughters of Men'. The two families of Dôn and Llyr were united by the marriage of Penardon, a daughter of Dôn, to the old sea god Llyr, signifying, no doubt, the fusion of two different religious systems, if not actually two peoples or cultures.

The Revd Edward Davies, writing in the late eighteenth and early nineteenth centuries, was convinced that Welsh mythology gave clear indications of the Biblical Flood and subsequent arrival on those shores of survivors from the 'old country' to the west, to which the collective unconscious of the Celtic race has ever been urging them to return.[5] Every reader to his or her own persuasion.

The symbology of the White Horse serves as a connecting link between the Gaulish Mother Goddess Epona, Macha of Ulster, Mebh of Connaught and the Welsh Rhiannon, but we will be covering the White Horse connection in more detail in Chapter 8.

The god Artaius, more generally referred to as Arthur, and subsequently designated a mortal king entered the mythological scene later. However, the picture of Arthur as presented in this context is not shared by all, as we shall subsequently see. A simple genealogical map is featured in Part II of this book to give the reader a clearer picture of the mythological background of the archetypes as presented in the *Mabinogion*.

The immortal personage of Gwyn ap Nudd is said to be the one that has truly fired the Celtic imagination and left a lasting impression on the Welsh collective unconscious. Equated with the Irish Finn, Gwyn, a mighty warrior and huntsman, assembles souls of the dead heroes in his shadowy Elysian-like kingdoms. Although a god of Light, Gwyn rules over Hades, his famous combat with Gwynthur ap Griedawl for Creudylad daughter of Lludd, which is renewed every May Day until the end of time, being ever a reminder of the recurring seasonal contest. Gwyn was later named as King of the *Tylwyth Teg*, or Welsh Fairies, in much the same way that the Danaans were allocated Fairy status after the arrival of the Milesians. Graves tells us that there was also a Gwyn cult in pre-Christian Glastonbury where this deity was known as Herne the Hunter, while in Scotland the same archetype went by the name of Arthur!

One of the Welsh Triads mentions that before Britain was inhabited it was called *Clas Myrddin*, Merlin's enclosure. Rolleston quotes an interesting tale of a Greek traveller named Demetrius, who was said to have visited Britain in the first century AD. An island is mentioned in the west, where Kronos was supposed to be imprisoned with his attendant deities, with Briareus keeping watch over him as he slept, 'for sleep was the bond forged for him'. Here we have a Hellenized version of the descent of the sun god into the western sea and his imprisonment there by the powers of darkness, together with his magical powers of light and life. Or dare we dismiss this suggestion and consider this tale as another version of the power of Merlin being buried under a stone, or the might of Arthur and his army secretly sleeping in some hidden cave, to be awakened by ....?

There is something here suggestive of a time capsule that will open when the right signal is given. Then, Merlin will cast aside his rock, Arthur will ride forth fully-armed at the head of his immortal army, the course of the sun will be changed and the yoke of darkness forever cast from this planet. But before I wax too Celtically lyrical I must take my leave of Welsh mythology at this point, to return to it in Part II of this work, when the god-forms of all Celtica will be submitted to occult scrutiny.

Endnotes
1. Peter S. Harper and Eric Sunderland (eds.). *Genetic and Population Studies in Wales.*
2. Gantz, Jeffrey. *The Mabinogion.*
3. Rolleston, T.W. *Myths and Legends of the Celtic Race*, p. 347.
4. Graves, Robert. *The White Goddess.*
5. Davies, Revd Edward. *The Mythology and Rites of the British Druids.*

5. THE CELTIC INFLUENCE IN SCOTLAND

The Belgic invasions appear to have effected considerable changes in the distribution of the earlier Iron Age tribes, forcing numbers of the older peoples to move far north into Scotland and across the water to Ireland. Ptolemy's geography, which was compiled in the second century AD, shows Cornavii on the Welsh Marches and in Sutherland, and Dunmonii in Devon and on the Clyde, neither being areas in which these tribes originated but where they were driven to by the Belgae. A similar fate must have met the Iceni, whose tribal area once extended from Wiltshire to Lincolnshire. T.C. Lethbridge opined that this tribe became the Epidii of Kintyre who were also great horse people, their modern descendants, the MacEacherns, claiming descent from a famous Horse Lord (or Lady). There had also been an immigration from Ireland into Argyll in early Christian times, but this did not, apparently, change the older Celtic beliefs that were established there.

Two miles from Kilberry, on the road to Tarbert, is the seat of Cailleach, onto which people still throw a stone to obtain a wish. Cailleach simply means 'old woman', but in fact what we are dealing with is the Crone aspect of the Triple Goddess. Among other things she controlled the winds, seas and seasons and also kept a beautiful maiden in a cave in Glencoe who ran away with Dairmid (or Dermot), the Gaelic Adonis. The maiden is obviously the New Moon, or her own Maiden aspect. Lethbridge saw her as 'black Annis' of Leicester and Gruagach, the Fair Haired One, which would be her middle-phase aspect.

Two hundred yards from Cailleach's seat is 'Slochd na Chapuill', the Hollow of the Mare, and below this is 'Glac na h'Imuilte', the Hollow of the Struggle. Although described in terms of clans, this struggle was a mythological rather than an historical one and involved one side trying to dismount Cailleach from her horse while the opposing side endeavoured to prevent this. The Celtic Horse Ritual is obviously inferred by this legend, Cailleach being the Scottish Epona, or an aspect of the Earth Mother, without whose blessing seamen could not double the Mull of Kintyre. This belief is further reinforced by the name given to the huge mounds that face this place, the Paps of Jura. To the north lies the whirlpool of Corryvreckan, where the Cailleach was said to wash her blanket.[1]

At the beginning of the Bronze Age, around 1800 BC, the British Isles was dominated by a race known as the Beaker people, and it is with these people that many of the old Scottish prehistoric sites are associated, rather than the Celts who arrived on the scene much later. The Beaker people were related by culture, if not by blood, to the Zoned-Beaker-Proto-Celts of central Europe, to whom Alpine ancestry is usually ascribed. These carried with them a pronounced form of religious worship which involved a triple-aspected Goddess attended by two males, one of whom was usually portrayed as a solar deity, and the other a god of the underworld skilled in magic.

The so-called 'Pictish' stone carvings are considered among the most interesting antiquities in Britain. There are a large number of these which are mostly carved on monoliths and found in all areas of Scotland. Their dating is still debatable, but their contents are of considerable interest to the student of the early religions of these isles. Although Christian symbols often appear among them, these were probably added later. Sickle Moons are the most numerous, and accord with similar sigils to be found on hill figures of Celtic and pre-Celtic origin throughout the whole of the British Isles. Sun discs are also in evidence, and many representations of animals notably the horse, horned deer, bull, boar, serpent, fish, eagle and hound. Although the Christians make claim to the fish symbol it must be remembered that it was also sacred to Astarte and Poseidon. All the other animals belong to the Moon Goddess, the boar, in particular, being sacred to the Cailleach, which is why many Scottish people eschew the eating of pork.

Among the Picts, the descent of rule through the female line apparently remained the custom for several centuries after the arrival of Christianity and traces of mother-rule are to be found among the people of Fife to this day.[2] As the Romans never succeeded in conquering this part of Scotland, the Scottish Druids were neither suppressed nor exterminated, and so were able to carry on a form of the old Celtic religion until, in later times, it became clothed in the dubious garb of what was erroneously referred to as 'witchcraft' and bitterly persecuted.

Scholars like Lethbridge have frequently questioned whether mythological beasts such as the Highland 'Water-Horse' were simply idle tales of imagination or whether they had, in fact, originated from descriptions given by earlier peoples who were familiar with, say, the hippopotamus. Perhaps they were even folk memories handed down from a time when a different kind of beast, the unicorn, for example, might have roamed the Earth.

It was the Belgae who apparently introduced the greater importance of male divinities into Scotland, and only the matrilineal Picts held strongly to the old, matriarchal ways. A Hebridean dance was formerly performed at wakes, symbolizing the dying year and the reviving spring. The English call this dance 'the Carlin of the Mill Dust', but Carlin is only another translation of Cailleach. The Mari Llwyd, with its horse's skull, which appeared in houses in South Wales on New Years's Eve was Cailleach's mare, Epona's mount, the White Horse of Uffington, as are all the hobby horses, hob-knobs, hoden-horses and their kin that are to be found the length and breadth of the country.

The worship of Cailleach covered the whole of the Highlands of Scotland where her people were the Caldones or Kaledonioi. She equates with Yellow Muillearteach and the Gruagach in the Triple Goddess context. The Cailleach has a blue-black face, one eye in the middle of her forehead and projecting teeth, somewhat after the style of the Indian Kali. She carries a hammer and thunderbolts, and is protectress of horses, deer, pigs, goats, cats and snakes, a sort of female version of Thor, if you like! Her husband is the sea god Mananan/Poseidon, which could account for her horse association. She is also said to be able to turn herself into a stone. The Gruagach, although fair of hair is also a destroyer, but there is a mystery concealed in the symbology of the destroyer archetype, which is concerned with the ever-changing pattern of evolution.

Black Annis, or Cat Anna of Leicester, was also a goddess of destruction, while partaking of a similar description to the Cailleach. She is said to be connected with the Irish Dana and the old Ephesian Diana. Annis was a tree goddess, the oak being particularly sacred to her. When the religion of the Goddess conceded to the Patrist onslaught which eventually overtook both religious and secular affairs, the attributes of these old goddesses were transferred to the gods who replaced them, in this case Zeus, whose cult appropriated the Oak Tree as its Oracle.

Another Scottish goddess was Nemon, or Nementona, who was also worshipped in the west of England, Ireland and Gaul. Nemon was the 'Pearl of Heaven', another name for the Moon and her husband was Neit, an Irish god of war and slaughter. Lethbridge sees her as Adraste, to whom Boudicca (Boadicea) sacrificed female captives, who probably shared some common origin with the Greek Nemesis, and conjectures that it was to her that white oxen were originally sacrificed when the mistletoe was found growing on the oak. Her association with the Sacred Groves goes back further than that of the male gods who later usurped her worship.

We may gather from the aforegoing that Scotland does not possess the same kind of mythological cycle as Ireland and Wales, but there is ample evidence there of both Celtic and pre-Celtic custom and worship for those with the time and interest to seek it. Any religion is naturally coloured by the emphasis prevailing in the relative ethos at the time of its introduction thereto. The Pictish legends that are written in stone and orally transmitted show clearly the effect of both Bronze and Iron Age cultures on their basic religious leanings. Later, when Christianity crossed the border, it too made a rather distinctive impression as the tales of the old Scottish saints bear witness. But beneath each overlay the intrinsic racial clock ticks quietly away, absorbing the lessons and influences of each time zone as it comes and goes. And so it is, of course, with every nation, tribe and ethos, which is why the same truth wears many national garbs, a fact that should not, if we possess any wisdom and insight at all, detract from its reality.

Endnotes
1. Lethbridge, T.C. *Gogmagog*, p. 73.
2. Ibid. Lethbridge, p. 136.

6. THE CONTINENTAL LINK

The old European Celtdom left its imprints on many parts of the continent, not the least of which was Brittany, once the Gaul about which Caesar commented so liberally. As no ancient Breton literature has been passed down to us, however, our only source of Celtic reference lies with French writers and it must therefore be borne in mind that there is some degree of speculation involved.

The Anglo-Norman poetess who wrote under the name of Marie de France circa AD 1150 produced, among her other works, a number of 'Lais' or tales which she is careful to emphasize were translated or adapted from Breton sources. Some of these, she claimed, were repeated exactly from the original:

> Les contes que jo sai lais,
> Dunt le Bretun unt fait les lais,
> Vos conterai assez briefment,
> Et cief [sauf] di cest coumencement
> Selunc la lettre è l'escriture.[1]

Most of her references are concerned with the Arthurian period and while certain details from the Welsh legends receive a degree of confirmation others appear in a different light coloured, no doubt, by the Bretons themselves and the events which took place subsequent to the dilution of the

Celtic influence which must have followed in the wake of the many wars and invasions. It would be correct to say that there is evidence to suggest that a somewhat diffused but nevertheless developed body of chivalric legends which feature the character of Arthur existed in Brittany and were transmitted orally, if not in writing, over the centuries. Rolleston is of the opinion that the 'Lais' of Marie de France point strongly to Brittany as the true cradle of the Arthurian saga, or certainly its chivalrous and romantic aspects. But as we hope to unfold in this book, with the Arthur archetype we are dealing with something more universal and less parochial than might be suspected at first glance.

Two other Bretonic sources remain for us to consider. The work of the French poet Chrétien de Troyes, whose Breton translations began in 1165 and who is said to be responsible for bringing the Arthurian saga into the poetic literature of Europe and giving it the outline and character that was eventually accepted. One of his works on Tristan was lost, but the introduction of Lancelot of the Lake into the story is attributed to him, and he wrote a *Conte del Graal* in which the Grail legend and Percival make a very early, if not initial appearance. The tale, however, was never completed and one is not told what the Grail really was. Another work entitled *Erec* contained the story of Geraint and Enid.

Chrétien's sources were most certainly Breton. Troyes is in Champagne, which was united to Blois in 1019 by Eudes, Count of Blois, and following a period of dispossession by Count Theobald de Blois was reunited again in 1128. There were close connections between Blois and Brittany as history confirms, and the suggestion is that many of the Breton 'Lais' found their way into the Court at Blois through visiting minstrels.

There would appear to be little doubt regarding the Breton contribution to the Arthurian saga with its Round Table and chivalric institutions that were later ascribed to Arthur's Court at Caerleon on Usk. So in order to understand the true nature of Arthur and all that his cult implies, the occultist must also take the Chivalrous French and Troubadour overlays (or underlays, as the case may be) into consideration, in addition to the ethnic colonizations of those other nations in whose folk literature these tales have featured prominently.

Our final Breton reference concerns one Gautier Denain,

who gives as his authority for the stories of Gawain one by the name of Bleheris, a poet 'born and bred in Wales'. Scholars believe this past Bardic personage to be one and the same as the *famosus ille fabulator, Bledhericus* mentioned by Giraldus Cambrensis.[2]

The Celts left a legacy of place-names throughout Europe and the British Isles. To cite them all would occupy too much space in this book, but here are a few examples. The word *dunum*, as in Dundalk, Dunrobin, etc., means a fortress or castle. It occurs frequently in France: e.g. *Lug-dunum* (Lyons); *Viro-dunum* (Verdun); in Switzerland: *Minno-dunum* (Moudon); *Eburo-dunum* (Yverdon); and in The Netherlands: *Lug-dunum* (Leyden). In Britain the Celtic term was often changed by simply converting it into *castra*, thus *Camulo-dunum* became Colchester, and *Brano-dunum*, Brancaster. In Germany the modern names Kempton, Karnberg and Leignitz were respectively *Cambo-dunum, Carro-dunum*, and *Lugi-dunum*, while we have *Singi-dunum* (Belgrade) and *Novi-dunum* (Isaktscha) in Romania — one could go on for pages. Major cities like Paris, Milan and Vienna, and rivers such as the Thames, Seine, Rhine and Danube can all lay claim to Celtic linguistic roots.[3]

In more recent times, researchers studying the history and background of the Knights Templars and Cathars have proffered some interesting observations. David Wood, for example, pursuing the theories of the Baigent/Leigh/Lincoln controversial book *The Holy Blood and the Holy Grail*, postulates a Celtic link with the standing stones at Narbonne, on the site of the old Celtic capital of Narbo. In his recent work *Genisis* which is concerned with the investigation of the Renne le Château area of southern France, he supplies a copy of the Henri Boudet map of 'Celtic Rennes', showing the concentration of standing stones in the area.[4] Whether or not these were actually erected by the Celts is open to conjecture, however, although we do know that the Celtic influence was very strong in those parts.

There is obviously much that could be added to our knowledge of Celtic beliefs and origins from other European sources, but this would require a series of books to do it justice. And so we are left with the myths and legends, so many of which have been severely corroded by the acid of time and the chemistry of prejudice. But then is this not the same with most, if not all of the truly interesting early cultures?

Endnotes
1. Rolleston, T.W. *Myths and Legends of the Celtic Race*, p. 339.
2. Ibid. Rolleston, p. 342.
3. Ibid. Rolleston, pp. 27/28.
4. Wood, David. *Genisis*, p. 230.

7. THE EDDIC LITERATURE

My search for Celtic clues among the myths and legends of the world has led me into many avenues of enquiry, some less obvious than others. A few years ago I came across a book entitled *The British Edda*, by Dr L.A. Waddell. The book was published in 1930 and gives no indication of the author's background and credentials other than supplying an impressive and scholarly list of his other works which include such titles as *The Makers of Civilization in Race and History, Phoenician origins of the Britons, Scots and Anglo-Saxons, Indo-Sumerian Seals Deciphered, A Sumer-Aryan Dictionary, Lhasa and its Mysteries* and many more, all of which are supported by excellent press notices from leading publications of the day.

Since it is my policy to leave no stone unturned in pursuit of truth, and believing in the right of every reader to choose his or her own path to this end I am prepared to give the man a hearing, but wish to make it quite clear that in examining Waddell's Sumerian setting of the Celto-Arthurian saga, I am neither setting out to prove or disprove the former existence of a British King named Arthur, but simply to imply, from information gleaned, the titular inferences contained in both the name itself and the nomenclatures of others attendant upon the Arthurian personage.

As his source of authority, Waddell draws upon a collection of disjointed lays and fragments known as *The*

Edda, or *Poetical Edda*. Although the Eddic Epic was previously thought to be the exclusive heritage of the Teutonic and Scandinavian peoples, the leading deities and heroes mentioned therein are referred to as 'Goths', which effects an immediate link with the Celts, one race having influenced the other as we have already established. The scene of the Edda is, we are told, located in Asia Minor, centring at Troy and Cappadocia, traditional home of St George. In *The British Edda* Waddell thoroughly substantiates his conclusions, but his detailed scholarship would involve more verbiage than I am able to spare for the purely historical side of my own line of enquiry, so it will be up to any reader whose interest is aroused by the ensuing information to pursue Waddell's work for him or herself. I will, however, try to condense his theories inasmuch as they provide a source of illumination on early Celtic origins.

Waddell first observed the Eastern connection with the Eddic literature while studying Hindu mythology and history during a stay in India. He was struck by the similarity between the name and exploits of the Eddic Eindri (Thor, also called Andvara) with his bolt and mace, and Indra of the Indian Veda who is also described as tall, fair, invincible and armed with a bolt. Both were red-bearded sky gods of giant proportions who led the Aryans to victory and fought against evil serpents and dragons of similar name. Of course, there were many other early deities who also tackled monsters: Zeus, Apollo, Horus and Marduk, for example, while the George and Dragon episode of Christian myth was undoubtedly borrowed from these earlier sources.

Links between Norse and Indo-Aryan mythology would appear to be unmistakable, and Thor's connection with the Grail legends bear much similarity to the Arthurian cycle. Waddell, however, draws a clear line of distinction between the English Christian King Arthur of popular legend and the earlier appellation from which he purports the name originated. Thor's Eddic title of Her-Thor is equated with Ar-Thur, 'Her' and 'Ar' being dialectic forms of the same root, and meaning 'Aryan'. In fact, his in-depth study of the early Sumerian culture of ancient Mesopotamia, said to have been the cradle of civilization, reveals some striking facts.

The Sumerians, history tells us, spread their civilizing influence to the lands of Egypt, Asia Minor, Crete, India and the prehistoric Danube valley of Europe. Their first King apparently bore the name of Indara, Dar-Danos or King Tur, from which the name Thor was derived. This monarch, who was later deified by the Sumerians, is represented as slaying a destructive serpent-dragon as early as 3380 BC. His warrior clans were known as 'Guts' or 'Goths', and their likenesses, which are chiselled on stones and sacred seals, show them wearing horned hats or head-dresses after the style of the later European Goths, Nordic people and ancient Britons.

Nor is Waddell the only scholar to note the similarities between the Nordic and Aryan-Indian pantheons. The Larousse *Encyclopedia of Mythology* cites many more examples of divinities shared between the two races: Varuna/Woden, Mitra/Tiw, for example, which are conclusively suggestive of a single origin. The first page of the section of Celtic Mythology (p. 235) leads with a photograph of detail on the Gundestrup Bowl (National Museum of Denmark, Copenhagen) which portrays the horned god Cernunnos surrounded by animals and grasping a ram-headed serpent. Somewhere in the distant past, a singular event would appear to have left its imprint on all the peoples who witnessed and recorded it, whatever it might have been, leaving their successors to render their own, doubtlessly embellished versions of the tale.

Taking into account the many mistranslations of the Eddic material, and in particular what Waddell refers to as 'Snorri's serious perversions of the theme', in the face of evidence from over a hundred ancient Sumerian, Hittite and Cappadocian Seals, sculptures and engravings, he was left in no doubt that the Edda was an historical and traditional text and not a mythological one. How he arrived at these conclusions and the material upon which he based them is contained in his book.[1]

According to the Eddic texts, roughly around 4000 BC the legends and beliefs of the Hindus and Aryans were basically identical, and it is only after then that the rift commenced. A race of tall, fair people whose menfolk were either clean-shaven or red-bearded suddenly put in an appearance. Upon their arrival in the Mesopotamian region these strangers encountered a cruel and barbaric race whom they proceeded to instruct in the arts and virtues of civilization. They abolished blood sacrifices, instituted marriage, taught agriculture and husbandry and introduced the religion of their god Asar or Osiris, Lord of Light and Justice who, with his Consort Aset (Isis), later became identified with their King-Leader. They also advocated a policy of pacifism which, no doubt, did not go down too well in those times and places. It seems to me that we are hearing the old Atlantean tale told in a different setting, or am I imagining things? David Wood seems to be in no doubt that the Celts and ancient Egyptians were both descended from the same root race, while I recall attending a talk in London some years ago when the speaker described the Celts as 'a group of Atlanteans escaping the Flood who settled in the Danube region'! Is there anything new under the sun?

Waddell is blatantly outspoken regarding the Adamic Biblical myth which he describes as 'spitefully mutilated' and containing 'Semitic calumnies against the ancient Sumerians', while the original Aryan/Sumerian Arthur, his consort and his people are spoken of in glowing Promethean terms as the progenitors of civilization.[2] Guinevere, we are told, was another name for Eve, while the son of this Sumerian Arthur and Guinevere (Her-Thor and Gunn-Ifa) was named Gunn, Cain, Gawain, Mikli or Miok, and later adopted by Christianity as the Archangel Michael or Mikaal. This same Miok did battle with the evil Loki (Lucifer) in much the way that Horus did with Set.

Waddell's *Edda* introduces us to many other recognizable characters from the Arthurian legend and other mythological sagas, including the Christian Bible, which he conveniently places into his own Sumer/Aryan context. The Arthur figure, he tells us later became deified, appearing in various pantheons as Indra, Zeus, Thor, Lugh, Mikaal and St George.

Whether it was, in fact, ancient Sumeria which gave birth to the culture of the Indian subcontinent or the other way round we will leave for the scholars to debate and science to prove or disprove in the fullness of time as the case may be. Students of the occult would no doubt distinguish two different cultures as contributing to the myths of the ancient past in the forms of the Mu/Lemurian from the east and the Atlantean from the west but, as we are constantly being informed, our views are purely conjectural so until the riddle of time-probing is finally resolved we are stranded on the storm-dashed rocks of historical scholarship with its accompanying prejudices.

As this chapter has been concerned with titles, and those of Arthur in particular, it is worth mentioning that there is another school of thought which designates the name Arthur as a derivative of Arcturus, and therefore a titular appellation of the Star Priests of Babylonia. Names similarly structured such as the Greek Artemis, the Celtic goddess Artio who was worshipped in the neighbourhood of Berne by the Helvetii, and the Christian St Artemidorus come from the same root, which has 'bear' associations. Arcturus is the brightest star in the constellation of Bootes, approximately thirty-six light years from Earth. Its name is derived from the Greek 'Arktouros', 'guardian of the bear', from its position behind the tail of Ursa Major (arktos — bear, ouros — guard). At Athens the little handmaidens of Artemis were called *arktoi*, 'she-bears', although the Greek scholar Professor Carl Kerenyi insists that Artemis herself was never associated with the bear, her original symbolic animal being a Lion. When the Greek gods were said to have flown to Egypt, hotly pursued by the monster Typhon, Artemis transformed herself into a cat and took refuge in the Moon. It was her much loved companion, Kallisto, who finally appeared in the sky as the Great Bear following her coupling with Zeus, to whom she bore a son, Arkas, the first ancestor of the inhabitants of Arcadia, or according to another source, the twins, Arkas and Pan. Either way we have the Arcadian connection between the Milesian Celts and their suggested Greek origins which cannot be ignored.

Endnotes
1. Waddell, L.A. *The British Edda*, Introduction, p. xlvii.
2. Ibid. Waddell. Introduction, p. lxxiii.

8. HILL FIGURES — THE CELTIC CONNECTION

Hill figures being so much a part of the British national heritage the question is bound to arise as to whether these do, in fact, constitute part of the Celtic legacy to these isles or whether they originated in an earlier age. Of course, many of these figures are fairly recent additions to our landscape but there are several that would appear to have roots somewhere in the distant Celtic past. Another fact to consider is that among the more recent appearances there are a few that have been cut in places where, according to local legend, something similar did exist in far-gone days.

The figure that makes the most frequent appearances is undoubtedly that of the white horse, so a magical examination of its significance, and the deities associated with it is called for. Two divinities from the Greek pantheon spring to mind: Demeter, who was pursued by the old sea-god Poseidon and in order to escape his attentions disguised herself as a mare and mingled among the horses of Oncios the Arcadian. Not to be outdone, Poseidon effected the guise of a stallion and covered her, which resulted in the birth of the wild horse Arion. Demeter as a mare goddess was widely worshipped under the name of Epona, or the 'Three Eponae' among the Gallic Celts, and remnants of this cult were to be found in Celtic outposts for several centuries after their decline as a world power.

This is borne out in an interesting account rendered by

Giraldus Cambrensis in his *Topography of Ireland*, where the relics of the old Horse Cult were still surviving as late as the twelfth century. He describes the crowning of an Irish petty-king at Tyrconnell, a preliminary to which was his symbolic birth from a white mare. The man was obliged to crawl naked towards her on all fours as though he were her foal, after which the poor beast was slaughtered and the pieces boiled in a cauldron. The man then entered the cauldron and partook of its contents, after which he stood on an inauguration stone where he was presented with a white wand and obliged to turn about three times from left to right and three times from right to left 'in honour of the Trinity', says the text. But we know better, of course, the mare goddess being an aspect of the old Triple Matrist divinity.

Poseidon was the other Greek deity closely associated with the horse. In addition to his aforementioned cohabitation with Demeter he also seduced Medusa in Athene's Temple. Infuriated by such profanation, Athene turned Medusa's hair into snakes, and when Perseus later decapitated her the warrior Chrysaor and the beautiful winged horse Pegasus sprang from the wound. According to Hermes Trismegistus the horse represents purified passion and, as the Goddess Athene is the epitome of reason and self-control, the moral of this tale must surely be obvious.

The Horse Cult, or a version of it, would appear to have been around prior to the arrival of the Celts, however, the only human figure represented in what survives of British Old Stone Age art being a man wearing a horse mask carved in bone, which was found in a Derbyshire pin-hole cave, a remote ancestor, no doubt, of the modern "obby 'oss' character.[1]

The horse goddess also surfaces as the Celtic Rhiannon in *The Romance of Pwyll, King of Dyfed*. When first setting eyes upon Rhiannon Pwyll fell in love with her and pursued her on his fastest horse, but (in the original story) she took the form of a white mare, allowing herself to be overtaken only when it suited her. Celtic horse associations being therefore indisputable, a closer examination of hill figures, and horses in particular, is called for. The following information may prove of some value to those readers who, after absorbing the contents of this book, might see fit to pursue the Celtic magical path.

From Kate Bergamar's comprehensive booklet, *Discovering Hill Figures*, I have compiled a list of the better known ones giving the dates they were cut, and separating the more recent additions from the genuinely historical sites which are suggestive of some sacred or magical past.

Whipsnade Lion — 1935; White Horse of Strichen — after 1773; White Stag of Strichen — 1870; Inkpen Horse — 1868; Plymouth Giants (now vanished, some records mention 1529, but the originals could have been earlier); Osmington Horse — date unknown, but could possibly be early;. Woolbury Horse — eighteenth century; Wye Crown — 1902; Watlington White Mark — 1764; Kilburn White Horse — 1857; Pewsey White Horse — 1937, but scoured over an earlier model; Marlborough Horse — 1804; Hackpen Horse — 1838; Devizes Horse — 1835; Broad Towen Horse — 1864; Alton Barnes Horse — 1812; Litlington Horse — 1838; Bledlow Cross — 1787 and Cherhill Horse — 1870 officially, but thereby lies a tale which I shall shortly relate.

This leaves us with the following antiquities to investigate: the Uffington White Horse, Whiteleaf Cross, Gogmagog Giants, Cerne Abbas Giant, the Red Horse of Tysoe (now extinct but the original was circa the Uffington Horse's period), the Long Man of Wilmington and the Westbury Horse.

Let us start with the White Horse of Uffington. Legend has it that if one stands on the Eye with closed eyes, turns round three times deoshins (clockwise), and makes a wish it will be granted within a '7'. Another oral tradition tells us that all places that fall on points calculated in multiples of seven from the Eye are of mystical significance or related to Earth energies.

It is interesting to note that the numbers '3' and '7' are sacred to Jupiter and Neptune. They are also said to be the sacred occult numbers of Britain inherited, no doubt, from our Celtic ancestors who used the triadic principle as a form of expression both secularly and sacerdotally. Neptune is, of course, Poseidon, Lord of the Sea, and arcane tradition holds that in the latter days of Atlantis the High Priests, in their efforts to placate the ever-invading tides that were eventually to inundate their land, gave great heed to the worship of this deity which included paying due deference to the symbology associated with his cult — the white horse!

For those who have not visited the Uffington site, it lies some quarter of a mile north-east of the Iron Age Fort of Uffington and two miles south of Uffington Village. Just below the north escarpment of the Berkshire Downs, about five hundred feet above the Vale of White Horse, the Horse is to be seen facing north-west on the thirty-degree slope. Considered by experts to be one of the most exciting monuments in Britain it faces the equally famous Dragon's Hill, where St George is said to have slain his notorious fire-breathing adversary. On the hilltop, where the Dragon's blood was supposedly spilled, no grass ever grows. To the west the land appears as a set of strange glacial terraces known as 'The Giant's Stairs' while the road up to the Castle sweeps across a deep combe known as The Manger. Half a mile westward lies the prehistoric chambered barrow of Wayland's Smithy which is linked to the Castle by a ridgeway. In fact we have at this site every indication of the Celtic influence superimposing, perhaps, on an even earlier cult.

Little is known of the origins of this hill figure. Who made it, how and why are still unanswered questions as far as the experts are concerned. There have even been suggestions that it is not a horse at all but a representation of a Dragon, or some strange feline. The first record of it comes to us from the reign of Henry II when the Manor of Sparsholt was described as 'near the place which is commonly called 'White Horse Hill'. By the fourteenth century the name 'Vale of the White Horse' was firmly established when a manuscript, now at Corpus Christi College Cambridge, included the Horse as one of the wonders of Britain second only to Stonehenge. By the seventeenth century scholarly interest was aroused and the arguments began. In his *Ballad of the White Horse* Chesterton makes King Alfred, who was apparently born near Wantage, scour a far older horse rather than create a new one as a memorial of his victory over the Danes in AD 871:

> Before the Gods that made the Gods
> Had seen their sunrise pass,
> The White Horse of the White Horse Vale
> Was cut out of the grass.[2]

In its official statement, the Ministry of Public Works suggests that it was probably made by the Belgae. It is in the non-representational tradition of Celtic art and mention is made of a strong resemblance to the stylized horses on the reverse of Celtic imitations of the gold staters of Philip of Macedon. These coins were first imported from Gaul but were later struck in Britain with a design of horses with beaked heads and disjointed bodies that faced to the right. Two horses, strongly reminiscent of the Uffington Horse, appear on *repoussé* buckets, one from Marlborough (now in the Devizes Museum) and the other from Aylesford (British Museum). The overall consensus of opinion is that the Horse was cut by the Celts in the first century BC.

As the Horse was obviously meant to be seen from a distance, it would seem logical to assume it to be a cult figure or tribal symbol. Animal worship was much favoured in the Iron Age, the horse being a particular favourite. It is some 360 feet long which figure may in itself have some magical significance representing, perhaps, the Druidic Circle or the 360-day cycle enjoyed on this planet prior to the orbital shift that brought about the inclusion of the extra five intercalary days. This would either suggest that the originators were familiar with the old Atlanto/Egyptian legends (see Chapter 9) or that the site itself, if not the Horse, actually went back earlier than might at first be suspected and was simply utilized by the Celts in the same way that they appropriated Stonehenge.

Local superstition says that the Horse is slowly moving up the hill, and although official photographs do show shadowy lines beneath the present outline there is no firm evidence to support this idea. Another tradition is that the shoes of the Horse are made by Wayland himself at his nearby smithy, in the Scandinavian legend Wayland having actually owned a white horse. The service of the smith was available for any traveller in need who cared to tie up his horse at the entrance of the smithy, place a groat on the capstone, and be on his way. On his return he would find the work completed for him.

Whiteleaf Cross is situated on a steep slope of the Chilterns facing west over the Vale of Aylesbury, near Monks Risborough. The Icknield Way passes below it, which could be significant as far as the Celtic connection is concerned.

Celtic roads were not, apparently, the unmade trackways we are led to believe, as the Celts were skilled charioteers. It can be seen from Headington Hill, Oxford and according to some authorities is also visible from Uffington Castle some thirty miles away. Its origins are obscure. In his book *Chiltern Country*, H.J. Massingham equated it with the Uffington Horse, the Long Man of Wilmington and the Cerne Abbas Giant as regards dating. He saw it as an astrological or phallic monument of the Bronze Age. It was latterly attributed to a religious order of which existence there is no clear record, and in a charter of AD 903 reference is made to a boundary mark in the vicinity of Whiteleaf known as Wayland's Stock, approached by a paved way. It is generally thought that the original phallic symbol was later shaped into a cross by the monks. As far as Celtica is concerned, this one, we feel, gets a plus.

The Gogmagog Giants were excavated in recent years by the late T.C. Lethbridge whose book *Gogmagog, The Buried Gods*, is a must for anyone interested in old sites. Lethbridge uncovered a series of huge figures including a Goddess mounted on a horse, a Warrior with sword uplifted, and a Solar God, each complete with symbol. Lethbridge was quite convinced of the Celtic nature of these discoveries and writes with considerable detail about the attributes and representations of the Triple Goddess, her solar mate, and the God of the Underworld, who together formed the Sacred Five of Celtic mysticism. Lethbridge dates the construction of the Iron Age fort at Wandlebury and start of the Horse Goddess Ritual Festival by the Iceni as circa 200 BC. Around 50 BC when the two male giants were added, the Iceni were displaced by the Belgic Catuvellauni, although in Lethbridge's opinion there was no evidence to suggest that Wandlebury itself was occupied by the Belgae. So while the site as a whole has not been established as being earlier than 300 BC the pagan sanctity of the place is unquestionable.

The figure of the Cerne Giant rests on Giant Hill, a quarter of a mile north-west of Cerne Abbas and eight miles north of Dorchester, and faces west. Behind the Giant is a rectangular enclosure known locally as the Frying Pan or Trendle which was the scene of maypole celebrations at Midsummer for centuries, and doubtless earlier fertility rites. One legend tells of how the people of Cerne drew the figure of the Giant around the body of a real giant whom they killed as he laid sleeping on the hillside after a heavy meal of their sheep. Another makes him a devourer of maidens while a third maintains that a girl who sleeps on the Giant will have many children. So strong is the fertility association that childless couples are still known to visit the Giant in the hope of attracting his energies.

According to William of Malmesbury, Cerne was the home of a particularly stubborn brand of paganism which suggests to us that the belief in the efficacy of the Giant probably lasted well into the Christian period. Since the Giant is near the Abbey, attempts have been made to connect it with the monks, but these have been denied. However, there must have been some strong reason why they did not destroy such a blatantly obvious pagan object, and it would seem that they were not averse to hedging their bets, as records tell that in 1268 the monks of Lanercost made a fertility figure of the Greek god Priapus for the local people whose cattle were diseased. Attempts were made to Christianize the old fellow in 789 when someone tried to scour the letters 'IHS' between his knees! In 1764 it was decided that the figure might represent Hercules, which view has been adopted by the National Trust and included in their Handbook. The club and other attributes reinforce this theory, the form being typical of Romano/British art, examples of similar figures having been found on pottery and altars of the period. A revival of the Hercules Cult took place at the end of the second century AD so there could be some Celtic connection here.

The Long Man of Wilmington is seen on the north face of Windover Hill, three miles north of Eastbourne and one mile south of the main Hastings–Lewes Road. It faces slightly east of north on the steep slope behind the village of Wilmington. Nothing is known of the history of this Long Man, which has also been known by the names of The Lanky Man and the Green Man, the latter being highly significant from a magical viewpoint. Unlike the muscular Cerne Giant the figure is slim and athletic, after the style of Hermes or Mercury. There have been many fanciful ideas as to its identity, Mercury, Mohammed, St Paul, a Roman soldier and a Saxon haymaker among them. A local legend tells how two giants once lived on Windover Hill and Firle Beacon, but they quarrelled, stones were thrown, the Windover Giant was killed and the figure lies where he fell. Flinders Petrie saw him as the Hindu deity Varuna opening the Gates of Heaven which would accord with the key motif so often encountered in this type of Celtic presentation, suggesting a Guardian or Keeper. The figure of a rooster is said to have originally been seen to the right of the Long Man around 1870 which apparently gave rise to the St Paul and Mohammed theories, both of whom included the cockerel in their personal symbologies. Saxon and Roman artefacts have apparently been found in the area so it would not be out of order to consider a stong, albeit later, Celtic influence than, say, that of Uffington.

No trace is now to be seen of the Red Horse of Tysoe, but it was eight miles from Banbury where the Banbury–Stratford-on-Avon road descends the Edgehill escarpment at Sun Rising Inn near Lower or Temple Tysoe and overlooking the village. There are many stories about how the original Horse was restored in 1461 to commemorate the Earl of Warwick's horse which fell in the battle of Towton in Yorkshire, but it is generally believed that it was after the style of the Uffington model, and therefore of definite Celtic origin. An investigator, who is both an archaeologist and an occultist whom I know personally as thoroughly reliable, has verified its antiquity, so it is certainly worth investigating from a magical standpoint.

And lastly we have the Westbury Horse, which is cut on the steep slope of Bratton Down about two miles from Westbury and one mile south-west of the village of Bratton. Above is Bratton Camp, an Iron Age fort with an earlier long barrow within its fortifications.

Lethbridge has a lot to say about this Horse, and *Gogmagog* contains a sketch taken from an aerial photograph of the 'phantom Horse of Bratton' close behind the existing model.[3] The original Horse was rather different from the one we see today. It had a long, heavy body and short legs. Both ears were shown but only one eye, placed oddly below the left ear. It wore a saddle cloth with two crescent-shaped marks and was clearly intended to look like some antique or mythical beast. Strangest of all was the tail, which curved upwards in a slim, reptilian way and ended in a forked tip. Lethbridge believes that this Horse, and those of Tysoe and Uffington, might not have been horses at all in the true sense. The new Horse was cut in 1853 but not over the old one, as

Lethbridge's photograph shows. A Mr Gee, steward to Lord Abingdon, remodelled it on Stubbsian lines, the older horse having in some way irritated him. The site is considered to be very ancient, however, and the original Horse, which was probably dedicated to the Triple Goddess in her three lunar aspects, was of the same period as Uffington or even earlier.

In spite of its more recent addition to the White Horse Stable, having been cut around 1780, the proximity of the Cherhill Horse to Silbury Hill raises a few questions. Its creator was a Dr Christopher Alsop, known as the 'mad doctor' because of his interest in white horses. Now did Dr Alsop know something that we do not? Perhaps a genuinely old Horse had existed there centuries earlier which he had learned about during his intensive studies of the subject. My reason for asking this concerns an experience I underwent in the company of four other people, when passing the present Cherhill Horse one dark and stormy night.

I was travelling in the back seat of a car that was being driven by the author, columnist and dream expert Nerys Dee. Two other ladies and a man were also in the car, making five of us in all. Just as we were passing the Horse, which was to our right, a strange apparition of a giant bird of pterodactyl-like proportions, seemed to emerge from the very hill itself, fly across our path and vanish into the darkness to the left of us. Naturally we were all mystified.

But as if that wasn't enough, as we proceeded on our journey, just as we were passing Silbury Hill, the figure of a man stepped out from the side of the road straight in front of the car. We were all able to see his apparel, if not his face, quite clearly illuminated in the glare of the headlights. His attire was more in keeping with that of either the Bronze Age or Iron Age and bore no resemblance to any clothing worn over the last few centuries. Nerys slammed on the brakes as hard as she could and the car skidded to an abrupt halt. She had actually felt the thud of impact as we hit the figure, so we all leapt out, anxious to help the poor victim in whatever way we could. BUT THERE WAS NOTHING AND NO ONE THERE! The road was absolutely empty, nor was there even a footprint on the wet tarmac. Nerys was naturally very shaken and it was suggested that we all seek the warmth and refreshment of the next hostelry down the road to calm our nerves and, perhaps, talk the matter over. When we arrived at the next inn we must have looked pretty shaken, as a couple of local men seated in the bar asked if we were all right. But before we could explain what had happened they were joined by a very chatty colleague who greeted us with the opening remark, 'From your faces, I'd say you'd seen 'ee up the road, no doubt. Well, you and plenty of others so don't let it worry you, 'ee's always about on a bad night like this.' Needless to say we made no comment but drank our coffee and hastily went on our way.

One should not forget that the word nightmare literally means 'Night Mare'. Robert Graves writes:

If the visitant is Nightmare, the poet will recognize her by the following signs. She will appear as a small, mettlesome mare, not more than thirteen hands high, of the breed familiar from the Elgin Marbles: cream coloured, clean limbed, with a long head, bluish eye, flowing mane and tail. Her nine-fold will be nine fillies closely resembling her, except that their hooves are of ordinary shape whereas hers are divided into five toes like those of Julius Caesar's charger. Around her neck hangs a shining poitrel of the sort known to archaeologists as *lunula*, or little moon: a thin disc of Wicklow gold cut in crescent shape with the horns expanded and turned on edge, fastened together behind her arching neck with a braid of scarlet and white linen. As Gwion says of her in a passage from his *Song Of The Horses*, which had been included by mistake in the *Cad Goddeu* (lines 206–209) and which is intended for the mouth of the White Goddess herself:

> Handsome is the yellow horse,
> But a hundred times better
> Is my cream-coloured one
> Swift as a sea mew...[4]

Endnotes
1. Graves, Robert. *The White Goddess*, p. 384.
2. Bergamar, Kate. *Discovering Hill Figures*, p. 8.
3. Lethbridge, T.C. *Gogmagog, The Buried Gods*, p. 80.
4. Op. cit. Graves, pp. 419–20.

9. THE CELTS AND THE MEGALITHS

The question of Celtic associations with megalithic sites is bound to arise. Did the Celts actually erect any of these, or simply utilize what they found already in existence on their arrival? There is obviously a degree of overlapping between the Megalithic, Bronze and Iron Ages which is easily identifiable by the trained eye. Sites like Callanish, for example, which exhibit evidence of an earlier culture in decline should not be confused with pure Celtica although in some cases there are suggestions of both infusions and superimpositions, especially in the religious context, the demarcation lines of which we will endeavour to define in Part II of this book.

Much has been written about Stonehenge, especially over the last few years, so the subject has been covered in more detail than I could hope to afford it in a single chapter. Connections between the pyramids and the megaliths have been noted and well documented, with scholars from many scientific disciplines contributing their opinions and the fruits of their research, most of which conclude that the site was in existence for a considerable period prior to the Celtic invasions. The Druids seemed to understand what it was all about, however, but then this is not surprising if their cosmogony and inner mysteries were as profound as many believe them to have been.

The original builders of the stone monoliths do appear to

have possessed an advanced knowledge of astronomy and mathematics, their method of preserving this wisdom in stone being suggestive of the remnants of a technologically advanced civilization used to more sophisticated materials utilizing what was available to them, to preserve or time-encapsulate their most sacred records.

Robert Graves had no difficulty in translating the Stonehenge message:

> The formula is plain. The Sun God of Stonehenge was the Lord of the Days and the Thirty arches of the outer circle and thirty posts of the inner circle stood for the days of the ordinary Egyptian month; but the secret enclosed by these circles was that the solar year was divided into five seasons, each in turn divided into three twenty-four-day periods, represented by the three stones of the dolmens, and each of these again into three ogdoads, represented by the three smaller posts in front of the dolmens. For the circle was so sited that at dawn of the summer solstice the sun rose exactly at the end of the avenue in dead line with the altar and the Heel Stone; while, of the surviving pair of the four undressed stones, one marks the sun's rising at the winter solstice, the other its setting at the summer solstice.[1]

Graves suggests that the altar stone and uprights were brought from Wales to break the religious power of the Pembrokeshire Death Goddess by removing her most sacred stones and re-erecting them on the plain. The number seventy-two would have been the main canonical number at Stonehenge, representing the seventy-two days of the midsummer season, eight multiplied ninefold by the fertile Moon having powerful solar connotations. He also mentions the five Stonehenge dolmens as having 'a broad gap between the two standing nearest the avenue (like the gap which contains the five holy days of the Egyptian or Etruscan year).

The number seventy-two makes its appearance as a significant factor in several other magical contexts; the Egyptian legend, for example, in which the five intercalary days were added to the ancient calendar of 360 days which was believed by many early cultures to have been the original measurement of one year. Thoth, Lord of Time, played a game of draughts with the Moon in which he won a seventy-second part of her light so that the births of the five gods Isis, Osiris, Horus, Nephthys and Set could be accommodated. A similar tale appears in Greek mythology with Cronus allowing the young Zeus to serve him a nectar that caused him to vomit up the stone that had been substituted for the infant Zeus, along with his two brothers and three sisters. That magical five again! And Cronus was also a 'time' deity. It is interesting to note that a seventy-second part of 360 is five. Once again we encounter this suggestion of a common knowledge which the builders of Stonehenge shared with those who erected the pyramids and the originators of the Hellenistic myths to name but two. The possibility of a single source from which all arcane knowledge originated must not, therefore, be discounted.

Graves produces a lot more evidence as to the original religious nature and flavour of Stonehenge which is certainly worth studying if one is intent upon getting to the bottom of the mystery, but a broad selection of reading matter is also suggested, as fact and conjecture need to be comfortably wed if anything resembling the real truth is to be arrived at.

Isabel Hill Elder comments:

Stonehenge the 'Greenwich Observatory' and great solar clock of ancient times, was pre-eminently an astronomical circle. Heliograph and beacon were both used by the ancient British astronomers in signalling the time and seasons, the result of observations, for the daily direction of the agriculturist and the trader. The unit of measure employed in the erection of Stonehenge, and all other works of this nature in our islands was the cubit, the same as used in the Great Pyramid.[2]

The said magical knowledge of the Druids might well be qualified as more scientific than mystical; Diodorus Siculus mentions the Druidic use of telescopes, for example, which no doubt gave birth to the superstition about their ability to bring down the magic of the Moon by enlarging her light!

Other stone sites round and about Brittany and the British Isles were obviously utilized by the Druids, some of which they were responsible for erecting and others not. It would seem logical to suppose, however, that if these very old centres, the Rollrights for example, were the encapsulators or keys to some ancient and unknown energy fields, the Druids and Bards, if they were as genuinely cosmically informed as might be supposed, would be aware of this and only too happy to plug in their power lines.

Another question that might well arise in relation to the subject matter of this chapter is the Celtic connection with Sheela-na-gigs, those female fertility symbols that appear in such improbable places as Christian churches. The meaning of the name is obscure, although it is said to have originated in Ireland where an old man, when asked whether there was a special name for these stone carvings, replied: 'Sighle na gcioch', translated by some as meaning 'Sheila of the Paps', although it is the genitals rather than the breasts that are usually featured. While 'Sheela-na-gig' is more generally used, I am assured that the correct term is 'exhibitionist'.

Another version suggests that 'Sheela' was 'Sithlach' (Holy Lady), while 'gig' meant 'god', so that we have 'The holy lady of the god', or even 'Holy Goddess'.[3] There are apparently forty of these carvings in England, Scotland and Wales and seventy-five in Ireland, the latter being found mostly in castles. Female exhibitionist figures do not appear elsewhere in northern Europe, the Celts being more inclined to emphasize the male sexual attributes when implying fertility. It would seem, however, that a display of genitalia of either sex was in some past age considered to ward off evil spirits, while in India it was believed to avert lightning! Had this ancient lore been passed down via the Celts it could, no doubt, account for the appearance of Sheela-na-gigs on churches, the spires of which are notorious lightning attracters. From the purely religious standpoint, these carvings probably represented the Earth Mother in her fertile, or her hag aspect, as the case may be. I do not feel that we can designate them wholly Celtic, however, as they are more reminiscent of Stone Age relics that were accommodated by the matrist-orientated Celts.

Fertility was, no doubt, an important issue to all the peoples of those early times, and its influence was visibly obvious both religiously and secularly, the success of their economy being contingent upon the healthy continuance of the race or tribe.

There are several comprehensive books on this subject which afford it the detailed analysis it deserves. These I have included in my bibliography.

In Part II of this book we will be examining the religion of Druidism itself, including the many subcults and overlays that it accumulated during centuries of Celtic residence among the early British and European communities. This will, I trust, help to clarify some of the questionable anomalies that have arisen concerning both overt and covert Celtic religious practices and mystery cults.

Endnotes
1. Graves, Robert. *The White Goddess*, p. 291.
2. Elder, Isabel Hill. *Celt, Druid and Culdee*, p. 59.
3. Bord, Janet and Colin. *Earth Rites*, p. 69.

10. CELTIC CHRISTIANITY AND THE CULDEES

There is a legend to the effect that when the first Christian missionaries arrived in Britain to convert the 'heathens', they were confronted by a highly civilized and more pristine version of the very faith they were there to preach. It would seem that the 'Church' they encountered was that of the Culdees.

But who and what were the Culdees, and from whom did they gain their knowledge? Some scholars are of the opinion that Druidism itself was the source from which the old Culdee belief sprang, but it is more likely that the first bringers of the Christian message were Judaean refugees fleeing the wrath of the more orthodox among their own people.

The obscure nature of the term 'Culdich', or to use its anglicized version 'Culdee', has left many writers speculating as to its meaning. A celebrated hagiologist named John Colgan translated Culdich *quidam advanae*, 'certain strangers' — particularly those from far shores, while Freculphus apud Godwin states that certain friends and disciples of Jesus fled to Britain in AD 37 to escape the persecution that followed in the wake of the ascension mystery. These 'certain strangers' were, we are told, hospitably received by Arviragus (Caratacus) King of the West Britons, or Silures, who was them housed in a nearby Druidic College. This same king later gave them lands equal to twelve hides or ploughs on which the first Christian church was built. The Domesday survey of AD 1088 confirms this fact: 'The Domus Dei, in the great monastery in Glastingbury. This Glastingbury church possesses in its own villa XII hides of land which have never paid tax.'[1]

Over the years much evidence has been collected to lend credence to the legend that the Glastonbury church was the first Christian edifice to be erected in this country, probably under the direction of those very people who had met and talked with Jesus at first hand and were, therefore, better able to quote his words and sentiments than later followers of the Christian cult whose views had been coloured by Roman, Greek and other external influences.

One much cherished but historically unsubstantiated legend tells how Jesus Himself actually visited Glastonbury and other parts of the West Country during the so-termed 'lost years' of His ministry, while the story of Joseph of Arimathea and his famous Thorn is well documented in all the official Glastonbury guidebooks.

The apostle Phillip, having preached to the Gaulish Celts, as Freculphus relates, there would appear to be no reason why his contemporaries did not visit the British Isles, in which case it would be logical to assume that their first converts might conceivably have been among the lettered class of the Druidic colleges. But where the stories of Jesus and Joseph are concerned I am neutral, so it will be up to my readers to make their own choice.

Much has been written concerning the similarity between the Druidic and early Christian doctrines which, we are led to believe, made it easy for one to incorporate or overshadow the other. From *Ecclesiastical Antiquities* of Cymry we learn that the Silurian Druids embraced Christianity early after its arrival in these islands, and that because of their existing priestly office they were immediately accepted as Christian ministers. One Welsh Triad mentions Amesbury as one of the three Druidic 'Cors' or colleges of Britain to be converted to Christian use. The Christian King Lucius, third in descent from Caradoc and grandson of Pudens and Claudia, apparently built the first minster on the site of a Druidic Cor in Winchester, and a national council held there in AD 156 established Christianity the national religion as a successor to Druidism.[2]

According to Eusebius of Cesarea: 'The Apostles passed

beyond the ocean to the isles called the Brittanic Isles', while
an imposing list of scholars and historians made reference to
the growth of Christianity in the British Isles in the first five
centuries. Gildas, the British historian writing in AD 542,
states: 'We certainly know that Christ, the True Sun,
afforded His Light, the knowledge of His Precepts to our
Island in the last year of the reign of Tiberias Caesar, AD 37.'[3]

Of course, not every Druid and Bard accepted Christianity,
just as there are those today who choose to espouse the old
Celtic Druidic beliefs in preference to the modern state
religion. In the same way, many statesmen, kings and princes
retained the services of Druids and Bards for centuries after
Europe became Christianized. The chief monarchs of Ireland,
for example, adhered to the old Druidism long after St
Patrick's time, but then the Irish did permit freedom of
belief, so Christianity was preached side by side with the older
faiths of that land.

Lewis Spence maintains that although the Culdees
practised a particular brand of Christianity, their inner
doctrines still retained a large measure of the old Druidic
philosophy. The Culdees who dwelt on Iona and professed to
follow St Columba practised a mixture of early Christianity
and ancient Druidism in spite of their outward acceptance of
the rulership of Christ.

What we have established, however, is that the early
Christian Church, as embraced by the Celtic Druids, was
known by the name of the Church of the Culdees, after the
Culdich, or refugees, the priestly caste of this establishment
who were mostly Christianized Druids claiming theirs as the
Mother church of Christendom. The infanthood of
Christianity has come under considerable scholastic scrutiny
over the past few years especially in the popular media, but I
am not sure whether these Culdeean claims have been
included in their dissertations and debates. Fortunately none
of this is my argument as I am not a follower of any organized
or established religious collective.

There are a few facts regarding the Culdee Church that
merit mention as they emphasize its independently Celtic
nature as against the later, Latinized version of the Christian
message. The Culdee Church was ruled by Bishops and Elders
— elder and priest (from *presbyteros*) being synonymous
terms.[4] The Culdees apparently saw no reason to alter certain

Druidic customs and terms of reference and they retained the traditional white Druidic garb. A superintendent among the Druids was referred to as a 'deon' or dean.

The early Culdeean clergy came into office through heredity, the principle of hereditary succession being part of Celtic custom. The Crown was hereditary within certain Celtic rules, the Bards were hereditary with little reference to qualification, while in Ireland there was an hereditary succession in the bishopric of Armagh for fifteen generations. Giraldus Cambrensis, Bishop of St David's in the twelfth century preferred the Latin Church to the earlier Celtic version, complaining that 'the sons after the deaths of their fathers, succeeded to the ecclesiastical benefices not by election but by hereditary right'. This Celticized version of Christianity flourished from the first to the seventh century AD, its accent of worship apparently being on the Trinity rather than the Virgin Mary, which information I find strange in the light of the 'Dowry of Mary' appellation that was applied to England prior to the Reformation.

The arrival of the Anglo-Saxons between 446 and 501 saw the Celts slowly forced back to the west of England, Wales and the south-west of Scotland, and with them the Culdee Church. Fleeing persecution from the Romans they established churches and monasteries in remote places such as Bardsey (off the Welsh coast), Lindisfarne, Iona, some of the islands off the west coast of Scotland where Gaelic is still spoken, and inaccessible parts of Ireland. Many of these spots became places of pilgrimage, while the local people carry to this day their own special brand of Christianity which is strongly tinged with the Culdeean and old Druidic ways.

In 597 the Augustinian mission sent by Pope Gregory to convert the Anglo-Saxons to Christianity arrived on these shores. The Celtic Christians were so taken aback at the version of Christ's teaching that was presented to them that one Columbanus later saw fit, on their behalf, to complain to Pope Boniface IV:

> Your Chair, O Pope, is defiled with heresy. Deadly errors have crept into it; it harbours horrors and impieties. Catholic? The true Catholicism you have lost. The orthodox and the true Catholics are they who have always zealously persevered in the true faith.[5]

But in spite of what the Culdee Church saw as blatant deviations, Augustine and his missionaries achieved a high degree of success with their questionable doctrines which greatly pleased Pope Gregory so that he despatched more missionaries, this time armed with church ornaments and vestments. From then on the story is an open one which may be read in any history book.

Conclusions? Every man and woman to his or her own belief, but many readers may see fit to adjust their perspectives in the light of the deeper Druidic and pagan Celtic mysteries to be revealed in Part II.

Endnotes
1. Elder, Isabel Hill. *Celt, Druid and Culdee*, p. 93.
2. Ibid. Elder, p. 96.
3. Ibid. Elder, p. 97–8.
4. Ibid. Elder, p. 104.
5. Ibid. Elder, p. 121.

PART TWO

RELIGIOUS, MAGICAL AND TRADITIONAL BELIEFS

11. GENERAL GOD CONCEPTS

There is considerable confusion as to the real nature of Celtic belief, many cults popularly dubbed 'heathen' or 'pagan' being conveniently placed under the Celtic religious umbrella. In order to discover its true teaching and tenets we need to go back a very long way, to the origins of the Celtic peoples themselves which takes us, if we are to accept the orthodox view, to the northern India and near Middle East of the Meso/Neolithic period. The main religion in those times and places was that of the Earth Mother, accompanied by a goodly sprinkling of shamanistic polytheism and set against a background of primitive sympathetic magic. As the first civilizing influences started to make their impression, wise men and women questioned and rationalized these beliefs, forming them into recognizable patterns which could be understood at one or other level by all.

Not all of the early matrist religions were lunar, however. Among the ancient Germanic peoples, for example, the sun and solar power were considered to be feminine by nature, as represented by the goddesses Sól and Sunna, and the rune ς .[1] Dominant sun goddesses were also to be found in Egypt, while among the deities of the Eskimos, Japanese, and Khasis of India the solar goddesses were accompanied by subordinate brothers who were symbolized by the moon.[2]

The earliest Celtic pantheon consisted of a Goddess in three roles — Nubile girl or Maiden, Virgin Mother, and Aged

Crone or Wise Woman — and a male god whose aspects were a benign Solar Deity of Light, and a Dark Tanist, Magician, or Lord of the Regions of the Dead. Just as the Christian Trinity consists of three persons in one God each of which is acknowleged singularly, so the old Celtic faith, we are told, held to its overtly pantheistic, but covertly monotheistic fivefold divinity. This deity was conceived of as both male and female, with each of the five aspects being individually recognized and yet constituting a single, cohesive whole. To these five identities individual personalities were assigned, as it is ever the way of mankind to fashion his gods in his own image and likeness, endowing them with his virtues, while at the same time projecting onto them the darker side of his own nature. The Druidic religion, therefore, could be many things to many people, its more esoteric aspects, however, being the exclusive domain of the Druids, Bards and those who studied with or under them.

In addition to their god concepts the Celts also held nature in great esteem and reverence. Trees, flowers, stones, streams, and other natural phenomena were accorded names and personalities and highly venerated. It is, in fact, this appreciation of these intelligences, as children of Mother Earth, that has designated the Celtic religion guardian of the Green Ray. Green is the sacred colour of Celtic magic and of the Earth Goddess herself.

Vestiges of these green eco-aspects of the old Celtic faith have survived in some parts of the British Isles to this day. In the Derbyshire hills, for example, the old worship of streams and wells continues, albeit under Christian guise, in the annual ceremony of 'Well Dressing'. Fully appreciating the necessity for a pure and reliable water supply, the Celts were careful to pay due deference to the spirits of streams and watering places to which they often erected stone altars.

In very early times there was not the religious intolerance that we are obliged to endure today. It was common practice for the traveller to equate the local gods that were worshipped wherever he or she might be passing through or staying, with his or her own special brand of belief, so that due deference was always paid to the divinity nearest to, or even identical with, one's own tutelary patron.

As time progressed, however, and the harsh hand of civilization exerted its ever-increasing pressure for conformity, the old concept of the Earth Goddess and her Consort, upon which the matriarchal society was based, was challenged by the patrist-orientated religions of those warrior peoples who drove their tenets home at swordpoint. Wholly male pantheons and all-embracing male divinities took charge, and with them came the over-emphasis of the animus with all that this implies in relation to the balance of the human psyche. And we still fight on. But the Goddess has invoked the Law of Rebound and sought the aid of The Keeper of the Divine Scales, with the result that mankind is reaping the dubious rewards of the rejection of Her principle. War, cruely, sexual imbalances, the worship of materialism and diseases associated therewith have plagued our planet.

Nor is the individual free to pursue the path of his or her religious inclination as the accusing finger of heresy, or non-conformity to the 'collective', is ever ready to make its dark mark. But the power of Creation is a double-edged sword — it can destroy just as easily as it can build — and sometimes the application of this principle is necessary for the cleansing of an undesirable condition, be it human or planetary. When we are sick we attack the offending organisms with whatever drug or medication we find expedient, without prior consideration as to *their* right to offend our bodies, or the validity of *their* free will. Place this principle into the macrocosmic arena, and the roles of Kali, Sekhmet and The Cailleach, to name but three similarly natured divinities, quickly fall into place.

Bearing in mind the numerous deities that have received mention in the earlier part of this book, how do these stand up as part of the Celtic religious heritage when viewed in the light of the Sacred Five? When the Celts commenced their westward wanderings they would have taken with them the names and natures of the gods that were worshipped in their land of origin, be that northern India southern Europe, Atlantis or wherever. Upon reaching each port of call they would have encountered the local divinities of that region, country or town. Some of these must have sounded very much like the deities they were used to worshipping, just as their gods doubtless found favour with the people they encountered during their journeyings. Names would be exchanged, and after a few years any one principle might end up with numerous nomenclatures.

Let us take a hypothetical example. A tribe of early Goidelic Celts travelling through Switzerland, decides to stop at a certain post to see the winter out. Several of the families accompanying them feel drawn to the location and are, therefore, reluctant to continue their wanderings when the spring air beckons the rest of the tribe to move on again. And so they decide to settle there and raise their children, eventually intermarrying with the local Alpine people. Now among those Celtic settlers are a Druid and Druidess who naturally proceed about their ministry. The local people become intrigued by the ceremonies and ask for more information. Upon receiving instruction they are delighted to note that an aspect of the Celtic Goddess appears to be one and the same as their own favourite deity, Artio, whose symbol is a bear. Slowly the two faiths merge and another name is added to the old Celtic pantheon.

Working on this principle, and moving forward in time and space, it is easy to see how the concept of multi-divinities became associated with Celtica as, indeed, it did with most other nations of these times who were wont to travel around a lot or colonize. In a religiously tolerant society it is very easy to equate principles, especially obvious ones.

And so we find ourselves with a list of god-names which varied according to the area, country, nature, customs and ethos of the peoples therein. Many of these were of no more significance than those Catholic saints who are prayed to in a specific context. As a child I was advised to 'pray to St Blaise' when I had a sore throat, ask St Anthony to find something I had lost, or seek the aid of St Thomas Aquinas prior to taking an important examination. Of course the ancient Egyptians would have turned to Anubis for help to find lost property and to Thoth for scholastic assistance, while for the former complaint the Celts, no doubt, would have sought Bardic aid with a poetic invocation or prayed to Bran, whose head was fabled for its pronouncements long after his body (the corpus of his faith) had ceased to exist. It must also be borne in mind that many of the old god-forms were purely representative of the seasonal cycles, one ritually 'dying' to make way for the festive 'rebirth' of another.

All pre-Christian beliefs were not Celtic, however. There were the Teuto/Saxon deities, those of Greece, Rome, and Carthage to name but a few. And, of course, the divinities which were worshipped in pre-Celtic Britain should not be forgotten. When the Celts arrived on these shores they found a flourishing form of worship which is broadly described as 'The Old Religion'. But what exactly was this ancient faith? It would appear to have been a combination of more than one belief, that of the Beaker people, perhaps, superimposed on an even earlier cult that was indigenous to these isles. What we do know is that the Horned God featured prominently.

One of the earliest known representations of this deity is to be found in the Caverne des Trois Frères in Ariège. It shows a man clothed in the skin of a stag with antlers on his head, and has been dated to the Palaeolithic (Old Stone Age) Period.

The Palaeolithic period was followed by the Meso/ Neolithic Age, the people of which left few artistic remains, and those they did were invariably of women. With the onset of the Bronze Age the Horned Figure returned to prominence, this time appearing in either male or female form, the Neolithic matrist emphasis having combined forces with the earlier Horned God.

Horned gods were quite common in Mesopotamia, Babylon and Assyria, as Waddell was quick to observe (see Chapter 7). They were also to be seen in Egypt; Amon with his ram horns and Hathor as the Divine Cow, for example. Horns were, for some reason, considered to be a symbol of divinity. In Babylon, when the King or High Priest appeared as the god Asshur with his Queen, or High Priestess as his Consort, Ishtar, the appropriate number of horns was worn on the royal head-dresses, the royal pair being regarded as incarnate deities.[3]

Nor was this phenomenon limited to the regions of Europe and the Middle East; the Indian figures of the Horned God Pasupati, found at Mohenjo-Daro, are of the earliest Bronze Age.

The horned trail leads us through the Greek Minotaurial labyrinth to the caves of the satyrs and Pans, and thence to our own Green Men or Robin Goodfellows. The Romans observed the preponderance of his worship in Gaul and called him Cernunnos, which simply means 'the Horned'. Chritianized history takes over at this point with its prejudices and persecutions, rendering further accurate observation impossible. He, like Pan and other nature or animal divinities became a symbol of 'the Devil', and from then onwards the state church saw to it that the populace was well and truly programmed out of the old beliefs.

The other side of the religious coin that the Celts would have found upon arrival in Britain was, of course, worship of the Goddess in her triple form, over which they were quick to impose their own Epona. Much nonsense has, in my opinion, been written about the Old Religion. For one thing this term has come to mean different things to different people. Those who would really like to know the truth about it I would refer to the writings of reliable and experienced experts such as Lois Bourne and Marian Green, or Michael Howard whose publication *The Cauldron* covers much of the subject matter of this book, and considerably more. As my work is not primarily about Wicca, I will leave that side of things in their very capable hands.

The question we must ask, however, is: were there any similarities between Celtic Druidism and Bardism and these older faiths? There must have been a crossroad in the dim and distant past at which several paths branched off, as all the signs indicate a single source. The Beaker people had taken the same road as their Celtic cousins, albeit a few centuries earlier, so each race must have read the signposts that had undoubtedly been erected by an even earlier migration.

The principle was broadly the same: the Goddess and her Consort. Sometimes she appeared in triple aspect as representing the three phases of the Moon, sometimes as a single deity who chose her 'King' at the appropriate time. Perhaps one aspect of the god stayed with her as a mate or companion, perhaps not, depending upon the flavour afforded to the religion by each area. But either way, we can say with surety that when the Celts did arrive in Britain the religious beliefs which they encountered were easily accommodated and absorbed into their own mythology and teachings. Maybe their Druids had retained more of the detailed esoteric and technical knowledge of the 'Old Country', which rendered their approach more scientific and their theogony more refined. But then one has to take into account the limitations imposed by climate and the availability of materials when assessing the obvious, or less obvious as the case may be, evidence of cultural development as expressed through overt religious practices. Many so-termed 'primitive' people adhere to beliefs of great inspiration, depth and sublimity, but do not build fine churches or richly adorn their places of worship. Equally, the material wealth of a religion is no guarantee of its spirituality or sublime content.

In spite of the monotheistic label that became attached to Druidism in the early Christian times it would be inaccurate to present a book about Celtic religion without detailing some of those deities that are known to be essentially Celtic. Whether these are viewed purely as theophanies of the Sacred Five, nature divinities, externally superimposed god names, the nomenclatures of past kings and heroes or simply old pagan appellations is irrelevant. Named they must be, or this work is not complete. Of course I may make the unforgivable mistake of omitting someones's obscure but meaningful favourite, in which case I apologize in advance.

History has left us somewhat in the dark when it comes to the names of earlier Celtic deities as the megalithic people did not always present their gods in concrete form. Stones, wells, rivers and other natural objects were frequently adequate symbols for them, being the embodiment of the supernatural forces they venerated. It is sometimes suggested that the Celts were incapable of satisfactory anthropomorphic representation which is said to account for the lack of human figures in pre-Roman iconography. The transitional period between the late Bronze and early Iron Age in the British Isles and northern Europe has, however, revealed a number of cult figures, some quite small but others more than life-size. Cernunnos and Tarranis, for example, were clearly portrayed on the Gundestrup bowl.

The imaginative mind of the Aryan Celt was capable of clothing its divinities in garbs recognizable and acceptable to other nations. Caesar reports that the Celts had gods equivalent to Mercury, Apollo, Mars and other Roman deities, while Lucan mentions a triad which consisted of Aesus, Teutates and Taranus (Tarranis). One translation renders Aesus or Esus as the Scandinavian Asa or Persian Ahura-Mazda, in other words a god of light; Teutates, from the Celtic root meaning 'valiant' as Mars while Taranus, who was a god of lightning was obviously Thor/Jupiter (Taran, in Welsh/Cornish/Breton means thunderbolt).[4]

Caesar naturally tried to fit the Celtic gods into the framework of the Roman pantheon just as the Gauls did after their conquest. Mercury was therefore named as chief of the Celtic gods, being the inventor of all the arts, patron of commerce, guardian of roads and travellers and guide of the spirits of the departed to the 'other world', his role of psychopompus being similar to that held by the Egyptian Anubis. Apollo was designated the Celtic god of medicine and healing, Minerva the initiator of arts and crafts, while Jupiter governed the sky and Mars presided over war.

It is obvious here that Caesar was trying to classify a number of Gallic divinities under five basic types and supply these with Roman names. One most notable Celtic deity was, he tells us, Dis or Pluto, God of the Underworld, from whom all Celts claimed to be descended. But it must be borne in mind that much of Caesar's commentary on the Celtic faith was based on his observations in Gaul, so basic Gaulish underlays need to be afforded consideration when weighing Roman evidence. The Romans were fairly tolerant of other peoples religious beliefs, however, and comfortably embraced local Celtic deities like the goddess Sul of Bath, rendering her Aqua Sulis in the Roman idiom.

Endnotes
1. Thorsson, Edred. *Futhark*, p. 52.
2. Stone, Merlin. *The Paradise Papers*, p. 18.
3. Murray, Margaret A. *The God of the Witches*, p. 25.
4. Rolleston, T.W. *Myths and Legends of the Celtic Race*, p. 86.

12. THE GODS OF THE TUATHA DE DANAANS

Let us return once more to the names of the old Celtic deities that have come down to us via the mythological cycles, starting with those from Ireland.

The Dagda

By his epithet *Eochaid Ollathair*, (Father of All), and *Ruad Ro-fhessa*, 'Lord of Perfect Knowledge', the Dagda obviously featured as one of the most prominent deities in the old Irish Celtic pantheon. He was not considered as progenitor of the gods, however, nor given special honours, but he does represent a patrist figurehead. His appearance was hardly prepossessing as he was spoken of as a gross, ugly peasant carrying a magic club that

> ... was so large that it would have needed eight men to carry it and was therefore mounted on wheels. When dragged along the ground it left a furrow like a frontier dyke. Under the club the bones of his people's enemies were like hailstones under horses hooves. With one hand he could kill nine men at a time and with the other restore them to life. He was Lord of Life and Death.[1]

He also possessed a cornucopia-like Cauldron that could never be emptied and from which no one ever went away unsatisified. This symbology is suggestive of a leader or god who was the nourisher of his people. His coarse appearance was, no doubt, manufactured by his followers who, for the benefit of their enemies, saw fit to present him in as terrifying an aspect as possible. In spite of this, however, and the acts of death and destruction he was supposed to have visited on their foes, the Dagda in his gentler mode was a master of music and magic as may be evidenced in the story of his fabulous harp.

Lugh

As I have already dealt with Lugh's appellations, all that remains is to recount his arrival on the Danaan scene. When he presented himself at Nuada's palace at Tara to offer his services, the doorkeeper enquired of him as to his special skill to which he replied that he was a carpenter.

'But we have an excellent one in Luchta, son of Luchad,' Lugh was told.

'I am a smith, too,' said Lugh.

'We have a master smith', the doorkeeper assured him.

'Then I am a warrior,' Lugh retorted.

'We do not need one while we have Ogma,' was the doorkeeper's answer.

And so the conversation went until Lugh had named all the arts and occupations he could think of, poet, harper, scientist, physician, spencer, and so forth, only to receive the reply that a man of supreme accomplishment in that trade was already in Nuada's service.

'Then ask the King if he has in his service one man who is accomplished in all these arts and if he has I shall stay here no more or seek to enter his palace,' Lugh insisted.

Upon this he was duly received.[2]

In spite of Lugh's solar connection this behaviour is more in keeping with the Mercurial archetype so a fusion of two deities must have taken place at some point, a clue to which may lie in the story of his arrival from what the myth refers to as 'The Land of the Living', from whence he came bearing many magical gifts. These included the Boat of Mananan, son of Lir the sea god, which 'knew a man's thoughts and could travel whithersoever he would', the Horse of Mananan that could 'go alike over land and sea', and a terrible sword named 'Fragarach' (The Answerer) that could cut through any mail. Thus equipped, Lugh appeared before the assembly of Danaan chiefs who all exclaimed that they felt 'as if they beheld the rising of the sun on a dry summer's day.' The myth would appear to be telling us quite blatantly that Lugh was an addition to their existing pantheon from this 'Land of the Living', the location of which we are afforded no clue. Lugh was the father, by the Milesian maiden Dectera, of Ireland's most heroic figure, Cuchulain.

Unlike the Dagda with his heavy club, Lugh's weapons were a spear and sling of great magical powers. He also contrasted strongly with the gross appearance of the Dagda, being more refined, and comely in face and form. Although he is counted among the Danaans, there is surely something more Milesian about his character. There are also time discrepancies here if you care to think about it.

Angus Õg

Angus Õg (Angus the Young) was the son of the Dagda by Boanna (the River Boyne) and his palace was said to be at New Grange on that river. Four bright birds that hovered over his head were spoken of as his kisses, their singing being forever an enchantment to youths and maidens, for Angus Õg was the love god of the Irish Celts. He was patron of all who were struck by Cupid's arrows, and restorer of life to those who relinquished their last breath in the cause of love. Associated with youth, beauty, music and charm this deity embodies the qualities of both Aphrodite and Adonis, which tells us a lot about the psychology of the Celts in relation to their anima/animus balance.

Len of Killarney

Brother of the Dagda, Len was a goldsmith by trade who 'gave the ancient names of the Lakes to Killarney — once known as Locha Lein, the Lakes of Len of the Many Hammers. Here by the Lake he wrought, surrounded by rainbows and showers of fiery dew.'[3]

Midir The Proud

Also a son of the Dagda, Midir is described in glowing terms as a youth of great physical beauty and refinement, very ethereal and almost fairylike in nature, appearing but seldom and then only to the chosen few. His tunic, we are told, was of purple, his hair a golden yellow and reaching to the edge of his shoulders, his eyes lustrous and grey. In one hand he held a finely pointed spear, and in the other a shield with a white central boss encrusted with gold and gems. Graves describes him as a Goidelic underworld-god who lived in a castle on Mananan's isle (the Isle of Man) with three cranes at his gate whose duty it was to warn off travellers. The cranes, which effect a link with Ephesian Artemis, were considered symbols of fertility as recently as Edwardian times when they were frequently depicted on vases or objets d'art.

Nuada of the Silver Hand

Nuada was the Keeper of one of the Fairy Gifts of the Tuatha de Danaans, the invincible sword which once unsheathed was so powerful that no enemy could escape it. This attribute would most certainly mark him as one of the really old Danaan deities. He was said to have been killed in the second battle of Moytura, but there is some confusion as to what really happened to him. The answer to this question is surely to be found in the arrival on the scene of Lugh, as representing the incoming solar cult which doubtless usurped the earlier, lunar orientated religion, silver always being associated with Moon.

Lir and Mananan

Lir is a somewhat vague nautical divintiy who first appeared in abstract form but later became more personalized when he was said to dwell invisibly on Slieve Fuad in County Armagh. His Poseidonian attributes were mostly transferred to his son Mananan, one of the most popular deities in Irish mythology. Mananan therefore became Lord of the Sea, beyond or under which the Land of Youth or Islands of the Dead were supposed to lie, which designated him the Guide to these places. He was a master of tricks and illusions, which is surely the myth's way of telling us that the human emotions, as represented by the Element of Water, are ever illusory and devious by nature!

Mananan also owned a variety of magical possessions. There was the boat 'Ocean Sweeper', which obeyed the thought of those who sailed in it and went without sail or oar; the steed 'Aonbarr', which could travel alike on land or sea; and the sword, 'The Answerer', which no armour could resist. How Mananan came to receive these gifts from Lugh (if in fact he did) is not made quite clear, which could indicate a fusion of two different cults. White crested waves were called the Horses of Mananan, and in later heroic tales it is mentioned as being tabu for the hero, Cuchulain, to watch them. Mananan wore a huge cloak which could take on every conceivable colour, and many were the tales of those who claimed to hear this great garment flapping as the god strode about in anger. His seat or throne was said to be on the Isle of Man, thus giving that island its name.

Ogma

Ogma, or Ogmius, whose appellations include 'the Champion', 'the Sun Faced' and 'the Lion Skinned', in addition to his prowess in battle, was also a deity of learning and writing. He is credited with the invention of Ogham script, which was named after him.

Dana, Anu and Brigid

Dana was considered by some as the greatest of all the Irish goddesses and known as 'Mother of the Irish Gods'. Sometimes she is mentioned as being the daughter of the Dagda, which is something of an anomaly since the Danaans were always referred to as the Children of Dana rather than the progeny of the Dagda, implying the predominance of the feminine principle in this Celtic pantheon.

The only descendants of Dana to appear in mythology are Brian, Iuchar and Iucharba, sometimes spoken of as the sons of Brigid, representing the triple concept of a single deity which is common in Celtic iconography. The name of Brian, who was the leader of the three brothers, is derived from a more ancient form *Brenos*, the god to whom the Celts attributed their victories at Allia and Delphi, mistaken by the Romans for a human general.[4]

Dana is frequently confused with two other goddesses, Brigid whom some say was her daughter and Anu, a local divinity after whom the Paps of Anu in County Kerry were named. In this context she could, of course, represent the maternal aspect of the Triple Goddess with Brigid as the Maiden and Anu as the Crone. Graves, however, sees the matriarchal trinity as Ana, Babh and Macha, who collectively form the character known as the Morrigan. Brigid is by far the strongest and most enduring of the great Irish Celtic goddesses, and the fact that she has survived to this day speaks for itself. Both Brigid and Dana were benign divinities and givers of plenty, who were loved and respected by the ordinary people. Brigid, however, had additional functions as a tutelary deity of learning, culture and skills, which equates her with the Greek Athene.

The Morrigan

Viewed by some scholars, notably Graves, as one of the destructive aspects of the Triple Goddess, Morrigan appears in the singular as both a war goddess and a rather perverse enchantress with considerable prognostic powers, after the nature of Circe, Kali or a female Loki, At times she presented a charming front, especially to heroes, while secretly she was intent upon their undoing. Morrigan, like her counterparts in other pantheons, however, could be a good friend, but a bad enemy.

Ainé

Patroness of Munster Ainé was the daughter of Owel, the Danaan, who was a Druid and foster son of Mananan. She was both a corn goddess and a giver of fertility and love. Her cult persisted for many years after the advent of Christianity, especially among the Irish peasantry who made torches of hay and straw which they lighted and carried round her hill at night. Afterwards they dispersed themselves among their fields and pastures, waving the torches over their crops and cattle to bring them good luck. One night, according to legend, the ceremony was omitted on account of the death of a neighbour, but upon looking towards the sacred site the people observed phantom torches in even greater number than usually circling the hill, and Ainé herself in front directing the procession. This is but one of the many fairytale-like or ghostly legends associated with this goddess. Nor did these appear to frighten the local people but rather reassure them as to her continued patronage and kind watchfulness.

Sinend

Sinend, the daughter of Lodan son of Lir, was wont to visit a certain well in fairyland at which, the Bardic narrative tells us, 'are the hazels of wisdom and inspirations, that is, the hazels of the science of poetry, and in the same hour their fruit and their blossom and their foliage break forth, and then fall upon the well in the same shower, which raises upon the water a royal surge of purple.'[5] We are not told what sin of ritual omission Sinend had committed on her visit to this sacred well, but the waters in their anger broke forth and overwhelmed her, washing her up on the Shannon shore where she died, giving the river its name.

The myth of the hazels of inspiration and knowledge and their association with fresh spring water runs throughout Irish legend, while the Sinend story expresses the Celtic veneration for science and poetry but warns that these gifts may not be attained without a degree of peril. Knowledge without wisdom is always a potentially dangerous weapon, as may be witnessed in our present day and age.

Macha

An eponymous deity of the capital of Ulster, Macha is generally reckoned to represent a survival of a Mother Goddess worshipped in parts of Ireland prior to the arrival of the Celts, She appears in the myths as the wife of more than one heroic or immortal personage and the best known story about her tells how she was forced, while pregnant, to run a race against the horses of Conchobar at Emain Macha. She succeeded in the contest, but died giving birth to twins. In dying, she put a curse on the warriors of Ulster which subjected them for nine generations to the pangs of childbirth for five days and four nights in the hour of their greatest need.

The tale is thought to refer to some collective ritual, but it immediately brought to my mind the story of the birth of Apollo and Artemis in which their mother, Leto, was obliged to suffer atrociously for nine days and nine nights before Iris was finally permitted to fetch Ilythia from Olympus to alleviate her suffering. And yet again we are faced with those five intercalary days that I emphasized earlier. In addition to its equine overtones, the Macha legend also exhibits signs of Graeco-Roman influences. Whether this was via the later Celts or from some earlier invasion, however, is open to conjecture.

Minor Deities

Minor deities such as the surgeon Diancecht, the woodland goddess Flidais, and Gobnui the Smith/Brewer are also mentioned in the immortal context, but accounts of their deeds are too brief and their roles too ill-defined to merit much emphasis other than in the wider framework of the Irish pantheon.

When considering how I should present these Irish gods, my first plan was to erect a genealogical chart of the Danaans similar to the three given for the British Houses. But unlike the Houses of Dõn and Llyr, the Danaan relationships lack definition and the information is too scant, so I was obliged to settle for these few brief descriptions. The bibliography includes several more comprehensive works on this subject, notably the Rolleston, for those readers who require greater detail.

Endnotes
1. Larousse, *Encyclopedia of Mythology*, p. 237.
2. Rolleston, T.W. *Myths and Legends of the Celtic Race*, p. 112.
3. Ibid. Rolleston, p. 123.
4. Ibid. Rolleston, p. 126.
5. Ibid. Rolleston, p. 129.

13. THE HOUSES OF DŎN AND LLYR

The fact that many of the Welsh deities correspond with those of the Irish pantheon has been attributed by some scholars to the influence of Irish settlers in Wales rather than to the single source theory. There would, however, appear to be too many parallels in the myths of other countries to account for these 'coincidences'.

These two great Houses of Dŏn and Llyr were united when Dŏn's daughter Penardun married the sea god Llyr, which obviously infers a fusion of two schools of belief, one probably more ancient than the other. There are some interesting personalities in these two pantheons as we shall see, the most notable of which was:

Gwydion
This heroic deity was certainly more than a simple echo of some primitive folk divinity. His nature and deeds are of such length and complexity, however, that I could not do justice to them in a short analysis. Gwydion, a divinity of science and light, was the slayer of Pryderi son of Pwyll, Head of the Underworld, and the goddess Rhiannon. His triumph over Pryderi, however, which started with his illegal acquisition of a herd of Pryderi's swine, was achieved by magical means and therefore deemed unfair, whereby Mãth set him a series of exacting penances which are reminiscent of the punishments meted out by Zeus in the Greek myths. The esoteric message

in this story would appear to be that those who posses occult skills are in violation of cosmic law if they employ these to give them unfair advantage over their less gifted fellow men.

Dôn

The mother goddess of an obviously matrist pantheon. Although her husband, Mãth, dispensed justice among his oft-times unruly brood they were essentially referred to as her children and carried her name.

Mãth

Mãth was a god of wealth or increase after the nature of the Greek Hades, or Dis Pater who also possessed unusually acute hearing. Although Mãth is not mentioned as being an underworld deity of the same calibre as Pwyll or Pryderi, his associations with the money principle tend to point him in that direction. It is interesting to observe how gods of the underworld are essentially associated with material possessions and the acquisition thereof, the obvious inference being, no doubt, that whatever we receive as a bonus on 'this side' has to be paid for in some other time zone or karmic scene.

Larousse remarks on how many of the Children of Dôn gave their names to constellations or astronomical phenomena and quotes three examples: Cassiopeia — Llys Don (The Court of Dôn); The Milky Way — Caer Gwydion and Corona Borealis — Caer Arianrod.

Llew

The solar deity of Dôn's children, Llew equates with the Irish Lugh. Llew's full name was Llew Llaw Gyffes. Born to the goddess Arianrod, Llew was raised from an early age by Gwydion, although the latter was not actually his father, which is reminiscent of the Merlin/Arthur story.

Arianrod

A dawn goddess, whose name is said to mean 'Silver Circle', Arianrod has obvious lunar associations, her son Dylan being a noted marine divinity. Her other famous son was Llew, whom Gwydion took from her at an early age, which is suggestive of the lunar or goddess cult conceding to the oncoming tides of solar emphasis engendered, no doubt, by reason (Gwydion) as against the anima (feminine) quality of intuition.

Gwyn ap Nudd

Gwyn, the Warder of Hades, is the Night Hunter, Herne who, like the norse god Ullr, always catches his prey before the light of dawn. Guardians of dark portals, or those gods like the Egyptian Anubis who have right of way though the underworld, represent a definite occult lesson which is concerned with the necessity for the initiate to negotiate the darker realms before he or she can approach the places of light. Of course there is a mistaken idea that this infers a free licence for hedonism. Should this be the conclusion drawn by the student, then he or she should give up right now as it is *not* what Initiation is all about, the Gwydion/Pryderi episode in itself supplying part of the answer. (The archetype of The Hunter is also highly significant and I have dealt with it, as applied to Artemis, in some detail in my book *Practical Greek Magic*.)

As may be observed from the chart (p. 107) there are several other Children of Dōn, whose deeds tend to intermingle with those already mentioned. Gwydion's brother Gilvaethwy, for example, who accompanied him on his journey to Hades prior to the Pryderi disaster. But the appropriate inferences are supplied on the chart, and any reader who feels drawn to one of these in particular is advised to read *The Mabinogion* for the finer details.

The gods of the House of Llyr are by way of being somewhat more human, while the fact that they are referred to as Llyr's family confirms the patrist nature of this pantheon.

Llyr and Manawyddan

This old sea god, like his Irish counterpart, appeared to relinquish most of his power to his son Manawyddan, a nautical god of enchantment who later married the horse goddess Rhiannon. Always there is this connection between the horse and the sea which cannot be a coincidence as it occurs in so many pantheons. According to a later legend, Manwyddan was usurped by another son of Beli named Casswallawn, also a magician who possessed a cloak of invisibility similar to that of the Greek Hades.

Rhiannon

Although she married Manawyddan later in the tales, Rhiannon's first husband was Pwyll, Ruler of Hades. Now Pwyll very much wanted an heir, but as no child was forthcoming he mentioned to Rhiannon his intention of seeking another bride for this purpose. Rhiannon, however, begged him to give her one more year and sure enough during that time a pregnancy occurred. The goddess, who was to be delivered of her child in the early hours of the morning was attended by six serving ladies. But the night was a long and painful one and all the ladies finally fell sleep, as did Rhiannon herself after the exertion of bringing forth her child. Although she had been delivered of a boy, when the women awoke there was no child to be found. Knowing how their negligence would invoke the anger of Pwyll, they set up a ruse by killing the cub of a staghound that had just littered, laying its bones by the still sleeping Rhiannon, and smearing the blood around her face so that when she awoke and asked for her child they told her she had devoured it.

And so the false story was told to Pwyll and sworn to by all six of the women. Pwyll, however, refused to put Rhiannon away, choosing instead to inflict a penance upon her. She was to sit every day by the horse block at the gate of the castle, tell the tale to any stranger that came by, and offer to carry them into the castle on her back, which she did for half a year.

How justice came to be finally done to Rhiannon is an important tale as it brings us back to the old Celtic Horse Cult. There lived at that time a man named Tiernyon of Gwent Is Coed, who was possessed of a most beautiful mare. Although the beast foaled on the night of every first of May the colt always mysteriously disappeared. Tiernyon finally resolved to get to the bottom of the matter and on the next May night that the mare was due to foal he took up arms and stationed himself in the stable to see what was happening. The mare duly foaled and as Tiernyon was admiring the colt's strength and beauty, a strange noise was heard outside and a long, clawed arm stretched through the window and laid hold of the young horse. Tiernyon immediately smote the offending limb with his sword, severing it at the elbow so that it fell inside the stable still holding its prey, while a great wailing was heard without. He rushed outside to see what was happening but only the darkness greeted him, his assailant having vanished as though into nowhere. Upon his return to the stable he found, to his amazement, a male infant, wrapped in swaddling clothes and a mantle of satin. He gathered up the babe and brought it to where his wife, who had no children, lay sleeping.

When she awoke next morning, upon beholding the child she immediately loved it and decided to bring it up as her own telling her friends that she herself had borne it. They called the infant Gwri of the Golden Hair, for his hair was the colour of yellow gold. The child, in keeping with all hero-figures, grew at a miraculous pace and was soon able to ride and master the colt that had been born on the same night.

In time Tiernyon came to hear of the tale of Rhiannon and her punishment and upon scanning the face of the young lad he was rearing, observed how identical his features were to those of Pwyll, Prince of Dyfed. After discussing it with his wife they agreed that the proper thing to do was to take the child to his father so that Rhiannon could be released from her labour. As they drew near to the castle they beheld Rhiannon sitting by her horse block and nobly carrying out her totally undeserved penance. 'As I have promised, I will bear each one of you into the Palace', Rhiannon told them, but they refused to allow her to thus burden herself. After they had related to Pwyll and Rhiannon the story of the boy and the colt, Tiernyon exclaimed, 'Behold, there is thy son, lady, and whoever told that lie concerning thee has done thee wrong.' All who saw the lad immediately recognized him as the son of Pwyll, whereupon Rhiannon exclaimed, 'I declare by heaven that if this be true there is an end to my trouble.' A chief by the name of Pendaran who stood nearby commented, 'Well hast thou named thy son Pryderi (Trouble), and well becomes him the name of Pryderi the son of Pwyll, Lord of Annwn', and from thenceforth that was what he was called.[1]

From the aforegoing we may surmise that there was a period when the followers of the Horse Cult were badly treated, perhaps even persecuted. But in the aftermath of what was considered to be some supernatural occurrence or miracle, faith in the integrity of the Goddess was restored and the people turned to her once again. This would also fit in with her later association with Manawyddan, her marriage to Pwyll representing, no doubt some 'troublesome' period when her cult was banished to the underworld or forced to go underground until it was re-established through the enchantments of Manawyddan at a later date.

Bran and Branwen

The tale of these two is certainly one that merits mention as it is thoroughly British in its context and evocative, therefore, of the Celtic patriotism usually associated with the Arthurian cycle.

Bran the Blessed, a mighty giant, had been crowed King of the Isle of the Mighty (Britain). He was in residence at his seat at Harlech in the company of his brother Manawyddan, his sister Branwen, and the two sons Nissyen and Evnissyen which his mother, Penardun, had borne Euroswydd. One day he looked out to sea and noted the arrival of thirteen ships from Ireland. Matholwych, King of Ireland, had evidently arrived to seek Branwen's hand in marriage so that the two countries might join to become a great force. The Irish were hospitably entertained, and after consulting with his lords Bran agreed to give his sister to the Irish King in wedlock. And so the wedding was arranged and the two were duly married.

The tale that ensues concerns the treachery of Evnissyen who, unlike his gentle and good-natured brother, was a contentious character who loved nothing better than setting one person against another. It would take more than a chapter to recount in full the mischief that Evnissyen made between the Irish King and his men and their British hosts, which forced Bran to give his magic Cauldron to Matholwych in atonement for his kinsman's misdeeds. I will, therefore, bypass the detail and pick up the tale at the point where a battle royal was being fought between Bran and his men and the army of the Irish King. Matholwych, however, made haste to heat the magic Cauldron and cast the bodies of his dead soldiers therein so that they emerged the following day whole and ready to fight again, but mute. When Evnissyen saw the dire straits in which his action had placed the men of Britain, he was so struck with remorse he hid himself among the Irish dead and was flung into the Cauldron with the rest of them at the end of the second day of battle. Once therein he stretched himself out so as to break the Cauldron, splitting it into four pieces, which also broke the evil spell. The effort, however, proved too great a strain on his heart and he died.

All the Irishmen were eventually slain and there were only seven British survivors, plus the giant Bran. Then Bran, who was severely wounded, commanded those present to sever his head, saying:

> Take it with you to London, and there bury it in the White Mount (where the Tower of London now stands) looking towards France, and no foreigner shall invade the land while it is there. On the way the Head will talk to you, and be as pleasant company as ever in life. In Harlech ye will be feasting seven years, and the Birds of Rhiannon shall sing for you. And at Gwales in Penvro ye will be feasting fourscore years, and the Head will talk to you and be uncorrupted till ye open the door looking towards Cornwall. After that ye may no longer tarry, but set forth to London and bury the Head ... .

The seven then cut off the Head of Bran and went forth with Branwen to do as they were bid.[2]

Branwen eventually died of a broken heart on account of the trouble her nuptials had caused. The Head was buried as instructed and remained so until Arthur dug it up for 'he would not have the land defended but by the strong arm.' There are numerous tales concerning the talking Head of Bran and many prophecies are attributed to it, but the whole tale assumes a fairy-like quality if read in its original and unabridged form. The magic Cauldron is reminiscent of that of the Dagda while the enormous size of Bran is in keeping with the giants and titans of many other ancient myths. Like the Dagda, Bran was also a skilled harpist and poet and possessed a singing voice of great beauty. Bran's love and devotion to his country were fulfilled in the ultimate sacrificing of his life for the protection of his people: shades of the dying king who goes willingly to the slaughter for the benefit of his subjects.

One of the strange but intriguing things about these myths is the mortality of these so-termed 'immortals', which is surely telling us nothing more esoteric than that these cults were eventually overriden by the oncoming tides of other, more forceful beliefs, Christianity, of course, adding the final headstone to their immortal graves. A paradox indeed! But then, as modern science is only too happy to inform us, nothing is ever completely annihilated, it simply changes frequency or ceases to manifest as the frozen energy of matter. The Old Ones are still there, albeit buried beneath their stones, but in the ultimate timelessness that is truth all stand equal in the light of cosmic law.

Endnotes
1. Rolleston, T.W. *Myths and Legends of the Celtic Race*, p. 365.
2. Ibid. Rolleston, p. 371.

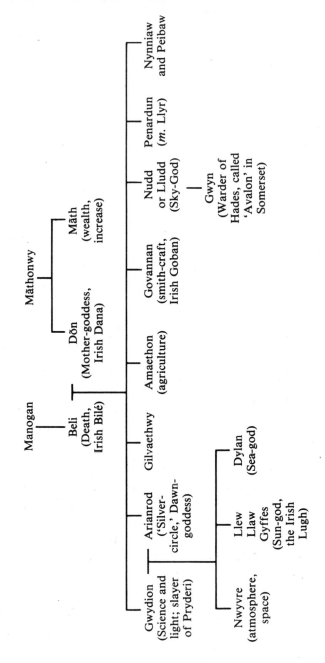

GODS OF THE HOUSE OF DÕN

Manogan

Beli
(Death,
Irish Bilé)

Mâthonwy

Dôn
(Mother-goddess,
Irish Dana)

Mâth
(wealth,
increase)

Gilvaethwy

Amaethon
(agriculture)

Govannan
(smith-craft,
Irish Goban)

Nudd
or Lludd (Sky-God)

Gwyn
(Warder of
Hades, called
'Avalon' in
Somerset)

Penardun
(m. Llyr)

Nynniaw
and Peibaw

Arianrod
('Silver-
circle,' Dawn-
goddess)

Gwydion
(Science and
light; slayer
of Pryderi)

Nwyvre
(atmosphere,
space)

Llew
Llaw
Gyffes
(Sun-god,
the Irish
Lugh)

Dylan
(Sea-god)

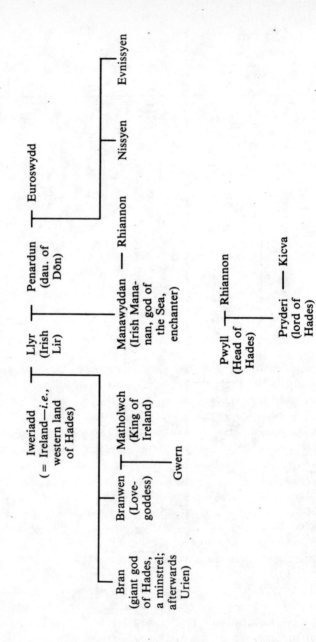

GODS OF THE HOUSE OF LLYR

14. THE ARTHURIAN SAGA

> Great Arthur still is sleeping,
> His warriors all around him,
> With grip upon the steel.
> When dawns the day on Cambry
> Great Arthur forth will sally,
> Alive to work her weal.[1]

Most of those who will choose to read this book will, on account of its title, be drawn to the fields of magic and the occult, and therefore fairly familiar with the history behind the Arthurian legends. But for those who are simply fascinated with anything Celtic but have not, perhaps, had the time nor inclination to seek out, let alone read, the vast area of conjectural literature of this subject, here are a few of the basic facts.

Mention King Arthur and the picture that springs to many people's minds is a Hollywood-tinted panorama against which backcloth are displayed the deeds of an heroic and chivalrous British king who lived somewhere around the sixth century AD, surrounded by virtuous knights who convened about a round table, and spent a lot of time searching for the Holy Grail. From what has already been said in this book, however, it must be obvious to the reader that there is far more to it than that.

In his preface to *Le Morte D'Arthur*, the eminent Welsh

scholar and historian, Sir John Rhys, mentions that in the *Annales Cambriae* dated AD 537, one of the oldest documents available in Britain, there is an 'Arthur' referred to, but not in the kingly mode, although the cross is mentioned as being his symbol and he was spoken of synonymously with St George. The *Book of Taliesin* also refers to him as *'Imperator Defectu Oraculorum'*, and states that he was regularly served by Druidic priests who prophesied for him.

Rolleston, however, tells us that the earliest extant mention of Arthur is to be found in the work of the British historian Nennius, who wrote his *Historia Britonum* around AD 800. His authority was derived from many sources including ancient monuments, some of the mythologies we have already examined, Roman annals, and the chronicles of the saints, especially Germanus. The result is a highly Romanized and Christianized view of British history which sees the British deriving from Trojan/Roman ancestry. His account of Arthur, however, is both sober and brief.

According to Nennius, Arthur did live in the sixth century AD but was not a king, his ancestry being less noble than many other British chiefs who chose him as their leader on account of his great talents as a military *Imperator* or *dux bellorum*. He led the British nobles against the Saxons, defeating them in twelve battles, the last being at Mount Badon.[2]

Geoffrey of Monmouth whose proper name was Grufyd ab Arthur, Bishop of St Asaph, was next to appear on the Arthurian scene with his *Historia Regum Britaniae* which he wrote in the early part of the twelfth century. Rolleston describes this work as 'an audacious attempt to make sober history out of a mass of mythical and legendary matter mainly derived, if we are to believe the author, from an ancient book brought by his uncle Walter Mapes, Archdeacon of Oxford, from Brittany.' (The Brittany connection we have already established in Chapter 6). Geoffrey, it would appear, wrote expressly to commemorate the exploits of Arthur, which character appears to have captured his imagination in some way.

The Arthurian personality thenceforth assumes the role of a king whose court was at Caerleon-on-Usk, the son of one Uther Pendragon and Igerna, wife of Gorlos, Duke of Cornwall, to whom Uther gained access in the guise of her husband, aided by the magic arts of Merlin. (This is reminiscent of Zeus assuming the shape of Amphytryon in order to lie with that gentleman's wife: result — Hercules!) The Red Dragon has always been associated with the British people. It was the crest of Uther and accounted for the title 'Pendragon', that is, 'Chief' or 'Great Dragon'. Some authorities, however, are inclined to view Uther as a fictitional representation of the old Celtic god Beli.

Geoffrey places the commencement of Arthur's reign in the year 505, recounts the Saxon wars and adds that Arthur eventually conquered Ireland, Norway, Gaul and Dacia, as well as the whole of Britain, while also resisting a demand for tribute and homage from the Romans. All rather fanciful if viewed against the cold light of historical fact, no doubt.[3]

However, the story continues: While Arthur was away on the continent carrying on his struggle with Rome, his nephew, Mordred, usurped his crown and wedded his wife, Guanhumara (Guinevere). In due course Arthur returned, defeated the traitor at Winchester, finally slaying him in the last battle of Cornwall, but not before he himself was badly wounded at his enemy's hand (AD 542). The Queen retired to a convent at Caerleon.

Prior to his death, Arthur conferred his kingdom on his kinsman, Constantine, and was then carried off mysteriously to the 'Isle of Avalon' to be cured and 'rest in silence'. (One cannot fail to be struck by the similarity between this myth and the Egyptian story of Osiris who, in his absence, was usurped by his brother, Set!)

Arthur's magic sword 'Caliburn' (Welsh 'Caladvwlch'), later known as 'Excalibur', is mentioned by Geoffrey who describes it as being made in Avalon, implying that it came from Fairyland or the 'Land of the Dead'. It was not until some time later that Avalon became identified with a specific place in Britain (Glastonbury). In Geoffrey's narrative there is no mention of a Round Table, the Holy Grail, or Sir Lancelot and, apart from the allusion to Avalon, no mystical element is present. Like Nennius, Geoffrey assigns a totally unrealistic classical origin to the British which should be enough to make anyone question the whole episode to start with.[4]

Lewis Spence tells us that Geoffrey's work was first written in Welsh, then translated into Latin, but retranslated to 'Kymraeg' later in his life, after which he comments to the effect that the facts differ materially from those of Nennius and the Cymric Chonicles. Arthur's residence is given as Caerleon-on-Usk while British sources designate it as Cornwall. It would also seem that details of Arthur's Roman battles are quite unknown to native legends.

Although Spence comments on the lack of Arthurian references in *The Mabinogion*, Jeffrey Gantz's translation includes 'How Culhwch won Olwen', 'The Dream of Rhonabwy', 'Owein, Countess of The Fountain', 'Peredur, Son of Evrawg', and 'Gereint and Enid', each tale being enacted against the background of a slightly varying Arthurian court.

Like other authorities, Gantz finds the Breton influences unquestionable.

Geoffrey was also the author of the *Vita Merlini*, or prophecies concerning Merlin but, as Spence observes not a word is mentioned in either of his works about Druidic training or practice. He alludes to Merlin, for example, as *'rex erat et vates'*, a king and a prophet, but Spence comments that without the Welsh version to check with there is no knowing from which word the term *'vates'* was translated.

Spence does, however, draw our attention to certain occult operations which are mentioned by Geoffrey, including an allusion to magical practices in the Temple of Minerva which coincide with similar Druidic observances.

A certain King Leir, who partitioned the kingdom between his three daughters, also comes into the picture and the manner of this monarch's burial in a tomb under the River Soar at Leicester, 'which had originally been built underground to the honour of the god Janus' cannot surely be anything other than the old sea god Llyr, his daughters the Triple Goddess and Janus the old giant Bran the Blessed whose triple-faced Head, like that of the Roman double-faced Janus, also possessed magical properties.⁵ After all, Leicester was Llyr's city as we have already established.

The next reference of interest concerns Merlin's consultation by Vortigern regarding the building of a tower in which he might successfully defend himself against the Saxons. Merlin, according to legend, never had a father, which is suggestive of a 'changeling' or fairly crossbreed situation, and Vortigern had been advised by his magicians to seek the magical service of such a man. But Merlin warns the ruler that the suggested tower will not stand because of two dragons, one red and one white which lie beneath it in a pool. The Druids were obviously familiar with ley lines!

In a later episode Aurelius, King of Britain, consults Merlin regarding the erection of a monument to the British nobles who had fallen to the Saxon armies whereupon the wizard advised him to send to Ireland for the Giant's Dance (Stonehenge) and erect it in Britain as a lasting memorial to the dead heroes. Aurelius apparently made light of this suggestion and was rebuked by Merlin thus:

I entreat your majesty to forbear vain laughter, for what I say is without vanity. There are mystical stones and of a medicinal virtue. The giants of old brought them from the farthest coast of Africa, and placed them in Ireland when they inhabited that country. Their design in this was to make baths in them when they should be taken with any illness. For their method was to wash the stones and put their sick into the water, which infallibly cured them. With the like success they cured wounds also adding only the application of some herbs. There is not a stone there which has not some healing virtue.[6]

Since we now know for certain that the Stonehenge monoliths were erected several thousand years earlier than the sixth century AD, Geoffrey's account must be discounted and doubt cast on the credulity of the remainder of his narrative. Spence is also careful to make clear his awareness of these facts, while emphasizing the African association with the old Stonehenge cult on the one hand, and the fact that certain of the stones were not local in origin on the other.

But to return to Arthur of British legend. We owe much of the popularly accepted picture of Arthur to Sir Thomas Malory (d. 1471). His epic work Le Morte D'Arthur was published in 1485 and was largely based on mythical and chivalric tales that were already around. Little is known of Malory himself, other than that he fought in the Wars of the Roses and sat in Parliament. According to Rhys who prefaced the work in recent years, the names used in the text have become Celticized and were originally continental in origin, which doubtless infers that Breton influence. He also commented that it was written in an obscure language which rendered accurate translation difficult.

But what of the romantic, albeit suspect, tales of the kingly Arthur? Following his birth he was taken by Merlin to his secret castle to be raised by one Sir Ector (Gwydion and Llew again!). Upon the death of Uther Pendragon, Merlin called all the knights and nobles together on Christmas Day. In the middle of the assembly hall there stood a huge block of stone upon which rested a large anvil; embedded in the anvil was a sword. Carved around the stone were the words: 'Whosoever pulleth out this sword from the stone and the anvil is the true born King of Britain.' Try as they might, none of the nights were able to dislodge the sword until New Year's Day when Sir Ector appeared on the scene with his sons, Kay and Arthur. Arthur withdrew the sword with ease, whereupon he was declared the true son of Uther Pendragon and rightful heir to the throne.

His feats in the field of battle followed his coronation and later the Fellowship of the Round Table was founded under Merlin's guidance, while his marriage to Guinevere was duly arranged. The rest of the story we have already considered, although in one version he is carried off in a boat by three women to be treated for his wounds, and is never seen again.

In spite of this thoroughly Christianized rendering of the Arthurian tale, as told by Malory and Geoffrey of Monmouth, it is easy to see, from reading between the lines, that Arthur and his associates are figures from Celtic mythology who have been given mortal status and attributes by mediaeval Bretonic story-tellers. Arthur's very birth is in keeping with the births of all the heroes of old who were half-god, half-man. His sword Excalibur, which, according to another version of the legend was given to him by the 'Lady of the Lake' and later returned thereto, possessed magical powers in keeping with Nuáda's Danaan fairy gift and Mananan's acquisition from Lugh. The Lady of the Lake is surely one of the three women who transport Arthur to Avalon and these three, in turn, are the triple personae of the Goddess. In Celtic mythology Avalon is another name for Gwyn's realm of Tylwyth Teg, that subtle dimension which houses the spirits of the Old Gods or Lordly Ones. The sacred boat upon which he is transported to Avalon is Mananan's 'Ocean Sweeper' (Charon's Ferryboat or the Egyptian Barque of Ra). Arthur has also been equated with the Brythonic deity

Artaius, who is also said to have stolen a sacred cauldron of knowledge (grail) from the gods.

The Tor of Glastonbury was once thought to have been placed on one of the secret entrances to that strange, timeless dimension which is nebulously dubbed 'the Underworld', where Thomas of Ercaldoune (Thomas the Rhymer) spent his missing years with Queen Mab.

Referred to as the 'once and future King', Arthur, it is believed, sleeps in some hidden place from which he will arise to lead his clan (the British) in some future hour of dire need. This alone implies a belief in his immortality, which immediately removes him from the context of earthly monarchs with limited life spans.

But we cannot consider the Arthurian tales without taking into account the nature, deeds and origin of the character known as Merlin. In the legend Merlin is Arthur's occult adviser and a magician of great power. But he carries the hallmark of the Celtic Druid or Indo/Aryan shaman, as we shall see.

His mother is mentioned by Geoffrey as being the daughter of the King of Demetia, and a nun (virgin) who had been visited by some angelic being who had fathered the infant Merlin on her, in keeping with magical or enlightened personages down the ages, thus endowing him with supernatural, or 'fairy' powers. Merlin has been identified with many earlier divinities: Hermes Trismegistus, the Roman Mercury, Hermes of the Greek pantheon, Thoth of Egypt, and the old Celtic Cernunnos. In later pre-Christian years the name Merlin assumed titular reference, appearing in the princely context as 'Myrddin Ab Morfryn', and as 'Merlin Ambrosius' or 'Merlin Emrys' in the *Historia Regum Britaniae*. Other authorities have different explanations. Canon MacCulloch regarded him as 'an ideal magician', possibly an old god like the Irish 'God of Druidism' while Rhys believed him to be a Celtic version of Zeus. In the famous poem of Taliesin's declaration, which will be featured in a forthcoming chapter, Taliesin is Merlin reincarnated, from which we may finally deduce that 'Merlin' is a title in one context and in another an appellation of one of the 'Old Ones', or 'Guardians of Cosmic Time', who is especially connected with the distinct flavour of the British ethos.

Most authorities, when writing on the subject of Merlin,

quote the famous Breton verses:

> Merlin! Merlin! where art thou going
> So early in the day with thy black dog?
> Oi! oi! oi! oi!
> Ioi! oi! oi! oi! oi!
>
> I have come here to search for the way,
> To find the red egg;
> The red egg of the marine serpent,
> By the sea side in the hollow of the stone.
> I am going to seek in the valley,
> The green water cress, and the golden grass,
> And the top branch of the oak,
> In the wood by the side of the fountain.[7]

There is a third verse to this but as it is so obviously a Christian travesty of the original, and as Graves says, 'The ancient poetic mysteries have been reduced to a tangle by the Church's prolonged hostility...' that I cannot find it in my heart to include it. Merlin's black dog must surely be Anubis, or his Celtic equivalent, who would guide him safely through the dark regions of initiation. The marine serpent is the Uraeus, or Eye of the Sun God, the wisdom mode of which has been deluged by the sea of man's deep emotional unconscious and, like the secret energies of Merlin himself, time-encapsulated in stone. This may not be the recognized interpretation, but it is how I see it.

One legend speaks of the abode of Merlin being a house of glass, a bush of whitethorn laden with bloom, or a sort of smoke or mist in the air, 'a close, neither of iron nor steel nor timber nor of stone, but of the air without any other thing, by enchantment so strong that it may never be undone while the world endureth.' Finally, he is said to have descended upon Bardsey Island, 'off the extreme westernmost point of Carnarvonshire ... into it he went with nine attendant bards, taking with him the 'Thirteen Treasures of Britain', thenceforth lost to men'.[8]

Other legends supply different versions of Merlin's final disappearance, however, including his being immured in a magic grotto into which he had been decoyed, transported to a joyous garden after being cast under a love spell by the fairy enchantress Vivien, buried under a large stone after having been put to sleep by a magic draught and conveyed to an idyllic island on a lake. The perpetrators of these acts are sometimes referred to as 'immortals', 'nymphs' or even 'admirers', but the one thing they had in common is that they were always female.

Similarities between the Celtic Annwn (pronounced 'Anoon') and the Egyptian Amenti would seem to demand attention. Osiris is frequently referred to by different authorities in the Arthurian context, which would place Merlin in the role of Thoth/Tehuti, the magician of the Egyptian pantheon who was responsible for the conception of Horus. Waddell also observed the links in the Asar/Osiris/Arthur chain of connections. Mordred is Set, by whose hand Osiris/Arthur was slain; the body is ferried across the Nile by Isis and Nephthys, the Ladies of the Lake, to the regions of Aalu (Avalon) in the west, the place where Osiris/Arthur, whose physical death(s) are unrecorded, ruled and who await glorious resurrection. Both Arthur and Osiris had associations with the Bull Cult, while Horus, son of Osiris, was depicted as a hawk and Arthur as a crow, 'For no Englishman in olden times would kill a crow lest it be the hero's spirit.' The name of Arthur's nephew Gwalchmei also means 'hawk'.[9]

One could go on quoting from this or that authority for pages, and giving endless examples of unquestionably obvious connecting links between the Arthurian saga and the myths and legends of much older cultures. Of course, readers will see what they want to in these stories, but in summary the author would like to take the following stand:

These fables are based on an ancient religious cult, the origins of which can be traced back to pre-Flood days. Some see this as originating in the east; others ascribe it Atlantean origins. Over the centuries it accumulated many different overlays, each being influenced by the nature of the ethos in which it flourished. Various persons throughout the history of many lands have appeared, either to those around them or to members of the resident priesthood of the period, as 'Chosen Ones'. Always with such characters there is a changeling story, which simply tells us that the person in question exhibits qualities that are partly of this world and partly of another (often labelled 'fairy', Devic, or in the case of Christianity, a virgin birth or heavenly visitation). The

Hollywood Arthur adds up to a combination of romanticized Breton heroic legend superimposed on a local Celtic leader who was highly favoured by his Arch Druid, and flavoured with the spices of occult mythology and mediaeval escapism.

The real Arthur, however, represents 'He of the Old Ones', who is the legitimate carrier of the Celtic cosmic message. And so he sleeps, but not for long. The hands of the cosmic clock move slowly forward towards the hour of Merlin/Thoth, when the horn shall sound and the eon of the new Arthur/Horus will herald the onset of the Aquarian Age.

Endnotes
1. Lewis, Elvet. From the poem *Arthur Gyda nil* ('Arthur With Us').
2. Rolleston, T.W. *Myths and Legends of the Celtic Race*, p. 336–7.
3. Ibid. Rolleston, p. 337.
4. Ibid. Rolleston, p. 338.
5. Spence, Lewis. *The Mysteries of Britain*, p. 111.
6. Ibid. Spence, p. 113.
7. Ibid. Spence, p. 116.
8. Op. cit. Rolleston, p. 355.
9. Loc. cit. Spence, p. 128.

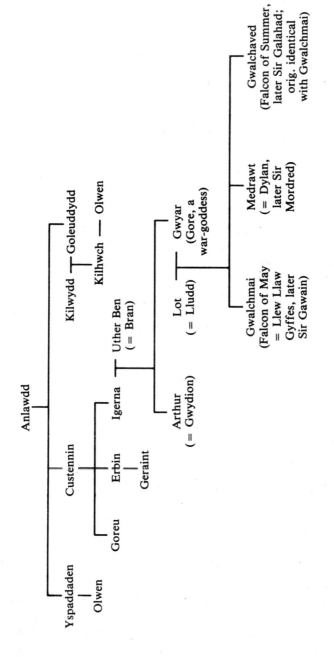

ARTHUR AND HIS KIN

15. THE MAGICAL SIGNIFICANCE OF THE GRAIL

One of the main themes of the Arthurian legends is the quest for the Holy Grail, which is closely linked with the Chivalrous Order of the Round Table. According to mediaeval traditions, Glastonbury was visited by Christ as a boy with his uncle, Joseph of Arimathea who returned a few years after the crucifixion to preach the gospel. With him, Joseph is said to have brought the Chalice that was used at the last supper, plus two cruets containing the sweat and blood of Christ, which were later buried at some secret place near Glastonbury.[1]

Another version designates the Grail as the Cup which collected the Blood of Christ which Joseph brought to these lands and handed into the safe keeping of one Bron or Brons, another name for Bran the Blessed, the superimposition or infusion inference being obvious.

But there were Grail stories long before the *Annales Cambriae* was penned, or Geoffrey of Monmouth's Arthurian tales made their appearance. The old Welsh legends tell us how Arthur set sail in his magic ship Prydwen to the shadowy regions of Annwn wherein Pwyll is Lord. Upon his arrival there he perceived a magic cauldron, guarded by nine maidens, which he proceeded to capture.

In the Taliesin poem *The Spoils of Annwn* the Cauldron is found at a place called Caer Sidi or Caer Pedryvan, the Four Cornered Castle, in the Isle of the Active Door. Likewise, the

Breton version sees the Grail in the keeping of Pelles or Peleur, a Normanized version of Pwyll, in the Castle of Carbonek, which is really Caer Bannauc, the 'peaked' or horned Castle, as referring to the points or corners of Caer Sidi. The vessel which Arthur and his companion recover is described in the poem as a cauldron, the rim of which is set with pearls. The fire beneath it was kindled by the breath of nine maidens, it spoke as an oracle and would not cook food for anyone that was unworthy. Again the Breton story is confirmatory of the poem, with the Grail supplying the knights with any kind of food they might desire, although only the worthy could approach the vessel. Those who worshipped at the Grail Chapel of Peleur remained young and were unaffected by the passage of time, while the Breton Grail also headed the sick.[2]

But magic cups and cauldrons are plentiful in Celtic literature from the Tuatha de Danaan gift onwards. We have already discovered how Bran's vessel could restore dead warriors to life while the Dagda's bowl was a never diminishing cornucopia that could feed an army and still be filled to the brim. And then there is Keridwen's fabled cauldron, which is due to make its appearance shortly in this book.

Nor are Grail legends the prerogative of the Celts; the Egyptian goddess Nephthys, to whom the Chalice or Cup is sacred, actually has this symbol incorporated in her headgear. Nephthys was essentially a goddess of all that is hidden or concealed and yet, paradoxically, she was also the Revealer, albeit sometimes of things that one would rather not know! But such is the path of initiation. Her silver Cup encapsulates all later Grail and Cup symbology as the sacred container or receptacle into which the waters of Light and Truth — the libations of life — are poured.

Another ancient legend tells how the Grail was fashioned by angels from the emerald that dropped from Lucifer's forehead when he fell from heavenly grace. In the East, god figures are frequently depicted with a jewel in the centre of the forehead — a third eye — said to correspond psychically with the pineal gland and the ability to 'see' beyond the five normal senses. Nephthys' colour was green, like the emerald, and she was goddess of hidden dimensions which would equate with the Celtic underworld, while green is also the colour of the Celtic ray!

The quest for the Grail carries a deeper significance than the generally conceived Christian concept of locating the Sacred Chalice. It is more of a search for the unknowable, things hidden or occulted, the knowledge of which opens the doors to enlightenment and spiritual status earned through suffering, self-discipline and perseverance. In Arthurian literature a prerequisite for finding the Grail or having it revealed to one was pureness of heart. The preparation for the Quest, therefore, involved a series of purification ceremonies which were seen in the context of the religion to which the seeker adhered. Christian knights prayed, fasted or attended retreats. Their pagan forebears performed their rituals of submission to a higher power or undertook severe penances that were guaranteed to give them mastery over their own lower or darker aspects, for unless the darkness, both of Hades and of the individual soul, is conquered the initiate cannot hope to understand the hidden mysteries of light and truth.

The Welsh version of the Breton story concerns one Peredur, whom Rolleston sees as the character *der reine Thor*, the valiant and pure-hearted simpleton reminiscent of The Fool in the Tarot. After proving himself at Arthur's court, Peredur set forth in search of the Holy Vessel and many were his adventures. His initial travels took him to a castle beside a lake where he found a venerable man fishing. This is the castle of the Grail, the home of the lame Fisher King, Guardian of the Sacred Cup, who also happens to be Peredur's uncle. The old man tells him that whatever strange events he may witness in the castle he must not speak of, which is indicative of initiatory rites if anything ever was!

Some scholars are of the opinion that the name of the 'Fisher King' originally had a deep significance which is now lost, but by all accounts he was one and the same as Gwyn Ap Nudd, Lord of the Underworld, although in subsequent Grail stories he is given the name Bron or Bran. The Greek Hephaestus, whose smithy was also in the regions beneath the earth, was likewise lame as was Wayland. We may therefore assume that the Fisher King was the Dark Tanist of the fivefold Celtic faith, considered by some occultists as the Hanged Man of the Tarot. His lameness had been caused by the thrust of a spear that had also rendered him impotent. Only when the true knowledge and understanding of the Grail message is grasped will the Fisher King be healed and the country restored to prosperity. One cannot help feeling that somewhere in this symbology is concealed the encapsulation of the Old Ones, the knowledge of whom is kept bound by the sins of ignorance, spiritual blindness and bigotry.

Peredur is faced with a series of enigmatic tests, plus a considerable amount of opposition from the 'nine sorceresses of Gloucester', whom he and Arthur eventually despatch.[3] But Peredur, or Percival as he was subsequently called, did not, it would seem, put the right questions to the Fisher King who was consequently unable to break his silence and speak the words of power that would have dispelled the enchantment that both rendered him lame and encapsulated the British Isles. (In case anyone has not thought of it already, what about an Arthurian Tarot?)

There are many other versions of the Grail story, that of Wolfram von Eschenbach, for example, whose Grail hero was the much sung Parsifal of Teutonic myth and opera. Writing circa the year 1200, some twenty years later than Chrétien de Troyes, he says of the knights of the Grail Castle:

> Si lebent von einem steine
> Des geslähte ist vîl reine . . .
> Es heizet *lapsit [lapis] exillîs*,
> Der stein ist ouch genannt der Grâl.[4]

The Cup was originally brought down from heaven by a flight of angels and deposited in Anjou, as the worthiest region for its reception. Its power is sustained by a dove which every Good Friday comes from heaven and lays on the Grail a consecrated host. It is preserved in the Castle of Munsalvasche (Montsalvat) and guarded by four hundred knights who are all, except the King, vowed to virginity ...! Of course there is much more than this, as anyone who is familiar with the Parsifal story will know, but it hints too strongly at Christianized romantic invention to merit serious occult consideration. After all, Wolfram himself tells us that he had the substance of the tale from the Provencal poet Kyot or Guiot, who in turn rather suspectly professed to have found it in an Arabic book in Toledo written by a heathen named Flegetanis![5]

Of the Cauldron of Abundance there are many versions but it is generally accepted that the Celts inevitably endowed their cauldrons with three virtues: inexhaustibility, inspiration and regeneration, which could be summed up in one word — fertility. All cauldron owners had fertility associations, the Dagda and Bran for example, but the original emphasis was undoubtedly a feminine one, the receptive symbology being essentially female.

The Grail legends are therefore simply Christianized versions of the old cauldron theme, dressed in the trappings of Breton chivalry and sanctified by the Last Supper legend which earned them the blessing of the Church and the respectability that this implied.

In a recent book entitled *The Holy Blood and The Holy Grail*, Michael Baigent, Richard Leigh and Henry Lincoln, after intensive research in the Rennes le Chateau region of southern France came up with the theory that the Grail represented something as fundamental as the blood line of Jesus which is carried through by his descendants in that area to this day. The earlier spelling of the word 'Sangreal', they believe was, in fact, more accurate than the more recent version which became erroneously hyphenated and should really read 'Sang Raal' or 'Seng Réal' — Royal Blood.[6]

Far be it from me to discount the diligent, and for all we know accurate, findings of these good gentlemen. After all, there is no valid reason why Jesus should not have fathered children and founded a dynasty that has survived to this day. So while his genealogy may well have, at some time in the past, become concealed by some secret organization safely within the Sangraal context, as I see it this in no way detracts from the old Cup or Cauldron legends that were in existence thousands of years before the emergence of Christianity.

Arthurian mysticism, and the Grail legend in particular, was never more popular than it is today thanks to the media. The righteous hero searching for the truth is an evergreen theme which inevitably assumes an added sense of urgency or importance in times of world crisis. While many may find their Grail within the confines of orthodoxy, others among us, like Peredur, seek outwardly ever pressing forward in our pursuit of the answer to the Fisher King's riddles. Our journeyings may take us into the regions of Pwyll or Gwyn, or we may be waylaid *en route* by the treachery of those we have trusted as friends and kinsfolk. But, like the Eternal Fool, we sling our simple knapsack over our back and make for the cliff's edge, our faithful 'familiar', like Merlin's black dog, anxiously tugging at our attire to warn us of possible danger. But it was ever the way of fools to rush in where angels fear to tread and, after all, innocence and a sense of childlike wonder is oft-times the best protection!

Endnotes
1. Mathias, Michael; and Hector, Derek. *Glastonbury*, p. 10.
2. Spence, Lewis. *The Mysteries of Britain*, p. 138.
3. Rolleston, T.W. *Myths and Legends of the Celtic Race*, p. 404.
4. Ibid. Rolleston, p. 407.
5. Ibid. Rolleston, p. 408.
6. Baigent, Michael; Leigh, Richard; and Lincoln, Henry. *The Holy Blood and the Holy Grail*, p. 267.

16. DRUIDIC AND BARDIC BELIEFS

I fully realize that in writing this chapter I am likely to disturb a few sacred cows. There are two schools of Druidism that are well known in this country, both of which differ, while to my personal knowledge there are many others who practise what they believe to be the old Druidic faith, or their version of it. So I shall stay with the traditional views as given by recognized authorities.

Regarding the etymology of the word 'Druid', it is suggested that the latter part connects with the Aryan root *vid* which appears in 'wisdom', in the Latin *videre* etc. This root in combination with the intensive particle *dru* would yield the word dru-vids, represented in Gaelic by *draoi*, a Druid, just as another intensive, *su* with *vids* yields the Gaelic *saoi*, a sage.[1]

All Celtic paths lead to Druidism, while Druidism, according to the historians, existed wherever the Celts settled. But although the Druids were often associated with the dolmens, there were Celtic settlements without dolmens and dolmens where there were no Celts. There already existed in western Europe and the British Isles an all-embracing religion with a powerful priesthood, steeped in magic and the Cult of the Underworld. In fact, so strong was this magical faith that it evoked from Pliny the comment that he believed it to be indigenous to neither Greece or Italy, as it was conducted in Britain with such elaborate ritual it would almost seem as if it was they (the Britons) who had taught it to the Persians!

The historial references, in fact, infer that Druidism was imposed upon the imaginative and sensitive Celts by the earlier megalithic population of Europe, or perhaps it would be fairer to say that the two religions fused to produce the brand of Celtic belief that we are now in the process of examining. What we do know for sure is that the concept of the immortality of the soul constituted the cardinal doctrine in Druidism.

Caesar wrote of the Druids, 'They discuss and impart to the youth many things respecting the stars and their motions, respecting the extent of the universe and of our Earth, respecting the power and majesty of the immortal gods.' But as the Druids strictly forbade the committal of their doctrines to writing, although their scribes were well acquainted with lettering, we are deprived of the details. This policy tended to surround their religion with an aura of mystery on the one hand, while on the other it protected their beliefs against controversy. The written word is so easily manipulated, as may be evidence with the Christian Bible of which there are innumerable interpretations, the followers of each believing their ideas and theirs alone to be correct.

However, Caesar's respectful words regarding the refined and sublime nature of Druidism stand in stark contrast to the historical reference to human sacrifice among the Celts whom, we are told, encased numbers of people at a time in huge frames of wickerwork and then burned them alive to win the favour of their gods. Something here does not seem to add up, although sacrificial practices of this nature were common to a certain stage of development in most peoples. The continuation of human sacrifice among the Celts after an otherwise fairly high state of civilization and culture had been attained has its parallel in Mexico and Carthage, and has been attributed by historians to the domination of a priestly caste. The ancient Egyptians, however, although greatly influenced by their priesthood, were not thus afflicted. Manetho tells us that human sacrifices were officially abolished there around 1600 BC, although they were viewed with repugnance by the Egyptians from the very earliest of time.

Spence is of the opinion that Druidism arose out of the Old Stone Age Cult of the Dead which became segregated in the British Isles because they were more culturally apart from the Continent during the Bronze Age. There was certainly a flourishing Goddess religion in Britain for centuries prior to the arrival of the Brythonic Celts, as we have already established, and the earlier Celtic beliefs would appear to embody much of this.

The similarities between the oral Celtic traditions and the old Egyptian faith are unmistakable. Ammianus Marcellinus says: 'With grand contempt for the mortal lot they professed the immortality of the soul', while Pomponius Mela writes:

> One of their dogmas has come to common knowledge, namely, that souls are eternal and that there is another life in the infernal regions. ... And it is for this reason, too, that they burn or bury with their dead things appropriate to them in life, and that in times past they even used to defer the completion of business and the payment of debts until their arrival in another world. Indeed there were some of them who flung themselves willingly on the funeral piles of their relatives in order to share the new life with them.[2]

Bearing this in mind it is little wonder that Christianity found so many converts among the Celtic people, especially prior to the 'tunnel period', when its simple doctrines promised a heavenly hereafter to the poor, sick and suffering.

The Druidic veneration for the dead and the regions they inhabited is well commented on by Caesar, Dion Cassius, Tacitus, Diodorus Siculus and other classical writers. As was the Egyptian custom, the Celts also left offerings for their departed. Cups containing milk, or various items of food were frequently deposited at sacred sites such as wells, groves and on special stones, which practice included ancestor worship as well as acknowledging and paying homage to the spirits that ensouled these places. The dead were also commemorated at fertility festivals, such as Lughnasa (Luguasad) and Samhain, which symbolized the birth and death of vegetation, the inference being, no doubt, that as the new season would bring the rebirth of the earth's bounty so would the souls of those departed also arise to be reborn.

Some authorities, however, believe that the Druids did not fully embrace the Pythagorean concept of metempsychosis, their idea of the hereafter being more in keeping with the old Egyptian beliefs. What they did believe, it would appear, was that the soul retreated to an underworld place where it resided for some considerable time before returning, when the rebirth could be in the body of an animal, as the Tuan macCarell stories well illustrate.

Confusion has also arisen regarding the souls of the departed and the denizens of the 'Middle Kingdoms'. Those occultly unread or untutored are inclined to lump the two erroneously together, considering the Fairy People as nothing more than ancestral spirits, which is far from the truth. Of course, the fays of old were frequently depicted wearing butterflies wings, which image has survived to this day which confusion arose, no doubt, from the old Celtic belief that butterflies represented the souls of the dead.

What one has to bear in mind when trying to establish the nature of the corpus of Druidic belief is that we are dealing with a fairly broad framework of time. The early Druidisim, which was doubtless coloured by the old megalithic beliefs, naturally contrasts strongly with the Christianized versions that surfaced from the tenth century onwards. As I see it, the earlier the purer. But then there are plently of people who like to hedge their religious bets!

History faces us with a confusion of ideas as to the hidden secrets of Druidism, most of which are pure conjecture or have been arrived at from scraps of incomplete information that found their way into Greek or Roman hands. To where, then, may we turn so that we may learn more of this 'secret and sublime cult?' The answer must be, to the literature of Wales.

One of the most detailed works on Druidism is undoubtedly *The Mythology and Rites of the British Druids* by Revd Edward Davies. I have been fortunate in that a fellow occultist trusted me with the loan of her very rare copy of this work that was privately published in 1809, an aged tome indeed! In spite of the severe criticism it received from scholastic quarters generally, I found it absorbing. Davies is frequently maligned on account of his 'Arkite' theories, in which he draws evidence from ancient Welsh literature to support his idea that people escaping from the Flood arrived on Welsh shores and it was from the ancient philosophies that they brought with them that much of British Druidism has arisen. Now, I see nothing outlandish in that supposition, but one would need to read Davies fully and decide for oneself as some of his conjectures are highly controversial. The Bardic poems he includes, however, are certainly worth studying and I shall be featuring several of these in later chapters.

Although the Druidic tradition was basically an oral one, three forms of writing were associated with the cult. The first of these, which was developed in Ireland, is called the Ogham Alphabet (see Figure 1), after Ogma or Ogmius, an old Celtic god of learning and writing, and consisted of a series of strokes written or carved on either side or both, of a dividing line. It is a very easy system to master, and although of insufficient range to allow for any depth of literary expression, it does carry strong magical connotations. There is another version of it called Virgular Ogham in which the strokes are indicated by a series of arrowheads, none of which intersect the medial line. Ogham was apparently favoured by the Druids of Ireland, Cornwall and Scotland especially in pre-Christian times, when it was used for magical and divinatory purposes.

THE OGHAM ALPHABET

B L F S N H D T C Q M G NG Z R A O U E I

Figure 1

The other system of writing employed by the Druids was called Boibel-Loth, or Tree Writing. In the old Celtic or Gaelic it was known as the Beth-Luis-Nion from the names of the first three letters; Beth — the Birch Tree, Luis — the Rowan, and Nion — the Ash. From this Tree Alphabet sprang a whole system of magic, which we shall be examining in ensuing chapters.

Another main source of information from Wales is a work entitled *Barddas*, a compilation made from materials in his possession by a Welsh Bard and scholar named Llewellyn Sion, of Glamorgan, towards the end of the sixteenth century and edited, with a translation by J.A. Williams ap Ithel for the Welsh Manuscript Society at Llandovery, in 1862. Its title purports it to be 'a collection of the original documents illustrative of the theology, wisdom and usages of the Barddo-Druidic system of the Isle of Britain'.

There has been considerable scholarly debate regarding the

contents of these works. Some felt that they were purely the invention of the Bards of the fifteenth, sixteenth and seventeenth centuries, while others designated them direct copies of the Brahmin teachings of India. The original pre-Christian Bardic concepts have obviously suffered severe editing somewhere along the line, the overtly Christian nature of this material being generally acknowledged by all authorities. However, many experts are of the opinion that a vestige of the old faith is contained somewhere within their structure, one triad in particular stating:

> There are three special doctrines that have been obtained by the nation of Cymry: the first, from the age of ages, was that of the Gwyddoniaid, prior to the time of Prydian, son of Aedd the Great; the second was Bardism, as taught by the Bards after they had been instituted; the third was the faith in Christ, being THE BEST OF THE THREE.[3]

The first book of *Barddas* is entitled 'Symbol' and deals with the origin of the letters, alphabet and secret writing of the Bards. Letters, it tells us, were invented by Einiged the Giant, son of Alser, and recorded on blocks of wood that were called *coelbren*. Bran the Blessed brought the art of dressing goatskin as parchment from Rome while the three original letters were given to Menw the Aged by God himself as manifested in three rays of light thus: $/ \mid \backslash$ in three columns. The sound 'O' was accorded to the first stroke or column, 'I' to the middle one and 'V' to the third. These were originally written $\Diamond \mid \lor$, which is not dissimilar to runic script and like the four letters of the Hebrew Tetra-grammaton (YHVH), may not be pronounced. These three mystic letters are said to stand for the godly attributes of Love, Knowledge and Truth, which three principles were represented in the three degrees that were conferred upon British Bards. From these three main letters sixteen other letters were formed, and all letters subsequently developed by the Bards formed the 'Abcedilros', a word composed of the ten primary letters. Later other letters were added to make the number twenty-four.

From the three original 'OIV' columns came the custom of casting knowledge into triadic form, although it must be remembered that the number three was sacred to the Celts long before the Christian influence made its presence felt.

Following a dissertation on the establishment of Bardism and the Gorsedd, enlightenment is supplied as to the principal Nature of Things being 'Power, Matter and Mode. The elements of Science are life, intellect and affection; of Wisdom, object, mode and benefit; and of Memorials, understanding from affection, distinctive sign and reverence for the better.' As regard the mysteries of the Bards the following quote may be of interest to those who value mystical ciphers:

> The mysteries of the Bards, that is to say, the secret *coelbrens*, are small *ebillion*, a finger long, having notches, so that they may be used by two persons or more, who are confidants. It is by placing and joining them together, with reference to what is secret, that words and phrases are formed; and by bundling them into words according to secrecy, missive epistles and secret books are constructed, the meaning of which no one knows but confidants; nor is it right, according to usage and troth, to divulge the same. They are called the Charms of the Bards, or Bardic Mystery.

> Secret *coelvains* are similar, made of small stones bearing the marks of mystery; and it is by disposing them, according to the arrangement and art of the secret, that necessary sciences are demonstrated. And where such *coelbrens* exhibit the number of the letters of the Historical *coelbren*, let them be made secret by changing one letter for another, so that it be not ascertained, except from the necessity and declination of the same letter twice in the same meaning and power.[4]

The last entry in the 'Book of Symbols' comes in the form of a question and answer:

Q. What is the *Dasgubell Rodd*?
A. The Keys of the primitive *coelbren*.
Q. What is it that explains the primitive *coelbren*?
A. The *Dasgubell Rodd*.
Q. What else?
A. The secret of the *Dasgubell Rodd*.
Q. What secret?
A. The secret of the Bards of the Isle of Britain.
Q. What will divulge the secret of the Bards of the Isle of Britain?

A. Instruction by a master in virtue of a vow.
Q. What kind of vow?
A. A vow made with God.[5]

The second book, entitled 'Dwyffyddiaeth', or 'Theology', which covers the mystical teachings of Bardism, postulates two primary existences, God and Cythrawl, representing the principle of energy as manifesting in all life forms and the principle of destruction or annihilation. Cythrawl is realized in Annwn which is seen in this context as the Abyss or Chaos. 'In the beginning there was nothing but God and Annwn, then the Word was pronounced and the 'Manred' was formed.'[6] (Shades of the Johannine Gospel!)

The third book, 'The Book of Wisdom', deals with the doctrine of the Elements. Manred, the primal substance of the universe, is conceived of as a multitude of minute particles, each being a microcosm, as God was complete within each of them while they, in turn, are part of the macrocosm which is God the Whole. The totality of existence is represented by three concentric circles, the innermost, which is called 'Abred' being the stage of struggle and evolution, the contest of life with Cythrawl. The next is the circle of 'Gwynfyd', or purity, in which life has triumphed in its battle with evil and attained to a state of joy and creativity while the last, and outermost circle is called 'Ceugant', or infinity, which is obviously a totally abstract state of eternal timelessness that is sublime, all-knowing bliss (see Figure 2). The Bards designated Ceugant as inhabited by God alone, but other esoteric schools of thought tend towards the doctrine that we all eventually return there, time itself being non-linear, but rather an 'eternal now' in which our present existence is only isolated from the whole by time-zone encapsulation.

Here is a catechismic extract from *Barddas* that conveys the ideas of the man who wrote the work or assembled its material:

Q. Whence didst thou proceed?
A. I came from the Great World, having my beginning in An-nwn.
Q. Where art thou now? and how camest thou to what thou art?
A. I am in the Little World, whither I came having traversed

THE CIRCLES OF BEING

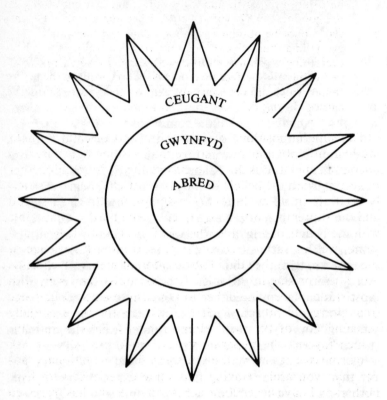

Figure 2

the circle of Abred, and now I am a Man, at its termination and extreme limits.

Q. Where wert thou before thou didst become a man, in the circle of Abred?

A. I was in Annwn the least possible that was capable of life and the nearest possible to absolute death; and I came in every form and through every form capable of a body and life to the state of man along the circle of Abred, where my condition was severe and grievous during the age of ages, ever since I was parted in Annwn from the dead, by the gift of God, and His great generosity, and His unlimited and endless love.

Q. Through how many different forms didst thou come, and what happened unto thee?

A. Through every form capable of life, in water, in earth, in air. And there happened unto me every severity, every hardship, every evil, and every suffering, and but little was the goodness or Gwynfyd before I became a man... Gwynfyd cannot be obtained without seeing and knowing everything, but it is not possible to see or to know everything without suffering everything... And there can be no full and perfect love that does not produce those things which are necessary to lead to the knowledge that causes Gwynfyd.[7]

The superimpositions of gnosticism and oriental thought are blatantly obvious here, so we may assume that pure and uncomplicated as this doctrine may sound, it is not altogether in keeping with the beliefs of the ancient Celts. Nor is it strictly accurate in its evolutionary assumptions, the patrist god and the supremacy of Homo sapiens being hardly compatible with the beliefs of a people who saw fit to acknowledge that a stone, well or sacred tree might possess more knowledge of the universe than they did. The question of metempsychosis is ever a thorny one in the side of the occultist, however, with most students stepping either to the eastern side of the fence (that we evolve through all 'lesser' life forms, eventually reaching 'top of the class' Homo sapiens) and the Sothian, (which favours the 'separate stream' concept, i.e. your oak tree or pussy cat may well be further up the evolutionary ladder than you are!). Having had some experience with hypnotherapy I have never come across anyone who has regressed back to a flower or a stone although I have encountered cases where the subconscious mind has yielded information of lives elsewhere in the universe, and even existences in the Kingdoms of Fairy. But then that would be the case with a changeling, would it not? Besides, had we all ascended through these various 'Kingdoms' we would carry in our deep subconscious a full understanding of and reverence for them, having experienced and suffered in their context. I see little evidence of this in the vandalism, cruelty to animals, and total disregard of the eco-environment exhibited by Homo sapiens as a whole today. In case I have not by now made clear to my readers to which camp I belong, may I say without hesitation the latter or Sothian school.

But is this Christianized Druidism so very different from its pagan predecessor? Hardly! God and Cythrawl, the dualism of light and darkness, for example, are surely none other than the King of Light, and the Dark Tanist, Gwydion and Pryderi; Llew and Gwyn; Lugh and Balor. Annwn is Pwyll's Mabinogion kingdom, although according to one version the former is more of a Summerland or Elysium than a purgatorial abode for the suffering dead. Nor does the Bardic Creation formula differ much from certain of the Egyptian, Greek or Amerindian versions, in spite of the Christian semantics. From Annwn the soul proceeds to Abred wherein it undergoes its trials, which would make Abred the earth plane or place of suffering and learning, the Bardic 'Little World'. From thence it eventually proceeds to Gwynfyd, or in occult terms rises above the world of matter to experience in more subtle dimensions that demand its understanding of their condition prior to its return to the Creator or Central Source of All Timelessness.

How one chooses to interpret any of these versions of the One Truth is a personal issue, of course, but the basic message is the same throughout them all. The mistake made by so many people is to decry the nomenclatures assigned to these constant cosmic principles by others. The Old Ones may appear in many garbs, yet not one of these man-created robes alters the basic nature of he, she or it whom man has seen fit to clothe therewith. Because one man or woman capitalizes the first letter of the word 'god', and another prefers to say Jesus instead of Llew, Apollo, Arthur or Horus, does not make him or her a better or more enlightened person, for in the final analysis it will not be the names, fashions, political expediencies or earthly dogmas of the human collective that will be the deciding factor, but the truth, light and love in the heart of the individual for his or her god or goddess.

Endnotes
1. Rolleston, T.W. *Myths and Legends of the Celtic Race*, p. 82.
2. Spence, Lewis. *The Mysteries of Britain*, pp. 48–9.
3. Ibid. Spence, p. 94.
4. Ibid. Spence, p. 96–7.
5. Ibid. Spence, p. 97.
6. Op. cit. Rolleston, p. 333.
7. Op. cit. Rolleston, pp. 334–5.

17. CALENDARS, TREES AND MAGICAL ALPHABETS

The Celts observed certain fundamental calendar feasts, dividing their year into four main parts, each of which was preceded by major religious celebrations that commemorated some god, hero or legend. These festivals were accompanied by fairs, markets, games, sports and revelries, as well as religious ceremonies and, in olden times, sacrifices.

The first division of the calendar year occurred on 1 February and was called Imbolc or Oilmelg. In ancient times it was sacred to the goddess Brigid or Brigantia, but was later taken over by her Christianized aspect, St Brigid. The origin of Imbolc is somewhat obscure, but is generally thought to have pastoral connections on account of its associations with the coming into milk of the ewes. Brigid in her fertility aspect was a pastoral goddess, although she is generally designated as an all-embracing deity and therefore probably honoured in many ways.

The second Celtic feast, which took place on 1 May, was Beltaine, *Bealltainn,* or *Cetshamain,* which carries the name of the old god Beli or Bilé, although according to some authorities it translates as *Bel-Tene*, a 'goodly fire'. As with all the festivals it had fertility connections and magical rites to encourage the growth of cattle and crops. Bonfires were lit and sometimes cattle were driven through them for purification purposes. Beltaine is still celebrated in parts of the Scottish highlands to this day.

The third festival, the Feast of Lughnasa, or Luguasad, took place on 1 August and was essentially an agrarian feast, being concerned with the harvesting of crops rather than pastoral economy. As the name suggests it was Lugh's feast while in Ireland it was sometimes referred to as Brón Trogain, 'Trogain's Sorrow'. It was also associated with two powerful Irish goddesses and there were traditionally two main assemblies held, one being Oenach Tailten, the other Oenach Carmain.[1]

There are two stories regarding the origin of this feast. According to one source it was established by Lugh himself in honour of his foster mother, Tailtiu, who died on 1 August, foster parents being treated with honour and devotion in the old Celtic society. A second account tells how Lugh founded the feast to commemorate his two wives, Nas and Bui. The Lughnasa traditionally lasted for one month, fifteen days before 1 August and fifteen days after.

The fourth festival, which marked the actual beginning of the Celtic year and the commencement of the Celtic winter was Samhain, usually considered the most important of the four. Although its official date was 1 November, it was traditionally celebrated on the evening before, when it was believed that the veil between the world as we know and see it and the 'other world' of the supernatural became very fine or could be momentarily withdrawn. At Samhain the Dagda ritually mated with Morrigan the war goddess, whose psychic powers were emphasized in all the early traditions.[2]

In some parts of Scotland at the Samhain festival, the last sheaf of corn or barley was cut and dressed in the guise of a woman known as 'The Carlin', another name for 'The Cailleach'. On certain hills in the highlands bonfires were lit into which each person present cast a white stone with his or her mark upon it. Failure to find that stone after the fires had died out presaged doom or bad luck for the ensuing year. For some, Samhain allegorically signified the encapsulation of the sun god Lugh or Llew who, for the season that followed, was under the spell of the powers of darkness.

There were several minor public feasts celebrated in the ancient world such as the Festival of Tea, divine Patroness of the Assembly of Tara, but most of these, if studied in detail, can be traced back to the Triple Goddess in one or other of her aspects, if not all three of them.

But in addition to these better known and documented feasts and sacred days there were the magical days which were frequently only observed by the Druids, initiates or those of learning. These were connected with the Tree Calendar. Tree Calendars are extremely ancient in origin and can be traced back as far as 5000 BC. They are therefore widespread and to be found wherever the old Goddess religion left its mark. When the Celts came to these isles they would have brought with them their own version of the old truths which in time fused with the existing beliefs from a former age to form the distinct flavour that is the Celtic magical ethos.

There is an occult teaching that each portion of the globe, be that land or sea, carries its own personality which is decided by the nature of the Elemental beings who originally fashioned and now inhabit those parts. So strong is this influence at times that people who have moved from one part of the world to another have been observed to exchange their former national characteristics for those of the new land.

While we are not dismissing the genetic pool concept completely, this theory of interaction between mankind and the land upon which he dwells and from which he draws his sustenance must make its mark somewhere. As modern nutritionists tell us, 'You are what you eat!'

Magic Alphabets and Tree Calendars did not come together immediately, however. The Calendar apparently arrived in Britain somewhere around the third millenium BC, whereas the Alphabet came with the Celts nearly two thousand years later when the trees were renamed appropriately in Gaelic. Here is Robert Graves' versions of the two Alphabets, with their corresponding Celtic names and sacred tree.

THE TREE ALPHABETS [3]

Letter	Beth-Luis-Nion	Boibel-Loth	Tree
B	Beth	Boibel	Birch
L	Luis	Loth	Rowan
N	Nion	Neiagadon	Ash
F(V)	Fearn	Forann	Alder
S	Saille	Salia	Willow
H	Uath	Uiria	Hawthorn (Whitethorn)
D	Duir	Daibhaith	Oak
T	Tinne	Teilmon	Holly
C	Coll	Caoi	Hazel

Letter	Beth-Luis-Nion	Boibel-Loth	Tree
M	Muin	Moiria	Vine
G	Gort	Gath	Ivy
P or NG	Pethboc/Ngetal	Ngoimar	Dwarf Elder/Reed
R	Ruis	Riuben	Elder
Q or CC*	Quert	Cailep	Apple
SS(z)*	Straif	—	Blackthorn
A	Ailm	Acab	Silver Fir
O	Onn	Ose	Furze
U	Ur	Ura	Heather
E	Eadha	Esu	White Poplar
I	Idho	Jaichim	Yew
Y*	—	Idra	(Mistletoe?)

* The old Irish Beth-Luis-Nion did not appear to include Q, SS or Y, as it only consisted of thirteen consonants and five vowels. Quert and Straif were later added by Graves, who also effected a connection between the Boibel-Loth 'Idra', the letter Y, and the hallowed Mistletoe which was considered too sacred to be accorded a written name.

Graves effects a critical comparison between the Beth-Luis-Nion and the Greek and Irish alphabets which emphasizes the Celtic Mediterranean and ancient Greek connections.

This Celtic calendar was lunar rather than solar and consisted of thirteen twenty-eight-day months with one extra day at midwinter. As the Moon's period does not constitute twenty-eight days exactly, which the ancients were well aware of, the extra day in the solar year means that the calendar months phase with the new Moon only once every twenty-one years, which is called the Great Lunar Year. The last Great Year was 1972 and the next one will therefore be 1993.

Their year was divided into five sessions of seventy-two days each, with five 'Dark' days extra, and punctuated by nine Great Days, each of which was celebrated by a week long festival. New Year was at the winter solstice, while Leap Year could be inserted as it fell in the spring, or as the sixth 'Dark' day before the extra day.

The months and days were named after trees appropriate to the time of the year, each resonating to, or having a mystical significance that was symbolized by a colour, stone, substance and number. These should be heeded by those who practise the old Celtic religion as the powers that build up at certain times will be based on the pattern set by the Druids of old, which will have made its imprint on the energy fields of the subtle planes.

The Seasons
These five seasons are far more in keeping with what actually happens in the countryside than the present four, which have become so blurred in recent years that one feels them to be grossly ill-placed if not ill-named:

Beginning 24 December: Sleep or Burgeoning. The time of rest and breaking bud.

Beginning 6 March: Spring or Flowering. The time of awakening and bringing forth.

Beginning 17 May: Setting or Ripening. The time of bringing to fruition and climax.

Beginning 28 July: Harvest or Gathering. The time of reaping the reward of good husbandry.

Beginning 8 October: Fall or Fading. The time of ending and settling of accounts.

Beginning 19 December: Winter or Sorrowing. The dead of the year, when time stands still (the Five 'Dark Days').

The month of Saille was shared with Quert, the Apple, and the month of Coll with Straif, the Blackthorn, making fifteen in all. Some authorities reverse this arrangement, however, allotting Quert to Coll and Straif to Saille. Quert had the Emerald as its stone and Straif the banded black-and-white Agate. Although the Holly is named for Tinne, the original association was probably the evergreen oak, but as this did not find its way into these climes until the sixteenth century AD, the early Celts took the Holly as the nearest equivalent. The allocation of the stones can be adjusted as long as the principles and colours are kept constant so I have given my own version of these.

The Nine Great Days
The Winter Solstice, being the extra day of the calendar, was not observed as a feast, the day on each side of it being celebrated instead, making a total of five quarter days which

The Months:

	Begins	Tree	Stone	Attribute
BETH	24 December	Birch	Crystal	Inception
LUIS	21 January	Rowan	Tourmaline	Quickening
NION	18 February	Ash	Aquamarine	Seapower
FEARN	18 March	Alder	Garnet	Fire
SAILLE	15 April	Willow	Moonstone	Enchantment
UATH	13 May	Hawthorn	Lapis Lazuli	Cleansing
DUIR	10 June	Oak	Diamond	Endurance
TINNE	8 July	Holly	Ruby	Blood
COLL	5 August	Hazel	Topaz	Wisdom
MUIN	2 September	Vine	Amethyst	Exhilaration
GORT	30 September	Ivy	Opal	Resurrection
PETHBOC or NGETAL	28 October	Dwarf Elder or Reed	Sapphire	Royalty (regality)
RUIS	25 November	Elder	Olivine	The Inevitable

were traditionally allocated to the five vowel sounds of the Tree Alphabet. These five, together with the four traditional Celtic feasts (also referred to as the 'cross-quarter days'), constituted the Nine Great Days.

The Nameless Day

The last day of the year when the Dark King was dead and the Bright King not yet born, was sacred to the Dark Queen in her destructive aspect. This was considered so sacred by the ancients that we have little knowledge of its appropriate rituals or sacred associations. The day was never mentioned aloud in public and its sacred tree never committed to print, but it is generally believed to be the Mistletoe, beloved of later Druids and emblem of Life through Death.

But how did the mistletoe come to be associated with Druidic tradition? Several explanations have been put forward, notably the idea that the berries represented the pearls on the rim of the Cauldron of Inspiration.[4] Pliny is generous with his comments concerning the use of mistletoe by the ancient Druids, informing us that as it was seldom found on the oak, when it did occur on this, the sacred Druidic tree, 'it was gathered with due religious ceremony, if possible on the sixth day of the Moon when the influence of the orb was said to be at its height.' After an elaborate banquet and sacrifice involving two white bulls, a white-clad priest cut the plant from the oak tree with a golden sickle while another Druid held out a white cloak for its reception. The Roman then adds, 'They believe that the mistletoe, taken in drink, imparts fecundity to barren animals and that it is the antidote for all poisons,' while it was also known by a name meaning 'all healing'. To cut oakwood, however, was always considered unfortunate.[5]

There are two sorts of mistletoe — mistletoe proper and Loranthus. The Greeks distinguish them as *hypear* and *ixos* or *ixias,* respectively. The Loranthus is found in eastern but not in western Europe, and unlike mistletoe proper, grows on oaks. Whether the Loranthus was native to western Europe or whether the Celtic Druids brought it with them from the east, grafting it onto the oaks from other host trees, such as the poplar and the apple cannot be determined.

The cutting of the mistletoe from the Sacred Oak by the Arch Druid typified the emasculation of the Old King by his successor, mistletoe being, among other things, a phallic emblem. There is also the suggestion here of the castration of Uranus by Cronos, signifying the end of an age or the inevitable hand of time that decides all. Its association with fertility can be linked to the cult of Hercules (or Helith, this being another name for the Cerne Abbas giant) through Hercules' famous attribute, his club, supposedly made from the branch of an oak. Mistletoe's sexual overtones have survived to this very day in the custom of kissing beneath a sprig during the Christmas period.

Its healing associations could be referenced in Paracelsus' *Doctrine of Signatures*, no doubt. But that is a subject in itself.

The ancients believed that on the Nameless Day, the universe would cease to be if they did not placate the Old Queen, through fasting and mortification, to persuade her to begin the year anew.

From the old Tree Calendar and Alphabet, thirteen magical 'stations' were derived, as shown in the table opposite.

The order of the stations is the order of the numbers sacred to them and not an order of priority. Since they are all equal aspects of the Celtic god concept more importance should not be accorded to one than another. The link with the months is by association and not therefore of ritualistic significance. Full details of the Celtic calendar and its complexities may be found in *The White Goddess*, by Robert Graves.

Endnotes

1. Ross, Dr Anne. *Everyday Life of the Pagan Celts*, p. 200.
2. Ibid. Ross, p. 201.
3. Graves, Robert. *The White Goddess*, pp. 116 & 165.
4. Spence, Lewis. *The Mysteries of Britain*, p. 166.
5. Spence, Lewis. *The Magic Arts in Celtic Britain*, p. 125.

The Thirteen Stations

1.	Absolute Deity	Power	White	Beth, 1st month	Birch
2.	Dual King	Justice	Gold	Duir, 7th month	Oak
3.	Triune Queen	Fate	Black or Dark Green	Ruis, 13th month	Elder
4.	Double Sun	Riches	Blue	Ngetal, 12th month	Reed
5.	Humanity	Strife	Red	Tinne, 8th month	Holly (Kerm Oak)
6.	Sacred Fire	Life force	Green	Luis, 2nd month	Rowan
7.	The Sea	Love	Turquoise	Nion, 3rd month	Ash
8.	Mind	Knowledge	Orange	Coll, 9th month	Hazel
9.	The Moon	Blessing	Silver	Saille, 5th month	Willow
10.	Earth	Mortality	Gold	Muin, 10th month	Vine
11.	Spirit	Immortality	Amethyst	Gort, 11th month	Ivy
12.	Divine Will	Royalty	Purple	Fearn, 4th month	Alder
13.	Chaos	Dreams	Midnight Blue	Uath, 6th month	Hawthorn

18. TALIESIN THE BARD

Of all the tales collected by Lady Charlotte Guest for *The Mabinogion*, the 'Book of Taliesin' is, from an occult viewpoint, by far the most interesting as it renders a truly profound insight into the deeper mysteries, and therefore the basic psychology of the Celts. It is taken from a manuscript of the late sixteenth or early seventeenth century, although some of the poetry it contains is believed to predate it by some centuries.

The story goes: During the reign of Arthur, there lived a man named Tegid Voel of Penllyn whose wife was an enchantress named Keridwen. They had a son named Avagddu whom the gods had ill-favoured with an ugly appearance, and in order to compensate for this disadvantage Keridwen resolved to make him a sage. As her source of instruction she sought the Book of Feryllt or Pheryllt.

Now 'Feryllt' is believed by some authorities to be a mediaeval appellation of Virgil's, but the Welsh word 'Pheryllt', according to Spence, has other connotations, appertaining apparently to a section of the Druidic brotherhood who were teachers and scientists skilled in all that required the agency of fire, which would indicate that they were alchemists or metallurgists. The sciences of chemistry and metallurgy were known as 'Celvyddydan Pheryllt', or 'The Arts of Pheryllt', and the headquarters of this Druidic Order was in the city of Emrys in the Snowdonia district, noted for its magical associations and also called The City of the Dragons of Beli.

Keridwen, however, having put together the necessary ingredients with accompanying spells and incantations, and with due attention to the hours of the planets and books of astronomy, then had recourse to that great source of Celtic magic, the Cauldron. The concoction she had specially prepared guaranteed knowledge, science and inspiration for Avagddu so that he might be accepted on account of his cognition of the mysteries and the future of the world.

But the Cauldron had to be kept boiling for a year and one day and only in three drops of its magical brew were the aforesaid virtues to be found. Not having the time to constantly attend to the matter herself, Keridwen put Gwion Bach, son of Gwreany The Herald of Llanfair, in Powys, to stir the contents, and a blind man named Morda to keep the fire going beneath it while she applied the necessary ingredients from time to time, as directed by the Feryllt's book. But one day, towards the end of the year, three drops of the magic liquid flew out of the Cauldron and lighted on the finger of Gwion who naturally put his finger to his mouth to cool the burn, whereupon he immediately became gifted with supernatural insight. Realizing that he had received that which was intended for Avagddu, and that Keridwen would therefore destroy him, he fled to his own land while the Cauldron, being deprived of the three sacred drops, now contained nothing but poison which caused the vessel to burst. The evil liquid, however, formed into a stream and joined with nearby waters, from which the horses of Gwyddno Garanhir were wont to drink. As a consequence, when the horses next came to take the waters they were immediately poisoned.

Upon returning to the scene, Keridwen realized that her year of labour had been of no avail. In a rage she struck Morda and then set out in pursuit of Gwion Bach, but as he was now the possessor of great wisdom he saw her coming and changed himself into a hare. Keridwen then became a greyhound and continued the chase, whereupon Gwion leapt into the water, becoming a fish. But once again Keridwen pursued him in the guise of an otter. He then became a bird and she a hawk, and finally turned himself into a grain of wheat, hastily mixing among the other grains on the threshing floor. Not to be outdone, however, Keridwen turned herself into a black hen, espied the grain and gobbled it up. Nine months later she gave birth to an infant which she would have killed had he not been so beautiful. So she wrapped him in a leathern bag and cast him into the sea in a coracle.

Now Gwyddno, whose horses had been poisoned, had a salmon weir on his strand where his son Elphin, who was not the most inspiring of individuals, was wont to fish. Noticing the coracle on the weir which had been cast there by the incoming tide, Elphin made haste to investigate and found the bag therein which he took to his father. Upon opening it they discovered the infant. 'Behold, a radiant brow!' exclaimed Gwyddno and they brought the child home and reared it as their own.

And so Taliesin, prime Bard of Cymry, came into existence, and in his poems he exalted those who had saved him and given him a home. As these poems were highly potent magically, Elphin and Gwyddno soon grew in riches and esteem while King Arthur himself looked upon them with favour and affection. Not being the most discreet of people, however, Elphin was inclined to speak out when he should not which landed him in trouble and eventually in prison.

About the time of these occurrences, the youthful Taliesin saw fit to make his way to the court on a day when the King's bards and minstrels were due to entertain their liege. Seating himself in a corner, Taliesin made the sound 'Blerwm, blerwm', with his lips pouted and his finger on his mouth, so that when the bards came to perform they could do nothing but make a similar sound. The chief of them, whose name was Heinin, protested in anguish, 'Oh King, we be not drunken with wine, but are dumb through the influence of the spirit that sits in the corner under the form of a child.' Taliesin was immediately brought forth at the King's command and asked to explain who he was, whence he came and what he was about, and these are the verses he sang:

Primary chief bard am I to Elphin,
And my original country is the region of the summer stars;
Idno and Heinin called me Merddin,
At length every king will call me Taliesin.

I was with my Lord in the highest sphere,

On the fall of Lucifer into the depth of hell
I have borne a banner before Alexander;
I know the names of the stars from north to south;
I have been on the Galaxy at the throne of the Distributor;

I was in Canaan when Absalom was slain;
I conveyed Awen [the Divine Spirit] to the level of the vale of
    Hebron;
I was in the court of Dōn before the birth of Gwydion.
I was the instructor to Eli and Enoch;
I have been winged by the genius of the splendid crozier;

I have been loquacious prior to being gifted with speech;
I was at the place of the crucifixion of the merciful son of God;
I have been three periods in the prison of Arianrhod;
I have been the chief director of the work of the tower of
    Nimrod.
I am a wonder whose origin is not known.

I have been in Asia with Noah in the Ark,
I have witnessed the destruction of Sodom and Gomorrah;
I have been in India when Roma was built;
I am now come here to the remnant of Troia.
I have been with my Lord in the manger of the ass;

I strengthened Moses through the water of Jordan;
I have been in the firmament with Mary Magdalene;
I have obtained the muse from the Cauldron of Caridwen;
I have been bard of the harp to Lleon of Lochlin.
I have been on the White Hill, in the court of Cynvelyn,

For a day and a year in stocks and fetters,
I have suffered hunger for the Son of the Virgin,
I have been fostered in the land of the Deity,
I have been teacher to all intelligences,
I am able to instruct the whole universe.

I shall be until the day of doom on the face of the earth;
And it is now known whether my body is flesh or fish.
Then I was for nine months
In the womb of the hag Caridwen;
I was originally little Gwion,
And at length I am Taliesin.[1]

Whereupon all previous evils that had befallen Elphin and the
King's bards, were immediately dissolved.

It is a great pity that this poem has suffered Christianization and I, for one, would loved to have seen the original. It would appear that even all those centuries ago there were scholars who felt the same way about alterations effected in the original Bardic writings. Giraldus Cambrensis complains that in his age 'the simple works of the Bards had been disfigured by such modern and ill-placed flourishes.'[2]

The Druidic Bards of old designated Keridwen as presiding over the hidden mysteries of their cult which represented their secret initiatory rites. Cynddelw, who flourished about the middle of the twelfth century sings: 'How mysterious were the ways of the songs of Keridwen! How necessary to understand them in their *true sense*!' Llywarch ap Llwelyn, writing between 1160 and 1220 requests, 'inspiration as it were from the Cauldron of Keridwen', and continues to say that he will address his lord 'with the dowry of Keridwen, the Ruler of Bardism'.[3] All Bards who aspired to the chair of song were obliged to taste the waters of inspiration from her Cauldron, or in other words, become initiated into her mysteries.

The magical city of Emrys, known in the Welsh tradition as the city of Dinas Affaraon or 'higher powers', was said to have been situated in the area of Snowdon. Therein dwelt a community of Druids and Bards who specialized in the magical arts. Mention is made of this in *The Black Book of Caermarthen*, and although no one is sure where it was actually located there is one reference to the 'panting cliff' on Snowdon itself and another 'upon the road from the promontory of Lleyn to that part of the coast which is opposite Mona' (Anglesey).[4]

In Emrys, we are told, were concealed in the time of Bilé, and in the time of Prydain the son of Aedd the Great, the dragons that are frequently referred to as being harnessed to Keridwen's chariot, which probably designates this area as housing important Earth energies as well as being sacred to her mysteries.

Taliesin's own account of the contents of the famous 'brew' are recounted in a poem which I have featured in Chapter 26 in which the Initiatory aspects are covered in some detail. The residue of the Cauldron's brew after the ceremony was said to represent the evil and pollution from which the Initiates had been ritually cleansed. The Cauldron was kept at Caer Sidi or Caer Pendryvan, and the nine maidens by whose breath it was warmed were probably nine Druidesses in the service of the Triple Goddess who were skilled in matters magical. Pomponius Mela says of them: 'they are thought to be endowed with singular powers. By their charms they are able to raise the winds and seas and turn themselves into what animal they will, to cure wounds and diseases incurable by others and predict the future.'[5]

Many scholars are of the opinion that these nine maidens are synonymous with the virgin priestesses of other cults such as those of Circe, Galatian Artemis or Demeter, while Davies sees them as Fairy people, whose good offices were always sought by the initiates of ancient magical priesthoods.

There is frequent reference throughout Druidic lore to a special kind of 'ball' or serpents egg (see Merlin poem in Chapter 14). An allusion to this egg which connects it with the Cauldron Rites appears in a poem by the Bard Aneurin, cited by Davies, which reads:

> The assembled train were dancing, after the manner and singing in cadence, with garlands on their brows; loud was the clattering of shields around the ancient cauldron in frantic mirth, and lively was the aspect of him, who, in his prowess, had snatched over the ford that involved ball which cast its rays to a distance, the splendid product of the adder, shot forth by serpents.[6]

Regarding this egg or ball, Pliny comments:

> There is also another kind of egg, of much renown in the Gallic provinces, but ignored by the Greeks. In the summer, numberless snakes entwine themselves into a ball, held together by a secretion from their bodies and by the spittle. This is called *anguinum*. The Druids say that hissing serpents throw this up into the air, and that it must be caught in a cloak, and not allowed to touch the ground; and that one must instantly take to flight on horseback, as the serpents will pursue until some stream cuts them off. It may be tested, they say, by seeing if it floats against the current of a river, even though it be set in gold. But as it is the way of magicians to cast a cunning veil about their frauds, they pretend that these eggs can only be taken on a certain day of the moon, as though it rested with mankind to make the moon and the serpents accord as to the moment of the operation. I myself, however, have seen one of these eggs; it was round, and about as large as a smallish apple; the shell was cartilaginous, and pocked like the arms of a polypus. The

Druids esteem it highly. It is said to ensure success in lawsuits and a favourable reception with princes; but this is false, because a man of the Vocontii, who was also a Roman knight, kept one of these eggs in his bosom during a trial, and was put to death by the Emperor Claudius, as far as I can see, for that reason alone.[7]

There is some conflict of opinion regarding this supposed 'serpents egg' however. In parts of Cornwall, Wales and Scotland prehistoric beads of blue and green glass, sometimes carved and inlaid with white paste are known as 'snakestones' while in Ireland they are called 'Druid's Glass'. These long predate the Christian era. Druids were also known to the Welsh Bards as *Naddred*, or 'Adders', the inference being that just as the serpent casts its skin so is the initiate reborn through the ritual observances of his or her cult. This sounds much more logical and in keeping with the Uraeus concept I mentioned in an earlier chapter.

The egg theme is common to several mythologies, however, especially in the cosmological context, so it is no surprise for us to find that the Druids also spoke of the universe being hatched from two eggs. The ancient Syrians used to speak of the gods who were their ancestors as the progeny of eggs, while Davies tells us 'in the temple of the Dioscouri, in Laconia, there was suspended a large hieroglyphical egg which was sometimes attributed to Leda and sometimes to Nemesis, the deity of justice. It was sometimes described as surrounded by a serpent, either as an emblem of that providence by which mankind was preserved or else to signify the renewal of life, from a state of death; as the serpent, by casting his skin, seems to renew his life.'[8]

To return to Keridwen: the question which must be asked is, as she is mentioned in mortal terms as living in the times of Arthur, how can she be associated with initiatory rites of great antiquity? The answer must surely be that the 'Book of Taliesin' is a fictionalized version of the old goddess rites which have been superimposed over a mediaeval setting in much the same way as the Arthurian legends. In commenting on this very point Davies remarks, 'The Arthur here introduced is a traditional character, totally distinct from the Prince who assumed that name at the beginning of the sixth century.'[9]

Towards the end of the last century, Druidism saw a partial revival in Wales when a group calling themselves 'The Druids of Pontypridd' made their appearance. Myfyr Morganwg, their Arch Druid, publicly proclaimed the beliefs of his forefathers after preaching Christianity for thirty years, and was apparently utterly sincere in the tenets he taught and believed in. He was broad-minded enough to see similarities between his own faith and the popular religions of the time, as well as classical mythology. He was followed by one Owen Morgan, better known as 'Morien', whose version of Welsh Druidism appeared in a work entitled *The Light of Britannia* published in 1898. This was followed with *The Royal Winged Son of Stonehenge and Avebury*, which achieved similar popularity. Like his predecessor, Morgan drew his information from a wide variety of sources, which is as it should be with any magical work. His version of Druidic beliefs were as follows:

The Druids named the Creator Celi (Concealing), and his Consort Ced (Aid), or Keridwen. They believed that the firmament was one vast wheel in which, seated in a chair, the sun made its daily round. Ceri and Keridwen were abstract deities and, like the archons of Ptah, the originators or manipulators of atomic particles from which universes are formed. Thus they created matter through the offices of the four elements which enabled them to induce the seeding and growth of the embryonic structures of life as we now know it on this planet. This creative essence is feminine and passive by nature, and was brought every spring across the seas in a sacred boat shaped like the crescent moon which moved by Keridwen's magical power, being one and the same energy as the fires that heated her Cauldron.

The active principle was designated by the Druids as Celi, and personified by Gwion Bach. They also believed that the Sun and the Earth had emanated from two separate eggs in Keridwen's boat, the Sun being the second born (as with the Greek myth of Artemis and Apollo?) Taliesin was the Sun's name, although he was also known as Hu Gadarn, Arthur and Hesus (or Esus). In his Arthur persona he was the cultivator of the garden of Earth, the original Adamic man referred to by Waddell (see Chapter 7). All titles of the sun except Hu Gardarn are contained in a triad — Plennyd, Alawn and Gwron. The Earth was also a triad which consisted of the three queens of Arthur, spring, summer and winter. The negative or evil principles were the three males Avagddu, Cythraul and Atrais, and their female counterparts Annhras, Malen and Mallt. The Sun, it was believed, was reborn to Keridwen as a babe on 22 December.

The Druids subscribed to the eternity of matter and also of water, and that the passive or feminine principle of the divine nature pervaded both. They had a zodiac of their own, the names of the zodiacal signs representing the various emanations of the deity which are cast onto the Earth with the guidance of the Sun. The vernal equinox they named Eilir (second generation), the summer solstice Havhin (sunny temperature), the autumn equinox, Elved (harvest), and the winter solstice Arthan (Arthur's season), when Arthur as the Sun Archer armed with bow and arrow is engaged in fighting the powers of darkness.

The whole Earth was known as Buarth Beirdd or the Bovine Bardic Enclosure, the Earth's fertility being symbolized by a white cow, and the generating Sun by the white bull. There were three cows and three bulls employed by the Druids as symbols in their sacred 'cattle pen' or circle. The three bulls bore the names of the aforementioned triad, Plennydd, Alawn and Gwron, and the three cows Morwyn, Blodwen and Tynghedwen-Dyrraith, who are also designated the three sister spouses of Arthur, being personifications of the three stages of the earth year.

The Sun as the first begotten of Keridwen, the feminine or passive principle, became the agent of the Creator, who died allegorically on 20 December (in keeping with several other major deities), falling into the sea at St David's Head!

The Sun's divinity was symbolized as a Wren, and it was the custom to solicit funds by carrying a wren through the village in a small box, while the bearer sang a sad song about its poverty. The people of the Isle of Man held a Wren Hunt at the winter solstice, the bird being fixed to a long pole with its wings extended and afterwards buried to infer the death and burial of the old Sun.

Of the Keridwen myth Morgan (Morien) says that it represents a cosmic allegory, as we might well have guessed. Avagddu is night or chaos, first born of Keridwen; Taliesin as the Sun was assisted in his appearance by the boiling of the Cauldron, or the arrangement of cosmic energy which creates the stuff of which stars are made, the significance lying in the period of one year and one day, from 22 December to the following 20 December, plus forty hours over. The Cauldron is therefore the receptacle for the divine essence, or that which gives form to the abstract energies of creation. The three drops that inspired Gwion are the Triune Word of the Creator (the three golden apples, three bulls, etc.)

The connections between Druidism and the old Bull Cults of Minos, Mithras and Apis, are obvious, while Hu Gadarn is undoubtedly one and the same as the continental Celtic god Esus. As neither Taliesin, Keridwen or Gwion appear in continental references, however, we may assume them to be localized in Wales, although Keridwen had far too much in common with the Irish Dana or the goddess Brigantia for these connections to be ignored. After all, the Dagda, Bran and Keridwen appeared to share the same Cauldron. However, it should be remembered that Taliesin referred to himself as being 'thrice born', once to his natural mother as Gwion Bach, once to Keridwen, and again from the Mystic Coracle, thus suggesting some common ground with Hermes Trismegistus, called 'Thrice Greatest', which would remove him from the exclusively Welsh environment!

One could summarize this school of belief roughly as follows: the Sun was regarded as the centre of divinity, with Hu Gardarn, Esus or Taliesin occupying the throne in the hub of the golden wheel. His demiurges, Celi and Keridwen, were responsible for the work of creating the material universe, which would designate the Earth itself as Keridwen's Cauldron, in which we all undergo the initiatory rites of spiritual maturation. Keridwen, therefore, becomes the Divine Mother who is fecunded by Celi. The Cauldron could also be seen as the sacred Coracle in which embryonic matter was conveyed to this planet through the waters of the oceans. As to the white bull and the white cow, as this theme appears in so many other early cults we are once again faced with the 'single source' theory.

Ship or coracle symbology is highly significant in both the occult and modern psychology. The primordial waters of the deep unconscious have to be negotiated and fully understood. In other words, the Initiate must face his or her own darker side, or descend into the regions of Pwyll before he or she can ascend to the higher spheres of truth and knowledge. You can give this process any name you wish, but in the final analysis it all amounts to the same thing. The intelligence or being who taught me always referred to the treading of the magical path as being likened to 'Looking for a gas leak with a lighted match.' Therefore one should check on one's 'leaks', or character deficiencies before one starts out, as we all have some serious defect somewhere in our natures. We may be cultured enough to keep it well hidden from the prying eyes of the world, but once the first steps onto the path are taken it must be brought to the surface, faced and expunged by our own will-power. Never may we rely upon help from others or those who have already travelled the path. We may read the signposts they have erected, but that is all. And, as is often the case with the human condition, however, we frequently choose to read only what suits us at that moment, to our later cost.

Endnotes
1. Graves, R. *The White Goddess*, pp. 81 & 82.
2. Davies, Edward. *The Mythology and Rites of the British Druids*, p. 55.
3. Spence, Lewis. *The Mysteries of Britain*, p. 79.
4. Ibid. Spence, p. 80.
5. Ibid. Spence, p. 83.
6. Ibid. Spence, p. 84.
7. Ibid. Spence, p. 85.
8. Op. cit. Davies, p. 208.
9. Op. cit. Davies, p. 187.

19. FAIRIES, ANIMALS AND MYTHICAL BEASTS

Although I have used the term 'fairies', I am including in this category all those devic beings and nature spirits who are normally classified under the somewhat ambiguous title of the 'Middle Kingdoms'.

Some researchers are of the opinion that the Celtic *Sidhe*, or fairies, are no more than the spirits of the dead, while others see them as either a tribe of Picts, or wailing cult priestesses in fancy dress. But nothing could be further from the truth. History designates them as residing in a dim, subterranean sphere or sepulchral barrow on the one hand, or in some unseen dimension that resembles an earthly paradise on the other. The Fairy Queen is said to have warned Thomas the Rhymer against eating the apples that hung in her gardens, for to partake of the food of the dead is to know no return. This is surely reminiscent of the Persephone/Hades incident in Greek mythology, and would appear to relate to an old folk memory passed down from a formerly highly civilized society who understood the nature of time-warps. The Celtic myths designate this 'Place of Apples' as Avalon, or Tir-nan-Og, the Land of Heart's Desire, which is hardly suggestive of the infernal regions.

According to Scottish legend, the wise women of old Scotland were originally taught their arts by a fairy, which is rather in keeping with the Irish concept of the Tuatha de Danaans assuming fairy identity in another dimension, from which they benignly watch over and offer help to the just.

The idea that fays were small in stature could have several origins. There is an old belief that prior to the Stone Age the indigenous inhabitants of these isles were short troglodytes. Oral tales of earlier days when small, dwarfish people dwelt in caves could well have found their way down the centuries to account for the hobgoblins and elves of some mythologies.

The fays of Celtic folklore are of normal height, however. The Irish *Sidhe*, Morgan le Fay, Vivien and the Welsh *Y Mamau* are much as we are, as were the Breton fairy folk and those Scottish fairies who carried off Tamlane and taught the witches and wizards their lore.

However, there is an aspect of fairy beliefs that is appropriate to Celtic magic: the subject of changelings. According to old legends, when a child was born, if it was not immediately attended to, or when its mother was in her first sleep following the birth, a fairy being would enter and exchange the baby for a fairy child, thus affording one of its own kind the chance to live in this world. Rubbish! The spirits of the Lordly Ones are not particularly interested in earthly life as they do not normally change streams, having an evolutionary plan of their own that they usually stay with. There are exceptions, however, one being where a spirit from these regions chooses to serve someone in human incarnation, although I prefer 'work with voluntarily' rather than 'serve'.

Now it is interesting to observe that many of the famous personalities of the past who have contributed in some beneficial way to the history, art or welfare of our planet, or who have left the kind of indelible marks that have aided its process towards the light of justice, reason and love, were rumoured as being the result of a union between an earthly woman and some immortal, supernatural or fairy father. Alexander the Great believed himself to have been born of a divine father to an earthly mother and even Shakespeare is said to have been part fairy and part mortal. Nor does one have to look very far in the histories of the religions of the world to find similar instances, albeit cloaked in the respectability of orthodoxy but nevertheless containing the same message. All the mythological heroes of old would also qualify as being partly immortal as they inevitably resulted from unions of this kind.

Fairy, magical or immortal origins suggest a link with the infinite which can raise the person above the rank and file of ordinary folk; and yet this does not necessarily imply a ready access to the high spiritual places or the powers therefrom. These have to be learned or acquired through initiation and a coming to terms with the various aspects of the psyche or self. So what the changeling myths are surely trying to tell us is that when someone is born who is — to use a term that I do not really like, but is expedient — an 'Old Soul', he or she is frequently from a more subtle dimension or a psychic frequency that is perceptible to the fairy people, or maybe even from the fairy genre itself. I have first-hand knowledge of someone who, when regressed back to his origins, was certainly not of the Homo sapiens breed at all, but a Salamander or spirit of the Element of Fire, so there are such beings among us! Nor is this person mentally lacking integration of character or personality, according to the yardstick set by accepted worldly standards, and he would certainly not wish anyone to know of his karmic or cosmic roots.

Spence opines that the fairy changeling legends are nothing more than a survival of an old belief that the souls of the dead return to inhabit the bodies of mortal children, but my own thirty-five years in occultism force me to disagree. In fact, as I (and others of my persuasion) see it, there are many levels of conscious beingness in the universe in addition to ourselves and the more obvious denizens of our planet. Apart from the spirits that inhabit the four Elements of Air, Fire, Earth and Water there are the other nature essences, as any good Wiccan will tell you: tree spirits or Dryads, for example.

There is an abundance of literature from continental sources on the subject of the spirits of the four Elements, notably the work of the Abbé de Villars, entitled *Comte de Gabalis*, published at the close of the eighteenth century. In his book *The Occult Sciences*, A.E. Waite devotes a whole chapter to this work which personally I have found to be one of the best reference books available on the nature and functions of the spirits of the Elements.[1] I have also dealt with this subject in *Practical Techniques of Psychic Self-Defence*.

In addition to those dimensions that exist side by side with our own, there are intelligently inhabited energy zones which actually interpenetrate the structure of our world, albeit at different frequencies — call them parallel universes if you wish — which can be perceived by anyone who has mastered the control of the right hemisphere of the brain.

It is sad that the word 'fairy' has acquired homosexual connotations, as the denizens of the Middle Kingdoms are strict observers of the basic cosmic Law of polarity. I was recently criticized for citing this law in one of my other books but, as I explained to this protestor, I do not write the rules I only quote them, and if these rules do not suit the lifestyle or morals of some people that is neither my fault nor my criticism.

The Middle Kingdom does exist, rest assured of that. And it is not peopled by the souls of deceased ancestors (unless you happen to be of fairy stock yourself — and I mean that in the occult and not the irreverent sense of the word). Its denizens are oft-times suspicious of people, and not without good cause: Homo sapiens hardly has a good record when it comes to relationships with other life forms. A vast majority of people refuse to acknowledge the existence of anything outside of their own cosy little blinkered world, so why should the Lordly Ones concern themselves with us? But the fact is they do help people, just as they are visible to the innocent and those who are sufficiently deprogrammed to keep an open mind regarding the fact that we do share this planet with other life forms and other dimensions. Of course, one can work with them, but there are rules which must be strictly observed, as we shall see in Chapter 22. Much as it may hurt some people to read or hear the word 'rules', these do exist in the cosmic scheme of things and to disregard them because one is of hedonistic inclination does not alter their validity, or the punishments that are subconsciously self-inflicted when they are broken. Why even our own legal system states that ignorance of the law is no excuse for breaking it!

Before we can analyze the magical significance and import of the four Fairy Gifts of the Tuatha de Danaans, it is essential to understand something of the nature of the inhabitants of the Elemental realms and characteristics associated with them. Specific qualities in human terms are ascribed to each Element. The Salamanders represent creativity, ardour, raw energy, valour and loyalty; the Sylphs, intellectuality, speed, communication, detachment and adaptability; the Ondines, the emotions, feelings, receptivity, understanding and sympathy; and the Gnomes, thrift, acquisition and wealth in all forms, conservation and practicality. The Four Humours, as cited by Hippocrates, are also aligned with the Elements thus: Fire — the Sanguine; Air — the Choleric or Bilious; Water — the Phlegmatic; and Earth — the Melancholic.

Each of these four Elemental Kingdoms are, in turn, represented by a magical attribute which should be employed in any ritual working into which beings from the Elemental Kingdoms are invited to enter. Fire is traditionally summoned by the Wand, Rod or Lance; Air by the Sword; Water by the Cup or Chalice; and Earth by the pentacles, Shield or a sanctified Stone. And what do we find in the Danaan gifts? The Spear — Fire; the Sword — Air, the Cauldron — Water, and the Stone — Earth; in other words; the gifts the people of Dana took to Ireland with them were not necessarily material objects that had been highly charged magically, but the knowledge of the nature of the four Elements, or the power of the Elemental Kingdoms, which was possessed in the Old Country.

According to arcane teaching, only when mankind has conquered those aspects within himself that are represented by each Element respectively, will he truly have achieved his fourfold nature and then be ready to break from the wheel of karma and ascend to the higher or subtler planes of timelessness. The Danaan offerings were, therefore, gifts of knowledge and understanding of the self, for just as each Element has its positive qualities there is the inevitable duality that is Darkness and Light or the double-edged sword.

Observe now, in the light of this understanding, the basic nature of the Celts as emphasized by their favourite symbol, the Cauldron or Grail Chalice, which is warmed either by Keridwen's fires, the breath of nine maidens, or the heat of the sun. Truly these people were of a Watery, emotional and highly impressionable nature, tinged with the ardour and creativity of Fire. The Celtic wizards, to whom the people were subject, were Airy and magical, while the Celts themselves were a highly mobile people. Why then did they lack the staying power that Caesar and his contemporaries so carefully observed? The answer lies in the Element of Earth which appeared to be absent from their nature.

The numbers they held as sacred tell us more: '3' belongs to

Jupiter, denoting their expansion; '5' is Mercury's and therefore Merlin's number implying intellectually expressed subconscious leanings; the martial '9' suggest their prowess in battle; and the Neptunian '7' their impressionability and unworldy romanticism. Only when '9' is multiplied by the solid '8', making the magical '72' does the necessary discipline appear, and this is always and only for the Goddess and her Consort, by whichever name they may be called.

Perhaps a quick glance at their sacred animals might afford us a further insight into the Celtic character. Birds were high on their list, headed by the wren. The eagle, hawk, heron, swan, raven, crow, dove, duck and even the humble hen feature in their symbology, while the crane, in spite of its fertility associations, was tabu in some tribes where its flesh was certainly not to be eaten.

Sacred animals included the ox, boar, bull, stag, ram, goat, dog, lynx, cat, hare, and lion; while among water creatures, the salmon was particularly venerated. Many of these were totemistic and varied with each tribe, while some were more honoured than others on account of their association with certain deities. The ox, for example, was sacred to Hu Gadarn and the hen to Keridwen.

One could not write a chapter about Celtic animals without including those mythical beasts that were so much a part of their oral tradition. Graves has a deal to say regarding the role played by fabulous beasts in the mythology of many earlier cults, that of the Celts included. He feels that it is essential to be able to think mythically, and in so doing divorce onself from the mundane patterns of programmed existence which cramp the poetic style and chain us to the eternal wheel of materialistic philosophy. Therefore, beasts such as the Chimaera, Cerberus, the Gryphon, the Dragon and the Unicorn can play a role, albeit an unconscious one, in unlocking the mind's door into the interdimensional universe.

The red dragon has long been associated with the British race. It was the crest of Uther, father of Arthur who, in the mythological or deeper sense, was himself a dragon and bore the title 'Pendragon' or chief dragon. The white dragon was not aways seen as benign, however, this being no doubt due to its later association with the invading Saxons and not because its symbology originally merited distrust.

C.A. Cirlot, in his *Dictionary of Symbols*, refers to the

dragon as 'a fabulous animal and a universal, symbolic figure found in the majority of the cultures of the world — primitive and oriental, as well as classical.' He then gives a further three pages of detail regarding its symbology.[2]

What more can one add except to say that as far as the Celts were concerned, their magicians were certainly aware of the Dragon Lines or ley lines, those veins of subtle energy that traverse our planet, which are part of the arterial and venal system of the Earth Mother herself. To understand these was to anticipate her very breathings which awareness in itself constituted a power factor.

But the ever-romantic Celts, in addition to their dragons, were also aware of unicorn power. The unicorn has a special significance as far as the British ethos is concerned, featuring regularly along with the lion in the heraldry of these isles.

Graves thought that it also made good calendar sense, representing the five season solar years of the Boibel-Loth Alphabet. The horn, he reckoned, was centred on the dog-days (Sirius) which rendered it a symbol of power. Ctesias, the fifth century BC historian, was the first to write about the unicorn in his *Indica*. He describes its horn as being coloured white, red and black, which are, according to Graves, the colours of the three aspects of the Triple Moon Goddess.

The unicorn probably had a spatial as well as a temporal meaning and has also been associated with the Egyptian obelisk, and therefore both Ra and Sirius. Cirlot says of this animal:

Symbolic of chastity and also an emblem of the sword or of the word of God. Tradition commonly presents it as a white horse with a single horn sprouting from its forehead, but according to esoteric belief it has a white body, a red head and blue eyes. Legend has it that it is tireless when pursued yet falls meekly to the ground when it is approached by a virgin. This seems to suggest that it is symbolic of sublimated sex. ... Jung, in his work on the relationships between psychology and alchemy, has studied a great many aspects of this fabulous animal, concluding that, broadly speaking, it has no one definite symbolic character but rather many different variants embracing single-horned animals, both real and fabulous, such as the sword-fish or certain types of dragon. He notes that the unicorn is at times transmuted into a white dove, offering the explanation that on the one hand it is related to primordial monsters while on the other it represents the virile, pure and penetrating force of the *spiritus mercurialis*.[3]

This is all very technical and hardly in the deeply poetic and romantic Celtic idiom. I have, however, been introduced to a book entitled *De Historia et Veritate Unicornis*, a facsimile and translation by Michael Green of an original manuscript. The work is supposedly taken from a fifteenth century diary kept by a member of a secret order of monks which came into the author's possession in somewhat questionable circumstances. As to the validity of his claims I leave the reader to make up his or her own mind, but the text contains some deep occult truths so someone has his facts right. The illustrations, which are submitted as genuine reproductions of old manuscripts, are works of art in themselves while 'The Prophecy of the True Horn' on the final page hints at both Celtic and Atlantean undertones.

Into darkness will I fade,
Into a night that Man has made,
But through that gloom shall gleam the Sun
When I am lost, and again am won.

Release! Release! I call to thee
In New Lands across the sea;
Let another, on narrow pathways, come to me.

Furthest and Highest,
Yet not beyond reach.
Choose thou well a path that will teach
How the Sunken is raised
And Emptiness is filled
And a wandering heart
Can finally be stilled.

Seek the Great Stone! Mark it well, with a sign,
That the one who shall follow
Shall see it is mine,
And, seeing, shall ponder and certainly know
As the Ancients have writ: 'As Above, so Below.'

And I shall guard the Source of Greatness;
Waiting by a teardrop

From neither joy nor sorrow born,
In silver bound, beneath the ground,
I am the Spiral Horn.[4]

Endnotes
1. Waite, A.E. *The Occult Sciences*, pp. 1–49.
2. Cirlot, C.A. *Dictionary of Symbols*, p. 81.
3. Ibid. Cirlot, p. 337–8.
4. Green, Michael. *De Historia et Veritate Unicornis*, p. 64.

20. THE ROLE OF MUSIC AND DANCE IN CELTIC MAGIC

Music is one of the most powerful agents in our lives. Those who serve the negative forces have realized its value as a 'money-spinner' and mind-dulling agent, while the Old Ones have used it as a canvas against which to daub the many hues of the higher spheres which we, in turn, translate into harmonious sounds.

The power of music to both heal and influence human affairs was well known to the ancients. David played on his harp and healed Saul, and when Elisha was 'much troubled by importunate kings' he called for a minstrel who, when he played, 'the hand of the Lord came upon him.' Apollo soothed Argus to sleep and Orpheus tamed wild beasts and charmed Hades. Asclepiades (100 BC) predated by two thousand years modern vibrational treatment for deafness. Plato emphasized the influence of properly chosen music. In the thirteenth century the Arabs used musical treatment for disease and even Galen recommended it for certain ills. The primitive shamans employed chants appropriate to the problems with which they were dealing. And, of course, the Celtic Bards were among the most skilled in its uses at all levels.

As the Earth has been called the Planet of Music and Healing, there is an obvious connection between the magical values of music and many of the imbalances to which we are subjected. Music is also closely allied to another science, that of sonics — the forces which bind together the atoms and molecules of matter are affected by certain sound frequencies or wavelengths. Coelius Aureliamus mentioned the trembling and palpitation of the diseased parts of the body when a flautist played. An unexpected sound can cause the spirit to be temporarily ejected from the body — we 'jump out of our skins', as the saying goes — when we hear a sudden loud noise. Sound creates an impression on the mind causing a reaction in the mental-nervous-physical system which music can counter. And so we see a pattern emerging. Music and its accompanying vibrations can build or destroy, which highlights its potency as a legitimate magical force or energy.

It is said that each individual has a personal sonic which can be ascertained by playing a scale on the violin so that when an appropriate note is touched a sensation will occur at the base of the neck. Nature also has a personal sonic which is said to resonate to the note of 'F', which would therefore relate the key of 'F' to the Goddess in her eco-aspect, the Green ray, the Anahata or Heart chakra and the Celtic ethos. The occult nature of music is something that I, as a musician, could write reams about, but for the purpose of this book I will endeavour to keep it within the Celtic magical context.

The secret power of movement in association with sound is also highly magical. All cultures have their dance rhythms that are appropriate to their tribal or national characteristics and religious or mystical inclinations. Echoes of the old Celtic songs and dances are to be found in the folk music and customs of these Isles and those parts of Europe where the Celtic hegemony was the strongest.

The fact that morris dancing, for example, has survived to the present and is as popular as ever in many walks of life speaks for the impression it has made upon the collective unconscious of the British people, while the Celtic influence may also be witnessed in the traditional dances of Ireland and Scotland.

According to tradition, morris dancing originated in old fertility rituals that were designed to energize the growth of crops, and its origins are both ancient and obscure. Ritual always involves a concentration of thought power which is channelled into a single wish or desire, which process can be aided by the use of bodily movement and the verbal repetition of set chants or verses. After all, religious movements have been practising power-generating rituals for years, either in their formal services or, in the case of the more fundamentalist groups, via their hymns. Anyone who has attended a morris dance or old traditional ceremony will be aware of the energy field that emanates therefrom, which must, and does, affect the subconscious if not the conscious thought patterns of those present.

The ceremony that takes place in Padstow on the first of May is a typical example of this. Those who have witnessed this ritual attest to the emotionally-charged atmosphere that it creates, thus confirming the fact that we have at our disposal a storehouse of natural forces available for our use if we but take the time and care to study and address them.

I recently visited Padstow and talked to some of the local people about the festival as a whole, and the Horse in particular. They hastened to inform me that although it is not unknown for young couples to make for the woods following the celebrations it was not primarily a fertility ritual, having far deeper connotations. They also expressed annoyance with so-termed 'folksong experts' who placed various interpretations on their May song, none of which were truly correct. The song appears to have changed considerably over the years, the popularly rendered version not being the original. Bearing in mind the antiquity of the verses and the energy overlays they have accumulated over the centuries, however, this is not surprising.

There are two 'Obby 'Osses, the blue which is the first to appear, and the old or red 'Oss which appears later. My attention was also drawn to the function of the Teaser, who dances ahead of the 'Oss waving a 'Club' or small shield-shaped bat with a handle, his function being to encourage the 'Oss to mimic his movements and gestures. In olden times it was considered bad luck for a woman to touch the Teaser's Club, the belief being that infertility would result. The 'Oss, on the other hand, was believed to be fortunate in this respect, which rather suggests that at one period the Teaser represented the masculine polarity and the Horse the feminine which is as it should be, Epona, Rhiannon, Magog and the majority of horse deities being feminine.

I have arranged a visit Padstow in 1987 to witness the festival for myself and my local informants advised me to pay particular attention to the Dirge, which they felt would 'tell

me something'. As this book is due with my publishers prior
to that time I shall not be able to include my own psychic
impressions thereof, but many of my readers will doubtless
wish to have this experience for themselves.

Cornwall is a veritable repository of the old Celtic arts and
as one very wonderful and knowing lady I talked to in
Padstow remarked, 'For this we can thank the fact that
Cromwell never made it here!'

I am including the words of the May song as given by Bob
Stewart, but bearing in mind the aforesaid, and in due
deference to the kind people of Padstow who gave of their
time and knowledge to put me right on a few facts, I would
request my readers to keep an open mind on these versions.

THE PADSTOW MAY SONG

Night Song

Unite and unite and let us all unite
For summer is acome unto day
And whither we are going we will all unite
In the merry morning of May

I warn you young men everyone
To go into the greenwood and fetch your May home

Arise up Mr .... and joy you betide
And bright is your bride that lies by your side.

Arise up Mrs .... and gold be your ring
And give to us a cup of ale the merrier we shall sing

Arise up Miss .... all in your gown of green
You are as fine a lady as wait upon the Queen.

Now fare you well, and we bid you all good cheer,
We call once more unto your house before another year.

Day Song

Unite and unite and let us all unite,
For summer is acome unto day
And whither we are going we will all unite
In the merry morning of May

Arise up Mr .... I know you well and fine
You have a shilling in your purse and I wish it were in mine

All out of your beds
Your chamber shall be strewed with the white rose and the red.

Where are the young men that here now should dance?
Some they are in England and some they are in France.

Where are the maidens that here now should sing?
They are in the meadows the flowers gathering.

Arise up Mr .... with your sword by your side
Your steed is in the stable awaiting for to ride.

Arise up Miss .... and strew all your flowers
It is but a while ago since we have strewed ours.

Dirge

Oh where is Saint George?
Oh where is he Oh?
He is out in his longboat
All on the salt sea Oh.

Up flies the kite
Down falls the lark Oh
Aunt Ursula Birdhood she had an old ewe,
And she died in her own park-O.

With the merry ring adieu the merry spring
How happy is the little bird that merrily doth sing

The young men of Padstow they might if they would
They might have built a ship and gilded her with gold

The young women of Padstow they might if they would
They might have made a garland with the white rose and the red

Arise up Mr .... reach me your hand
And you shall have a lively lass with a thousand pounds in hand

Arise up Miss .... all in your cloak of silk
And all your body underneath as white as any milk.

Repeat Dirge

> Now fare you well and bid you all good cheer
> We call no more unto your house until another year.[1]

Stewart also tells us that these old songs seldom, if ever, have a 'God the Father' image and are often cited as being 'matriarchal', which associates them immediately with the matrist Celts and their predecessors in these isles.

Any follower of magical music should put in a special study of this old folk music and the way it was originally sung without paying too much attention to the 'experts'. The preponderance of certain rhythms and keys, together with the recurring modal themes, produce frequencies calculated to release the power potential in the human spiritual or psychological economy. In other words, they did not happen by accident! Most genuine folk tunes are half memories of a musical ethos in which the power and true nature of sonics was fully realized and utilized. The Celtic Druids carried a great deal of such information in their oral tradition which they employed in both the musical and poetic modes.

Among these powerful musical-cum-magic sequences one has to include plainsong or plainchant. I first became aware of the occult energy generated by plainchant when I encountered it at boarding school. I later made a special study of it and have used it in ritual magic. It was interesting to observe, however, that not everyone could take the type of energy it generated. In fact, some people I know found it quite disturbing. And yet, it has served the major orthodox religions faithfully for centuries, monastic orders of great discipline and mortification finding particular solace in its tones.

There is a reason for this. Plainsong is essentially a music of the higher chakras and does not in any way link with the lower or more physical aspects of human nature. For example, gentle people who dislike noise and strife are frequently attracted to plainsong, while the type of person who cannot be left alone in a room for a few minutes without turning on a radio or television set 'for company' is rarely drawn to the elevating strains of this musical form. When used correctly and understood for what it is, plainsong can prove a potent force in magic for the attraction of somewhat loftier energies than those primarily concerned with the satisfaction of the needs and gratification of the human desire nature. And the fact that the plainsong theme appears in so many ancient folksongs that have Celtic or pre-Celtic links certainly says something of occult importance. For those interested, I give as an example the 'Victimae paschali laudes' and 'Terri tremuit', being the Sequence and Offertory from the Proper of the Tridentine Mass for Easter Sunday. Compare these with the modal pattern of the familiar folksong 'Scarborough Fair', for example, and you will see what I mean.

Folk music is evocative of those mythical characters who appear with striking regularity within its words and music who can usually be dissolved into the twofold Celtic god: the King of Light and the Dark Tanist. Known by a variety of names: the Green Man, Jack-in-the-Green, Jack-in-the-Bush, the Garland, Robin-of-the-Wood, Robin Hood, May Man, and King of the May, this enigmatic character embodies the duo-fold concept of life following death, while emphasizing the creative power of the ancient Tree Magic. Janet and Colin Bord are of the opinion that such diverse figures as the mediaeval Wild Man of the Woods, and the Green Knight of Arthurian legend (which also re-echoes the theme of annual death and resurrection) also have their mythic origins here, as well as many ancient, and unquestionably 'unChristian' church carvings!

As for the hobby horses and other equines from Epona's stable, the inferences are obvious and the old beliefs shine through the cobwebs and mists of subsequent religious infusions that have never managed, in spite of persistent persecution, to kill off the belief in the existence and efficacy of the old gods of nature.

Other links between folksongs and the Celtic religion occur in both ship and wren symbology. Certain lines in the Padstow song suggest that there might have been a ritual ship or coracle involved at some time in the past:

'The young men of Padstow they might if they would
They might have built a ship and gilded her with gold.'[2]

This ship symbology occurs in the myths of many nations, notably ancient Egypt. Dr R.E. Witt, in his book *Isis in the Graeco-Roman World*, describes the Isian Ship procession in some detail, and I have personally taken part in a modern version of this old ritual. Although at first glance there would appear to be similarities between the Egyptian Isis and the Celtic Keridwen, I personally connect Keridwen with Nephthys who was the Hidden or Dark aspect of the Egyptian triplicity.

Hercules, with his oak club is considered to be synonymous with Ogmius, inventor of Ogham — he who binds through the magic of words (poetry) — who had a similar attribute. This club also appears in the form of a staff or spear which is said to equate with St George's lance and the judgement stick of the Egyptian Anubis. The Ogham alphabet was also closely associated with the magical chant system used by the Druids.

The wren was sacred to Bran the Blessed and the old ritual significance of the Wren Cult is to be found in the folksong 'The Cutty Wren'. It is a sad song for an animal lover like myself to stomach, but then so is many an ancient ritual. But there are, however, worse cruelties being carried out in this day and age under the banner of popular religious orthodoxy, the 'might is right' principle, which implies that if enough people follow a way of thought or belief then it must be correct, still holding strong. As far as its value and historical validity are concerned, 'The Cutty Wren' has to make its appearance in this book or I would be unfaithful to my task:

THE CUTTY WREN[3]

(abbreviated after the second verse)

Oh where are you going? says Milder to Malder.
We may not tell you says Festle to Fose—
We're off to the wild wood, says John the Red Nose
We're off to the wild wood, says John the Red Nose.

And what will you do there? says Milder to Malder,
We may not tell you says Festle to Fose.
We'll hunt the Cutty Wren says John the Red Nose.
We'll hunt the Cutty Wren says John the Red Nose.

How will you shoot her? ...
With bows and arrows ...

That will not do— ...
What will do then? ...
Big guns and big cannons! ...

How will you bring her home? ...
On four strong men's shoulders ...

That will not do— ...
What will do then? ...
Big cart and big waggons ...

How will you cut her up? ...
With knives and with forks.

That will not do— ...
What will do then? ...
Big hatchets and cleavers.

How will you cook her? ...
In pots and in pans.

That will not do— ...
What will do then? ...
In a bloody great brass cauldron!.

Who'll get the spare ribs? ...
We'll give it all to the poor.

One of the most popular of the old folksongs is undoubtedly 'The Dilly Song', more popularly known as 'Green Grow the Rushes, Oh!' Numerous 'experts' have tried their hand at interpreting this piece and the English Folk Dance and Song Society have actually issued a leaflet entitled *The Mystery of 'Green Grow the Rushes, Oh!'*. Although I have not seen this myself, I am assured by other occultists that it bears no resemblance to the mystical truths that lie concealed within its verses. It is usually accorded Qabalistic interpretation there being ten Sephiroth on the Tree of Life while the song features the numbers one to ten inclusive, commencing with the line 'I'll sing you One song, Green grow the rushes Oh; What is your One song....' etc. The numbers are then explained as follows:

One of them is all alone and ever more shall be so
Two of them are lily-white boys all clothed all in green Oh
Three of them are strangers o'er the wide world they are rangers
Four it is the Dilly Hour when blooms the Gilly Flower
Five it is the Dilly Bird that's seldom seen but heard
Six is the Ferryman in the boat that o'er the river floats oh
Seven are the Seven Stars in the Sky, the Shining Stars be Seven
   Oh
Eight it is the Morning's break when all the World's awake Oh
Nine it is the pale Moonshine, the Shining Moon is Nine Oh
Ten Forgives all kinds of Sin, from Ten begin again Oh.[4]

The meanings of some of these lines are so blatantly obvious when viewed in the light of the old Celtic religion that one fails to understand why this has not been commented upon outside the occult fraternity. Well, for what it is worth here is my interpretation:

1. The Creative Force or single deity into which all other god-forms dissolve.
2. The two Celtic male deities, the Lord of Light and the Lord of Hades or Annwn.
3. The mobile Celts themselves whose sacred number was '3'.
4. The fourth tree in the Tree Alphabet is the alder, sacred to Bran the Blessed, whose sister Branwen 'White Crow' is the Gilly Flower.
5. The voice of wizardry or Merlin, the sacred number of the Celtic gods.
6. Keridwen's Coracle, Charon's ferry, the Egyptian Anubis, initiation or the right of way through the waters of the deep unconscious.
7. The sacred number of the sea gods who guide the mariners via the stars.
8. The number of judgement or resurrection.
9. The Triple Moon Goddess thrice emphasized. The Nine Maidens who guard the sacred Cauldron.
10. The necessity to return to our basic origins, or find the 'self' in order to understand the Mysteries.

All the clues to the aforementioned are to be found in the various chapters of this book.

Endnotes
1. Stewart, Bob. *Where is Saint George?*, pp. 129–31.
2. Ibid. Stewart, p. 67.
3. Ibid. Stewart, p. 15.
4. Ibid. Stewart, p. 81.

PART THREE

CELTIC MAGIC FOR TODAY'S WORLD

21. GODS AND ARCHETYPES

In order to understand any magical system it is essential for the student to thoroughly familiarize him or herself with the history, customs, overt religious practices and ethos of the people responsible for its conception, while also bearing in mind that god-forms or archetypes relate to corresponding aspects in the human psyche. In the first two parts of this book I have outlined as much of this as space will allow, and in so doing have also tried to show how the fusion of Celtic mysticism and magic with the old religion of the indigenous populations of these isles in particular has produced something of a distinctive and immensely powerful occult energy field that is closely related to nature, the Fairy Kingdoms, the Earth Mother and the deep unconscious. What we now have to do is to apply this knowledge to practical magic.

My first statement is one that might well evoke a few cries of disagreement: Celtic magic is NOT a role-playing system. In other words, when working on its ray one does not assume the role of one of its gods or goddesses, as with Egyptian magic, for example. Nor is it like Greek magic, where the student chooses the deity he or she feels most drawn to and proceeds from there. In the Celtic system one simply tunes into the 'Green ray' and waits. Of course, one studies all the relevant literature, meditates on whichever aspect one feels drawn to and practices with one's *coelbrens*, if one feels so inclined. But as regards the deity, he or she will come to you when they deem fit, and it may not be exactly what you expect, so dispel any preconceived ideas to start with.

Perhaps you are a fiercely patriotic British male who sees in Arthur the spirit of the race, so you sit patiently hoping for him to appear — armour and all! You may well find the gods have decided that you are too 'macho' for your own good, for remember: the Celtic ray is matriarchal, so it could be the gentle Branwen who calls upon you during your meditations, or Morgan the Enchantress. Or, perhaps you are the typical Earth Mother type, a fully-fledged member of the Green Party and devoted to the education of the young. A visit from Gwydion, who tells you to use more of your mind and less of your emotions, might therefore come as a surprise. Or it may be Morrigan who whispers to you that you are not truly being yourself in allowing others to dictate your lifestyle so you must stand up and fight for your rights as an individual, change your pattern of living, throw out the old and bring in the new!

In earlier chapters I have outlined the better known Celtic deities, including a number of aspects of the five main principles. Which of these the aspirant eventually works with will be governed by the tutelary deity's choice of pupil, prior to which it will be up to the inclination of the individual. Names do not matter as long as the principle is intact. For example, the Triple Goddess may appear in any of her three aspects, the way in which she chooses to make herself known being utterly personal to you, the student. The Solar or Light King may appear as Arthur, Llew or Taliesin and the Wizard as Merlin, Gwyn or Pwyll, but these are only nomenclatures with which we have endowed them, and it is not the names that are important, but the comprehension of the true nature of those principles which constitute the essence of the old Celtic magical system.

Let us analyse the Triple Goddess archetype. In terms of modern psychology she represents the three aspects of the human psyche: the Natural or Instinctive, the Rational or Practical, and the Intuitive or Inspirational, the latter issuing from the deep unconscious, hence the 'Dark Goddess' or hidden aspect of the third person in this trinity. The dual-aspected male deity is suggestive of the right and left hemispheres of the brain; or the higher Transpersonal Self, and the lower nature or Id which needs to be controlled by the Heroic aspect (Gwydion versus Pryderi, etc.). The fact that there are three goddesses in one, and only two gods tells us that the Celts were orientated towards the feminine or intuitive, although overtly they displayed the characteristics of the Warrior as seen in the Gwydion/Arthur/Llew/Lugh archetype while adhering strictly to the religion of Merlin/Pwyll/Gwyn, the Magical Lord of the Underworld. The male Gods of Light express both anima and animus extravertedly, often being both poets/musicians and warriors, while the Dark King or Magician aspect is also both anima and animus, but expressed introvertedly. The three Goddesses are frequently seen to express more animus than anima; even the maternal types were adept warriors who thought nothing of taking their places beside their menfolk when it came to battle, as may be evidenced in historical accounts of the nature of the Celtic women. The first or Maiden aspect of the Goddess is extrovert, the Mother can be either according to the inclination of the devotee, while the Crone or Wise Woman is obviously introvert.

Add all these together and you have the Celtic ray, for the Celtic character is but a reflection of that from which it emanated at a finer or higher level: As Above, So Below!

Numerology and astrology should also be observed in any workings with the Celtic deities. The Celts could be described as emotional, literary warriors, which would indicate strong Fire, Water and Air influences, but as we have no set astrological chart for them as a people we must simply bear these observations in mind when thinking astrologically.

Let us now assume that you have been visited by your god or goddess and are all set to proceed. Where do you go from there? In Celtic Magic one has the choice of working with a group or individually, either pattern being acceptable to the deities. In my own case, I have been chosen by Keridwen the Enchantress in her Dark Aspect (with Brigid and Rhiannon assuming the other two roles) which also links me to her son Taliesin.

From the Initiation inference in Chapter 17, it may be observed that in this aspect Keridwen is a water divinity representing the deep unconscious, wherein lies her power. Her colour is silver, her association lunar and her symbols are the Cauldron (again a water symbol), a Coracle or small boat, and an Ear of Corn. If I were working in ritual magic, which I am not as I prefer the direct mind approach, I would have a Cauldron in evidence and all symbols associated with the element of Water. Although traditionally the Dark or Crone aspect of the Triple Goddess is portrayed in silver and black I do not care for black, so she has shown me a shade of deep misty grey-green that is acceptable to her. But remember, Keridwen, as with all of the deities, is only masked according to our concept of how she ought to appear and she may well choose to show herself as *she* wishes to be known. I see behind her mask a Maeve-like goddess whose long, luxuriant flowing tresses, which are a pale auburn in colour, reach down to her waist. Her eyes are green-grey, like a broody sea; her face, typically Celtic, is fair and slightly golden in hue. But then these are only my impressions and yours may be entirely different. As is said of the Egyptian Isis: 'She is all things to all men.'

Brigid I perceive in her Athenian mode rather than her maternal aspect, as the teacher of truth and guardian of righteousness. She stands tall and erect, not unlike the figure of Britannia, although in colouring she is similar to Keridwen. Her element is Fire and her colour is orange.

Rhiannon's symbol is the Horse, her element Water and her colour green, and she is the goddess to whom one can pray for justice and an airing of the truth. Those who have borne life's ills and injustices with patience, but who are nearing the end of their tether, may turn to her for solace and strength.

The Taliesin archetype appears to me as a tall, strongly built and handsome male in his prime, fair of hair and blue eyed, and representative of all that is artistic, but music and poetry in particular. His element is Fire, his symbol a Harp. The Fire/Water emphasis in this grouping is obvious and suggests the sacred '3' in its expansive mode, and the mystical, artistic and intuitive '7', as resonated in the planetary rays of Jupiter and Neptune and the signs Sagittarius and Pisces.

In both my previous magical books it has been my method to outline each deity, giving associated colours, emblems, descriptions, etc., but in this discipline my instructions from my tutelaries are not to do this. The Celtic ray is essentially one of creativity which is hardly encouraged if all the information is supplied in detail beforehand. By seeking the finer points for him or herself, the student will become receptive to the creative mode which is absolutely essential in this magical tradition, as one must be able to write one's own poetry or compose one's own tunes or chants. These need not be works of art according to accepted literary standards, as it is the effort which counts. And in that effort lies the Initiation.

The story of Keridwen tells us that we need to delve deep into our own subconscious minds, and thereby draw from the collective unconscious of the Celtic race and those from whom they in turn descended, before the doors of creativity will be opened to us. Like the true artist we must mix our own paints, fashion our own brushes, and weave our own canvas before we can withdraw our personal Excalibur from the Stone of Destiny that is our innate self.

22. WORKING WITH THE MIDDLE KINGDOMS

The ability to work with the denizens of the Middle Kingdoms is a must for anyone wishing to pursue the Celtic magical path. Fortunately, the gods have supplied us with the keys to the entrance to these realms in the form of the four Fairy gifts of the Tuatha de Danaans. But there are four doors and four keys, and to insert the wrong key in the wrong door will not only prove unproductive, but it may also annoy the Fairy folk — which is never a wise thing to do.

The most essential ingredient in Fairy magic is a thorough and honest assessment of the self. It is no use courting the good offices of the Fire Fairies, or Salamanders, if you are a person lacking in courage and unable to hold steadfastly to an ideal, or if you are totally uncreative and simply flow with the collective. Equally, if you have difficulty controlling your emotions to the extent that you are continually tossed about in the flotsam and jetsam of life's tides, then steer clear of the Ondines, for they will have no respect for anyone who cannot handle those very principles which they represent. People who are thoroughly impractical, unable to handle money and lack stability should think twice before summoning the Gnomes, while the slow thinker who is cosily esconced in one of life's inevitable ruts will not be welcomed by the Sylphs.

However, should the aspirant make a positive effort to overcome these faults through the employment of magic, then that will be a different matter, for the Fairy people are nothing if not admiring of the hero or heroine who strives to conquer the dark forces within his or her own personality, and will willingly lend their magical aid in this quest.

There may be those who would like to specialize in this particular aspect of Celtic magic which is also closely allied to an understanding and communication with all the forces of nature as manifested through the Green ray. Streams, sacred groves, magical stones, and ancient trees which in themselves are the repositories of great knowledge and wisdom are there to be communicated with, acknowledged and loved, and in return they will exchange their energies and give of their bounty.

All this may be effected either through ritual or through normal patterns of living, as we shall see. For the benefit of those who feel safe within the discipline of a structured framework, let us first consider the ritualistic approach.

Facsimiles of the four Fairy gifts must be present and the altar coloured according to the predominant natural force with which communication is being sought. Let us say that you, the student, are anxious to improve your mind. You find the imbibement of knowledge difficult, you cannot retain facts and lack energy to do the things you would like to do. So you have decided to seek the good offices of the Sylphs or spirits of the Element of Air to aid you in your quest for self-improvement.

Set your altar for all four Elements, remembering that the appropriate symbols must face the correct points of the compass: Earth to the north, Fire to the south, Air to the east, and Water to the west.

Each Element is associated with a metal and a colour. Gold or similarly coloured metals belong with the Elements of Fire and Earth, and silvery metals with Air and Water. The Elemental colours in their purest form are: orange for Fire, blue for Water, yellow for Air, and Green for earth. But bearing in mind that you will be working on what is primarily an artistic ray you will be allowed licence to effect whichever tint or shade of the basic hues that you feel to be appropriate to your own personal frequency. Flowers are also closely related to the Element of Air and although some practitioners like a vase of cut flowers, I personally prefer a potted plant that has its own life force. By talking to your plants for a period of time beforehand, you will soon come to know which one is your special friend. I have a spider plant who frets if he is not in my personal study or close to me in the living room. I have moved him from time to time to various other locations which were sunnier or allowed him more space, but he always hastened to let me know when he was unhappy. Your plants should have names, after all they are individuals, and there are many things they can teach you, as well as give you healing.

There are also appropriate musical notes or keys that resonate to each Elemental frequency. These are as follows: Fire — D, Air — E, Water — G, and Earth — F. Those with musical inclinations can effect variations with the use of minor keys depending upon the nature of the working and the deities invoked, but the normal procedure would be to employ major keys for the Solar Gods and the first two aspects of the Triple Goddess, and melodic minors for the Dark King or the Crone aspect of the Goddess.

So you are about to perform a ceremony to evoke the four Elements, but Air in particular. You should therefore have a yellow or similarly-shaded altar cloth and yellow candles. Flowers should either be purely green and leafy or with yellow or white blooms. If you wish to invoke an attendant tutelary deity a good choice would be Gwydion or Merlin, but avoid the Dark Kings in this particular working.

The room in which the working is to be held must be physically clean and also psychically cleansed either through ritual or by mind magic. I have given precise directions for this procedure in my book *Practical Techniques of Psychic Self-Defence*, but for the present purpose I will add a few Celtic hints. The most effective method would naturally be a versicle or short poem in keeping with the true Celtic mode. Any working should always be prefaced with an invocation to the appropriate tutelary deity. I am including two examples, one to Rhiannon and one to Gwydion, followed by a short triadic cleansing verse.

To Rhiannon: Swift on the heel thou comest
                Rhiannon fair, whose steed
                Defies the power of blame.

To Gwydion: Come as thou wouldst, fair Bard
                In garb as suits thy role
                To blessed make this place.

A protective and cleansing triad:

> Thrice round this place to weave,
> Thrice blessing in thy dance,
> Thrice cleansing in thy fire.

Having placed your four instruments in their appropriate positions, light your yellow candle and stand it in the centre of your altar. Now, place your plant in the position occupied by the Sword, which is the symbol for the Element of Air. (These symbols do not need to be massive affairs, small versions will do, so it will not be necessary to borrow some super-large refectory table for this purpose.) Place your Sword in front of the lighted candle and in your own words invite the Elemental and Fairy Kingdoms to be your guests at this working. *NEVER COMMAND OR ORDER!* Ask in love and peace. If you are not used to working with the Fairy people they will naturally be suspicious at first, so you will need to gain their confidence by showing your sincerity and anxiousness to learn from them.

Raise each of the Elemental symbols in turn, face the appropriate point of the compass, and request their entry into your sacred circle. Sometimes there will be phenomena. I know of one person who always has problems with the Element of Fire, while Dion Fortune herself publicly admitted that she had trouble with the Sylphs most of her life as a working occultist. But do not let this worry you, simply speak to the Elementals in question with love and respect and admit to them that you have not as yet mastered the necessary principles, but humbly seek their help to so do. They will read your heart and know whether you are simply using empty words or whether there is a true, sincere and humble desire within you.

Leave the Element for whom the working is primarily intended until the last, but in a normal invocation to the Elemental Kingdoms the correct order is Fire first (that being the senior Element), followed by Air, then Water and finally Earth. In this particular ceremony which we are now discussing the invocatory order would therefore be Fire, followed by Water, then Earth and finally Air.

Raise the Sword well above your head and request the help and presence of the Sylphs. You should really write your own verses, but here is a sample to give you the general idea.

> Fast darting, winged brother, come,
> Quick thinking, knowing sister, come,
> Message bearing, active beings, come!

The remaining content of your ritual will be up to each of you as individuals. It may be by way of seeking a favour (in which case you must always exchange an energy as this is the rule with the Elemental Kingdoms); for special healing; to learn from them; or purely devotional. But once the working is complete the energies that have been summoned *MUST* be dismissed in peace and love, and above all, *THANKED* for their good offices. And this means *sincerely* from the heart, and not in the ritualistically perfunctory manner that some people boringly recite prayers.

Dismiss first of all the last Element that you called, and then the other three in their correct order (Fire, Water and Earth), always facing to the appropriate compass point. You should write your own dismissal verses for that is the way it should be in Celtic magic. Finally, the tutelary god or goddess must be thanked in your own words, but preferably in poetic form.

This is but one example of how to work with the Fairy people, but there are other, and in my opinion, better ways. One of these involves going out to a pre-selected location, preferably in the country where the nature spirits have been allowed to live undisturbed by the onslaught of modern technology. If you can possibly choose a place where you will not be disturbed, then so much the better. You may use the Pan Call if you wish, but with the customary caution. (For details see *Practical Greek Magic*.)

If you are working with the Crone aspect of the Triple Goddess or the Lord of Annwn, you may prefer a night working. A lonely seashore is ideal for the former; a rocky domain, especially with caves or standing stones, is best suited to the latter. But avoid the better known sites as these have, sadly, been sullied by bad 'vibes' from people who started off meaning well, but have lost their way along the labyrinths of mental confusion and become subject to the power of the Dark King (the Id). In other words, they are not in control of themselves, being influenced externally by drugs, alcohol, or

simply undisciplined hedonism so that they lack the will to
cope with those energies whose good offices they try so hard
to court. Remember, the occult — and this goes for any
system therein — is mastered by will-power, which means one
must be ever-vigilant and in control or we are back to that old
lighted match/gas leak situation that I mentioned earlier.
'Doing your own thing' is not necessarily 'doing the right
thing', so, aspirant to the Celtic path, beware! As beautiful
and poetic as the scene may appear on the surface, there are
no short cuts, because beneath that artistically emotional
exterior lies the real hard 'nitty-gritty' of Initiation within the
deep sea of the unconscious, which is Keridwen's territory.
Take care that you do not get out of your depth therein, for
we all know what happens to the highly artistic or creative
person who loses mental control — history is generous with
its examples!

But to return to our Elemental beings and other inhabitants
of the Middle Kingdoms. The Fairy people possess great
healing gifts which they may dispense through herbs, flowers
or simply through the qualities which they themselves
represent. So you can effect a ritual or an out-of-doors
communication session strictly for healing purposes. A
person who is suffering from renal problems, for example, is
obviously having difficulties with the Element of Water,
which tells you that something in their emotional thought-
patterns is misfiring. Seek the aid of the Ondines to solve the
problem or ask the balancing Elemental force, i.e. Fire to help
put matters right. Sometimes, these deficiencies do not stem
from our bodies, but from our souls or psyches, so the
healing should be applied directly to that level.

Perhaps you are having financial problems which are
seriously affecting your health — ask the Gnomes for help.
They may not place a crock of gold on your doorstep, but
they will help you to cope with that aspect of your personality
that has caused you to get into financial difficulty in the first
place.

I have personally worked with the Elemental Kingdoms for
over thirty years; I have learned many lessons from them and
they have highlighted my weaknesses. Like many other
occultists I have formed special friendships from among
them. There will always be the one Element that proves
difficult, however, for few of us, if any, are in perfect

Elemental balance. Perhaps our emotions are the culprits; or it could be lack of concentration, or an inability to stand by a friend in need. Seek the appropriate Elemental antidote and you will find it will work wonders!

How the Fairy Kingdoms appear to the Initiate will be a very private thing, so do not rely too much on traditional images, such as elves, goblins, pixies, hobbits, mermaids, etc. These are but the clothes with which mankind has seen fit to garb his brothers and sisters from the Middle Kingdoms. A Fire Elemental who is very dear to me has no form at all, while my Airy friend shows herself in a very distinctive mode. They are not like us, and they live in a finer, less perceptible dimension. Bear all these things in mind, approach them with a clean and open heart in the spirit of love and giving, and they will respond equally. Besides, they are particularly fond of the Green ray, so you are halfway there to start with if you approach them through the good offices of Celtic magic.

23. TREE MAGIC

There are many other life forms with which we share this planet, some of which are more perceptible to our five senses than others. So while the less sensitive among us may have problems with the spirits of the Elements or the denizens of the subtle spheres, the tree spirits manifest themselves in forms which can be easily seen and communed with. Tree spirits are called 'dryads' and tradition tells us that there are several classifications of these intelligences which vary with the nature and functions of different types of tree. Some trees, for example, are noted healers while others are guardians, protectors, recorders, or dispensers of innate wisdom (for those wise and sensitive enough to effect the right communicatory connection). As the Celts were so close to nature, they became aware of the role trees could play in their everyday life and religion, hence the Tree Alphabet and the many magical offshoots therefrom.

Apart from the obvious occult connotations it does no harm to take into consideration the more practical applications of Tree Lore, especially where healing is concerned, after all, herbalists have used tree bark for centuries for the relief of many conditions.

RED CHESTNUT — is said to remove fears and apprehensions;
WHITE CHESTNUT — disperses persistent worrying thoughts;
ELM — removes frustrations and the inability to cope with life's

problems that so often bring on digestive disorders;

BEECH — from this tree, we are told, one learns the value of tolerance;

LARCH — helps one to absorb physical strength and promotes a feeling of general well-being;

OAK — soothes the motor nervous system and helps you to pick up the thread of some knotty problem;

FIR — pines are highly beneficial for bronchial complaints, as many people who have recuperated in Swiss clinics will know.

Getting to know your trees is a must for the aspiring Celtic magician. Next comes the process of making friends with the dryads, which might not be so easy if you fall into the category of those highly materialistic people who see trees as an inferior form of life to themselves, and therefore not really in a position to dispense wisdom and knowledge. Nothing could, in fact, be further from the truth.

The Tree Kingdom, or domain of the dryads, exists in what is occultly termed the 'observation mode'. In other words, trees are immobile (on this planet, anyway); they simply root to a certain spot, watch and record. That which they record, and this applies especially to long-lived trees like the sequoia, is relayed to the cosmic memory bank as valid observation, for unlike the thoughts and experiences projected by people, tree recordings are totally impartial and uninfluenced by the tides of human affairs.

Let us assume, then, that the aspirant has learned about his or her trees and made friends with the dryads. What next?

Once again we come to the question of working magic either according to a system, through nature, or via mental transmissions; the choice being up to the individual. Let us start with the ritualistic approach.

The student is advised to copy out the lists given in Chapter 17 for the Months, the Seasons, and the Thirteen Stations. Path working rituals can be created from the Thirteen Stations, but there are things to bear in mind. These Stations are placed in the order of the numbers sacred to them and not in a form of priority, and, as I have already mentioned in the chapter cited, one should not be accorded more importance than another. The essential thing is to know oneself and one's capabilities, always bearing in mind that one will naturally be more in tune with some trees than others. But at the same time, in order to gain an all round occult experience, all aspects must eventually be tackled and understood.

Path workings can commence at any point, of course, except Absolute Deity, but that again is a question of common sense and being aware of one's own limitations. Starting at chaos and working upwards would be the best approach, as is often recommended in Qabalistic practices. But on the other hand, if one should feel an affinity with one tree in particular then entrance can be effected at that point. I have constructed a simple diagram of a ritualistic tree which students may find easier to follow than working from a list.

Some occultists place the planets at the Tree points, so in case you, the aspirant, are also an astrologer I have included the planetary symbols. As there are thirteen points and only ten planets accepted in modern astrology including the Lights, I have seen fit to incorporate the Earth herself, as symbolized by $\oplus$, and the two planets which are not as yet generally accepted, Vulcan $\female$ (near to the sun), and Pan $\pm$ (beyond the orbit of Pluto). Should this be unacceptable to the purist, secondary rulings from the more orthodox system are also given.

If a short path working is needed, keep strictly to the number '5' using either the 13/10/7/4/1, or central ascent, or zigzagging from 13 to 12/11/10/9 inclusive. Another method would be to work from 13 to 12/9/6/3, or 13 to 11/8/5/2, using the side ascents. There are several other obvious variations.

The extent to which this system can be used will be governed by the spiritual awareness of the user. As with all magical formulae, there is always the risk of 'blowing a fuse', so it is advisable to accept one's limitations with humility and love. Crossing the central points in my diagram will always involve a power surge that can prove unbalancing to the psyche, especially if the student is under any form of stress at the time. For example, one should refrain from contacting the energies of The Sea or The Triune Queen if one's emotions are in a state of instability, and The Mind if one is in any kind of mental turmoil. Meditate well beforehand and search your mind for any of the above-mentioned psychological factors so that you avoid stepping into possible areas of occult disaster.

Each level must be approached with a courteous knock and request for entry. Never assume that you will automatically be

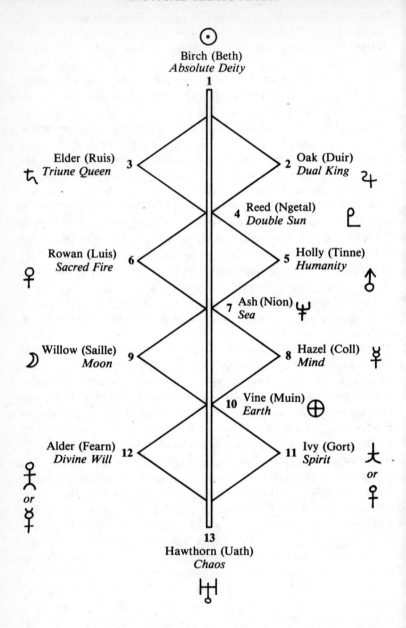

accepted. In magic one has no rights until one has earned them. Return by the route you came, closing and sealing each door safely and securely behind you, using the Tree symbology connected therewith, plus your own personal keynote or sigil (see *Practical Techniques of Psychic Self-Defence*), as the last thing you want is to bring back with you some force that is either unwelcome, or out of tune with the present frequencies of this planet. *Never leave a vacuum*, and always close your aura and 'earth' yourself well upon your return. Celtic magic is the same as any other system in that good manners are appreciated by the Old Ones, thanks always being in order.

Before attempting to tackle the Tree Calendar, however, it would be advisable to work through and thoroughly familiarize yourself with the Fairy Kingdoms, or Elemental beings, as suggested in Chapter 22. Use appropriate incenses, flowers and perfumes in you wish. In ritual all these can help, but in mind magic they are not essential.

For those unfamiliar with the story behind the ritual year it is as follows: The Queen is the Creatrix who bears the King, a babe at the New Year; at Candlemas, 2 February, she names and arms him; on 23 March he rides forth in splendour; on 30 April he becomes her lover; on 24 June he is sacrificially crucified by his own Dark Self and all his domains confiscated; on 2 August he is symbolically eaten as the grain that sprang from his seed when he was killed (the origin of the Eucharist); on 22 September he is mourned by the Queen as all the earth begins to fade towards autumn; on 31 October he is conducted to the Tanist Underworld, or Annwn, from which his soul escapes in the form of an Eagle; and on the 22 December his Tanist persona awaits death, its work completed while the Queen awaits the birth of the New Year. Following the Nameless Day the newborn babe slays the Tanist and the New Year cycle begins once again.

This is all allegorical, of course, and based on the seasons and the effect they have upon the earth as a whole and on all who dwell thereon. Only the Queen remains constant. The whole picture presents a highly poetic and deeply moving concept after the style of the old 'miracle' or mummery mini-dramas that were enacted ritualistically by such characters as St George and his Dragon, Jack-of-the-Green, Robin Goodfellow, and Maid Marian.

The second approach to Tree magic is through actually visiting trees and thus effecting a direct tree-to-person communication. This is especially beneficial for healing purposes. The simplest method is to press oneself close to the trunk of the tree and relax, breathing slowly and easily, while making a mental effort to unite with its spirit or consciousness, thus allowing its energies access to one's mind and body. Trees can help to open up the conscious mind to the full realization of the Transpersonal Self, thus aiding and accelerating the process of individuation that is essential to true spiritual progress. There are certain occultists who are specialists in Tree magic, Dusty Miller, for example, who knows more about trees than your author will probably ever know, in this life anyway.

Tree magic can also be used in *coelbrens* (see description in Chapter 16). These small divinatory or magical aids can either be inscribed with the Tree Alphabet or Ogham, but I shall be dealing with *coelbrens* and their construction in a subsequent chapter.

So, good pupil, go to your Trees and learn, for although every tree (as every person) is not at the same stage of evolution or spiritual development, there are many that are elderly in spirit as well as body, and some gnarled old male or female specimen (they *can* be of either polarity), may well be able to afford you the very impetus and you need for your poetic future as a Celtic Bard of the Magical Order of the Trees.

24. ARTHURIAN MAGIC

This subject is complicated by the involvement of two different occult levels and two differing religious emphases. The reason for this lies in the fact that many who are devotees of the Arthur Cult see it in the later Christianized form, rather than its earlier and truer context, while others find the symbology of the Breton chivalric mode easier to negotiate than the portrayals of ancient god-forms. And as far as many people are concerned the Arthur saga, at its mundane level, has a nationalistic content which is guaranteed to stir the emotions in many a Celtic heart.

However, we must abide by the facts and not allow our fancies to get the better of us, so I will commence with the distant past and the significances of the old Arthurian or Arcturian god-forms.

Arthur was known by many names prior to the advent of Geoffrey of Monmouth's epic work. Although he appears in human context in *The Mabinogion*, we have already established him as an archetype of considerable antiquity, probably dating back to the Old Country. According to Davies he was Hu Gadarn, who with the help of his oxen dragged the monster Avanc from the depths of the Lake of Llion, thereby containing the Flood and saving the people from further inundation. In fact Davies, in his Arkite theory, sees Hu as a kind of Welsh Noah who appeared on our western shores around the time of the final sinking of

Atlantis. Hu Gadarn, or the ancient Arthur, dates back to antiquity if we are to trust the scholarship of Davies, and after reading his book I must say that he raises many valid points: the Egyptian and Hellenistic connections between the Rites of Keridwen and those of the Apis Cult and the Eleusinia, for example. But then, I belong to the 'single source' school!

The Arthur archetype, therefore, is contacted through the Rites of Keridwen and his glories are sung by Taliesin. Sometimes he is given as Keridwen's husband with Taliesin as their son, the three ruling the heavenly regions together, while in other versions, notably *the Mabinogion*, Keridwen appears in a more earthly context. But surely most of these tales that were subsequently placed into the drama of everyday existence in which kings, queens, lords and priests played their customary roles, were memories of earlier deities, folk heroes or, as Davies suggests, survivors from the Flood who possessed knowledge technologically ahead of that understood by the people of the lands to which they escaped from the inundation. One thing that does appear to be consistent as far as the Arthurian ray is concerned — and this applies to whichever religion or occult level through which it is approached — it carries the peculiar flavour of the Celtic ethos.

Let us leave the pure archetype for the moment, and concentrate on the better known and probably more favoured version as rendered by Malory. Seeing Arthur in the role of an early Celtic king in no way diminishes the magical symbology which he and his attendant personae represent, but it must be remembered that Arthur himself was no magician. He was simply the temporal representative of the power of Merlin, who was the occult force or manipulator of the cosmic energies behind the Celtic ray.

According to tradition, there were twelve knights of the Round Table who together with the King made the number thirteen. Any good tourist shop in Tintagel will provide a list of these knightly personages, plus a diagram of the mythical Table giving the positions occupied by each knight. In case this interests some of my readers I will include the names of the knights and the virtues with which they were particularly associated. Sometimes they are accorded shield designs by speculative dealers anxious to sell their wares, but as we have no way of verifying such detail it is best omitted. Needless to say, they are also assigned planets and signs of the zodiac, but since some of the planets needed to make up the twelve are slightly suspect, I have kept it to the zodiacal signs which are inserted as appropriate.

Knight	Zodiacal sign	Attribute
Sir Tristram	Aries	The Honourable Knight
Sir Galahad	Taurus	The Gentle and Loyal Knight
Sir Lamorak	Gemini	The Noble Knight
Sir Bors	Cancer	The Virtuous Knight
Sir Gawain	Leo	The Charitable Knight
Sir Gaheris	Virgo	The Sincere Knight
Sir Percival	Libra	The Courageous Knight
Sir Bedivere	Scorpio	The Chivalrous Knight
Sir Lancelot	Sagittarius	The Gallant Knight
Sir Gareth	Capricorn	The Sober Knight
Sir Geraint	Aquarius	The Helpful Knight
Sir Kay	Pisces	The Humble Knight

Now in addition to the above and King Arthur himself, we have several other *dramatis personae* to include: Guinevere, Morgan le Fay, the Three Ladies, the evil Mordred, and Merlin himself. Bearing in mind that Celtic magic is not of the role-playing variety, how then may we tackle this veritable array of personalities? Easy. Take the Knights for the qualities they represent — Honour, Gentleness, Nobility, Virtue (which in those days had obvious connotations), Charity, Sincerity, Courage, Chivalry, Gallantry, Sobriety, Helpfulness and Humility. Mordred is the dualistic energy which, if not kept under control, assumes power by force, thus killing the King of Light. In other words, he is the dark side of the nature — the Id — which ever lurks within each one of us, awaiting the opportunity to burst forth and effect that takeover that will inevitably cause our destruction. The Three Ladies can either represent the Triple Goddess or the three aspects of the self; the Instinctive, Rational and Intuitive, which also need to be kept in balance, while the jealous enchantress Morgan le Fay, Arthur's half-sister, who was said to be secretly in love with him, expresses the destructive power of the emotions that is inevitably the downfall of so many.

When Arthur is surrounded by his knightly retinue, as represented by the aforementioned virtues, he reigns supreme. But during what are referred to as his periods of absence when he is separated from these finer qualities, he is vulnerable to his own dark self.

We are told that Sir Lancelot of the Lake was a later Breton addition to the Arthurian court. As the 'ladies man', Lancelot obviously symbolizes the romantic love syndrome which holds the balance as far as Arthur is concerned, the Queen's seduction by Lancelot (according to one version) being, figuratively speaking, one of the nails in Arthur's coffin.

My advice to those who would like to work Arthurian magic using these Christianized historical-type figures is to set up a chart in which all of the characters are listed, numbered and placed in order. Including the twelve Knights and those other characters I have already detailed, we find ourselves with a total of twenty, the number of letters in both the Ogham alphabet and the Boibel-Loth. Or, if the Triple Goddess or Three Ladies are counted as '1', we can accommodate the eighteen letters of the old Beth-Luis-Nion. Should the aspirant wish to individualize the three aspects of the Triple Goddess, Quert and Straif may be included, in which case Saille, Ailm and Straif would accommodate the Maiden, Mother, and Crone respectively, with Sir Galahad moving down to Quert.

Using either the Tree Alphabet or Ogham, construct a set of *coelbren* and carve or paint a representative word or notch on each together with the name of the knight, king or immortal. To make this task easier I have erected an appropriate Tree Alphabet list:

Beth-Luis-Nion	*Character*
Beth	Arthur
Luis	Sir Bors
Nion	Sir Kay
Fearn	Sir Gaheris
Saille	Sir Galahad
Uath	Sir Geraint
Duir	Sir Lancelot
Tinne	Sir Tristram
Coll	Sir Lamorak
Muin	Sir Bedivere

Gort	Sir Percival
Pethboc/Ngetal	Sir Gawain
Ruis	Sir Gareth
Ailm	Three Ladies/Triple Goddess
Onn	Guinevere
Ur	Morgan
Eadha	Merlin
Idho	Mordred

These arrangements are purely offered as suggestions/ guidelines, however, and it will be up to the individual to effect the placings and interpretations of his or her choice.

As the Ogham is more obscure and magical, it needs to be individually executed by the student, so I am not permitted to interfere here. There are some things in Celtic magic which have to be worked out by the practitioner alone, and this is one of them. To the ancient Druids, the Ogham *coelbrens* were highly secret and very personal, which is how it should be today.

There is more in Arthurian symbology that merits consideration, however, the Round Table for example. There are many explanations as to the significance and origin of this concept aside from the old historical reference to the equality of all who sat around it. It is mentioned as being emblematical of the thirteen Stations of the Cross, symbolic of the eternity of God, and even representative of the sphere of the Earth itself, although the latter strains the credulity somewhat if viewed in the light of the fact that it was many years after the kingly Arthur was reputed to have lived before it was generally accepted that the Earth was round!

The more logical assumption would be that it came to these isles from Brittany along with several other chivalric additions to the old Arthurian tales and was probably associated with some secret religious or magical code which involved the gnostic symbology of the rhombic dodecahedron. In his treatise on Aeonology, G.R.S. Mead writes:

It is a curious fact that if we were to imagine space filled with spheres all of equal diameter and in mutual contact, we should find that each sphere was surrounded by exactly twelve other spheres; moreover, if we should imagine the spheres to be elastic, and that pressure be brought to bear on one of such systems of twelve, on every side at once, the central or thirteenth sphere would assume a dodecagonal form — in fact, a rhombic dodecahedron.[1]

The rhombic dodecahedron is a semi-regular solid having twelve faces, each a rhombus of angles 70°32' and 109°28'. This particular rhombus is related to the √2 rectangle and the 'circle squared'.

In addition to the twelve faces, there are fourteen vertices and twenty-four edges, which numbers are of particular occult interest in that they correspond with the numerical harmonies of the planet Earth. Valentinius, one of the great gnostic masters, adopted this geometrical solid as a paradigm for the expression of his particular interpretation of the Gnosis. The twelve faces were seen as signifying the twelve-fold aspects of creation evident in this solar system: twelve signs of the zodiac, twelve Apostles of Christ, twelve tribes of Israel, twelve Knights of the Round Table, twelve Olympians, and twelve planets in our solar system (if one accepts the existence of the two as yet generally unrecognized).

The number fourteen signifies the duality of the sacred '7' and the fourteen pieces into which the body of Osiris was dismembered after his assassination by Set, while the number twenty-four refers to the Elders around the celestial Throne.

The numbers twelve, fourteen and twenty-four, when added together equal fifty, the sacred number of the binary star Sirius, fifty years being the orbiting period of Sirius 'B' around Sirius 'A' (see *Practial Egyptian Magic*, Chapter 20).

The Gnostics, Jews and Essenes also accorded the number fifty more than a degree of magical import. Their sacred number was seven; so $7 \times 7 = 49$, represented an important cycle, the following or fiftieth day being celebrated as a feast day (i.e., Pentecost, was celebrated on the fiftieth day after the Jewish Passover.) This number also figures in the sum of the squares of the sides of the three, four, five triangle which is known as the 'perfect triangle', which numbers when added bring us back to the twelve. These numerical frequencies represented to the Gnostics and Essenes the connecting link between the universal archonic forces and the manifestation of their energies in the form of matter.

An interesting geometrical relationship exists between the rhombic dodecahedron and the octahedron. The octahedron, one of the Platonic solids, has eight triangular faces, each a perfect equilateral triangle, which appears to be a direct expression of the Gnostic Ogdoad. The octahedron can be contained within the rhombic dodecahedron so that the edges of the octahedron align with the major axes of the twelve rhombic faces, illustrating how the archetypal forces blend and work through the twelve zodiacal rays which appertain to this solar system.

The Knights Templar were very much involved in this school of occultism so it was probably via their Order that the concept of these geometric paradigms found their way into the mythology of the Bretons and thence into the British Arthurian saga.

Here is a diagram of the traditional Arthurian Round Table giving the positions occupied by each knight. Place the Thirteen Stations and/or the Tree Alphabet correspondences I have effected in the appropriate positions, and you have a suitable vehicle for ritual working which must, however, commence at Sir Percival and proceed to Arthur, always moving deoshins (clockwise).

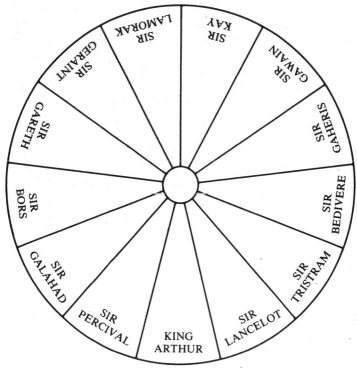

Our next consideration must naturally be Excalibur, as we have already analysed the Grail legends in some detail in a previous chapter. Sacred swords or weapons of war are as old as time. After all, the Tuatha de Danaans brought one to Ireland as a gift, if we are to believe Tuan of the Long Memory. The sword is therefore a symbol of a subtle energy which cannot be described in terms readily comprehended by the uninitiated. To most people in times past the sword represented a weapon of either destruction or victory, so in the hands of the right person it constituted a force or energy that could easily be perceived or understood. Excalibur is the power of Merlin manifest in matter, while Merlin himself is the magical force or occult ray which colours the Celtic ethos.

The Merlin archetype embodies the eternal magical principle of the taming and channelling of imperceptible energies for use at more easily perceptible levels. The nature and quality of these frequencies can constitute a danger and may therefore need to be withdrawn from time to time. Sometimes, however, this withdrawal is effected against the will of the magician through the Law of Equalities. The Merlin tale has many strange and inconclusive endings as we have already seen. Was the wizard really overpowered by his Fairy adversary and buried involuntarily beneath a stone? In other words, have the energies he represents been withdrawn from our benefit by some alien force and time-encapsulated until there are those among us who will eventually achieve Merlin status and be able to roll back that stone and release them? Or is the story of Merlin's long rest in some shaded and beautiful island the truer version, indicating that when we are ready Merlin himself, or a representative of his archetype, will cause that island to surface once again in the consciousness of mankind? We may all take turns at guessing, but in the final analysis none of us really knows for sure!

Just as Excalibur was handed back to the Spirit of the Waters, so the knowledge of these old truths now lies buried within the deep sea of our collective unconscious. But the theory is that one day it will resurface, and when it does those who have always believed will find their Excalibur. Perhaps it will rise like the Kundalini serpent from their own subconscious, or become perceptible to the Transpersonal Self in the wisdom context. Or maybe it will appear, as before, in the stone (the practical world of everyday living) to be withdrawn only by he or she who through merit of initiation has earned the right of spiritual kingship.

Endnotes
1. Mead, G.R.S. *Fragments of a Faith Forgotten*, p. 325.

25. EARTH RITES, FOLK MUSIC AND THE GREEN RAY

Celtic magic had, and still has, many faces, being by no means limited to the Druidic or Bardic mode of expression. In fact, it was, like the Egyptian system, open for all to approach at the level appropriate to each individual. Earth Rites and Folk Magic, therefore, constitute a major part of its expression, as these were more easily negotiated by the ordinary, unlettered person who lived and worked near to the land and the elements.

People who are not inhibited by the over-accentuation of left brain hemisphere programming are more easily able to effect contact with natural forces or energies, which is certainly to their advantage especially where mental health is concerned. Much of city neurosis and violence is caused by the lack of ability to exchange energies with nature, either psychically or physically, which is a great pity. But then, we are slowly approaching the top of the circle once again, and when the Ouroboric point is reached a new cycle is destined to begin, with all that that implies both spiritually and somatically.

But before we involve ourselves too deeply in eschatological waters, let us take a look at the old Celtic ways of contacting the forces of nature, and how these can be applied in this day and age.

First and foremost, it is essential to acknowledge the existence of our planet as an entity in its, or *her*, own right!

Just as we each have a heart, skeletal system, nerves, major organs and blood flowing through our veins and arteries, so also does our planet. She has chakras just as we do: seven of them, although some say eight or even nine, which are located in various parts of our globe. These constitute major power centres, while her venal system is the network of ley lines, dragon lines, fairy lines, or whatever one cares to call them, along which the pulses of her energies flow. Now regarding these chakric points, I am frequently asked when lecturing on this subject whether well known places, such as Glastonbury, Stonehenge, the Great Pyramid, etc. are Earth chakras. I feel not, and with good reason.

When the High Priests of the Old Country realized the planet was doomed to experience an axial alteration that would change its position in relation to the Sun and introduce the five intercalary days, they also knew that it would be many generations hence before somatic evolution would offer bodies advanced enough for the rebirth of the Wise Ones who could handle the powers of the Earth's chakras. So they time-encapsulated these chakric points, sealed them magically and placed guardians at each entrance so that none but the initiated, or representatives of the Old Ones, might recognize or enter them. The story of the burial of Merlin beneath the stone, therefore, relates to the knowledge of that particular chakra that is posited in these isles and programmed to be revealed during the Aquarian Age. The energy that will be released when the time is right is represented esoterically by the concept of Arthur and his knights, armed and at the ready, waiting for the sacred Horn to be sounded.

What can we learn from this and other similar world myths? That the energies of the Earth's chakras are related to the forces of time, gravity and sonics. Master these energies at the practical level and mankind will finally unite the physical with the metaphysical, the esoteric with the exoteric, the conscious with the collective unconscious!

As much as I am in sympathy with those who feel strongly about places such as Glastonbury, my occult experience precludes me from accepting that the really powerful subtle energies are so readily accessible. Unless we are to be counted among the harbingers of the cosmic future, if we step too near the edge to peer into the next level, like the foolish man, we stand to topple.

So, what energies are there to be drawn at the mundane or Earth level? There are many! The elemental forces can provide information regarding weather conditions, the sowing of crops, the right time to commence any undertaking, the nature of disease — all things that affect people today as much as they did when the Celts first arrived in these isles. And the fruits of Mother Earth can feed us, heal us, clothe us, provide us with housing and warmth, and all this on the purely practical side. Esoterically there is even more bounty, so do not dismiss the accepted power spots simply because they are not chakric points, but at the same time seek elsewhere for your own individual sacred grove, which will more likely be unsullied by the litter of tourism and the aura of self-gratification that surrounds so many people who are supposedly seeking spirituality.

When next you consider contacting Earth, ask youself what *you* can give to *her*, not what you can take from her. After all, those people who regularly visit so-termed places of power to 'recharge' themselves or 'imbibe the vibes', seldom think of what they can give in return and, as a consequence, the energies they have stolen circulate in their auras in ever-decreasing spirals causing them to develop appetites for anything that looks as if it might assuage their needs. If they but realized the necessity to comply with a fundamental occult law which decrees that an energy must always be exchanged, and give something back to Earth, this would take care of their complexes and afford them an outlet for their pent-up and insatiable emotions.

How then, does one 'give' to the planet? First of all, by acknowledging its being as a unique and total entity. How can you render a gift to anything if you are unaware of its existence? Come to know Earth, have reality of her presence, breathe with her, weep for her, feel her pain and her joy. If you are young and energetic, put in some time with the Green Party. Tidy up old rubbish dumps, clean out polluted streams, plant a tree and watch carefully over the saplings that others have planted so that they are not destroyed by hooligans. 'But these are all obvious, practical things,' some of you will say. Well, we live in a practical world, do we not? By all means meditate and give your love and your tears to your Earth Mother. Were your own mother sick, hungry and uncared for, would you not minister to her needs rather than sit by her bed meditating on her ailments and bemoaning your lot?

In ancient times there was a respect for the soft, quiet, secret places of the Earth. Hidden dells in which the fairy people could happily manifest were not unknown. Each stream had its resident entity who welcomed the humble gifts of flowers and grain that were oft-times scattered lovingly on its waters. The saucers of milk left out for the 'wee folk' probably were drunk by a hedgehog seeking food in the chill of the night, but surely that is as it should be, as all nature shares. Was it not Ramakrishna who said, 'The Divine Mother revealed to me in the Kali Temple that it was she who had become everything — that is why I fed the cat with the food that was offered to the Divine Mother.' What we give to her she shares with all, unlike mankind that seeks but its own physical gratification.

To became 'Celtically Aware' one needs to enter the emotional world of romantic surrealism wherein dwell the dragons, fairies and unicorns. The Celts of old were strong, brave and fearless in battle. Not even Caesar considered them cowards. And yet, in their quieter, softer moments they were aware of the sweet voices of nature and of the subtle dimensions wherein dwell the Lordly Ones. Their music was of the healing harp and their songs of the lyrical stars and those regions of the mind that harboured their enemies — their own lower natures — which needed to be mastered before they could comprehend the mysteries of the Old Ones and behold the Light of Ceugant!

Welcome the seasons with gratitude and rejoicing. Watch the movements of the hobby horse when he appears with your local morris men and know that the spirit of Epona or Rhiannon is being remembered in those prancing gestures. Hang a corn dolly somewhere in your home. Believe, as the Celts of old believed, for the fertility implied by these ancient symbols is not limited to the growth of the harvest, or the number of lambs born, or the milk yield; it can be applied to anything in today's age, from the plants in your greenhouse to the money in your bank account. The fertility emphasis so often placed on the Green Ray simply implies the multiplication principle, and it should therefore be borne in mind that the Ray itself also manifests at the higher frequencies and is not limited purely to the expression of human emotion. The doors upon which you may knock for help have not changed over the centuries, they are still there, albeit hidden by the overgrowth of neglect, but you may still draw nigh to them and on the other side may lie that which you seek.

All the Green Man and May Queen symbology is embraced in the understanding of Earth Rites. The aspirant may approach these in the traditional mode by using old songs and poems, or in the manner I have just suggested, which constitutes the modern portal to the Green ray. No, this side of Celtic magic is not limited to those of the Druidic caste, or occultists of dedication and exact discipline. It is an aspect of Celtica that belongs to you, the people. So use it, and use it wisely!

26. INITIATION

The remote antiquity of Keridwen and the Rites she represents is highlighted in the following lines by Taliesin:

> I implore my sovereign,
> To consider the inspiring muse (a title of the
>   goddess)
> What did *necessity* produce,
> More early than Ceridwen!
> The primary order in the world
> Was that of her priests.[1]

There is a mistaken concept that Initiation is synonymous with the examination procedure wherein one presents oneself at a certain place, answers a lot of questions, recites a few facts by heart and is then left in a darkened pyramid or barrow for three days and three nights after which, if one emerges sane, one has become an Adept!

As far as the occult is concerned, Initiation is a never-ending process; one never does reach that exalted stage where one has all the answers. The reverse, in fact, for with knowledge and awareness also comes the realization that one knows very little or even nothing compared with what there is to learn and know. Nor is knowledge synonymous with wisdom. We have all met those people with computer-like brains who can absorb any fact put in front of them. But given a human situation, or something that was not covered in the textbooks from which they have studied, and they are floored! The reason for this is that they lack either wisdom or creative imagination which, together with resilience, constitute important factors in the psychological make up of any true occultist. Essential prerequisites for the aspirant include the ability to pick onself up after those inevitable falls, to adjust one's much cherished views in the light of new evidence, and to adhere firmly to that which one knows in conscience to be right, although the fashion, customs or accepted behavioural modes of the current 'collective' point in the opposite direction.

Initiatory Rites vary with each age and ethos. In old Celtic magic, they came under the jurisdiction of the goddess Keridwen and her retinue. These included the characters of Hu Gadarn or Gwydion, Avagddu, and the Bard Taliesin himself. The only trace of role playing to be found in ancient Celtic magic appears in these Initiatory Rites, when the officiating priest or priestess assumes the part or character relevant to the Initiation. According to Davies, Hu Gadarn represents the old truths as they were brought to these isles from somewhere across the water; Keridwen is the goddess who dispenses them, while the Taliesin role is that of the Recorder. The fourteenth century Bard Iolo Goch writes of Hu:

Hu the Mighty, the sovereign, the ready protector, a king, the giver of wine and renown, the *emperor of the land and the seas*, and the *life of all that are in the world was he. After the deluge, he held the strong beamed plough*, active and excellent; this did our Lord of stimulating genius, that he might shew to the proud man, and to humbly wise, the art which was most approved by the faithful father; nor is this sentiment false.[2]

From the aforesaid, plus the introductory verses at the commencement of this chapter, we would not be out of line in ascribing considerable antiquity to these Rites.

In order to understand the role played by the Goddess in this context we must re-examine the legend of Taliesin's birth. During the time when Keridwen pursued Gwion Bach, many form changes took place, each represented by a sacred animal or bird. While these could be interpreted as symbolizing certain stages in the development of the soul there is another aspect as we shall see. Some authorities, notably Davies, are of the opinion that there was an actual Cauldron in which certain concoctions were brewed and later imbibed by the Initiate. In fact, the story has so much in common with certain elements in the Eleusinia, right down to the Nine Maidens whose breath supplied the heat for the Cauldron (in the Eleusinia it was the Nine Muses), that Davies and other scholars of this day were forced to conclude that one rite originated from the other, or was simply the Welsh version of the Greek original, Keridwen being one and the same as Demeter or Ceres. While this cannot be discounted, as there is doubtless more than a grain of truth in the idea, one must accept that the national imprint on these ancient rites renders them a uniquely Celtic flavour, and it is therefore in this context that we must consider them.

According to Davies' account of the Keridwen story, the Goddess rode in a chariot drawn by dragons, which suggests that one of the tasks to be mastered by the Initiate was the harnessing of Earth energies. The old Celtic priesthood was well aware of the general deficiency of Earth Elemental qualities in their national character, which lack they compensated through their dedication to the Green Ray in its earthing aspect. In this version the Goddess is given a daughter, Creiwy, in addition to the ugly Avagddu, the latter being purely a description of the spiritual state of the aspirant prior to the Initiatory ceremony, the ugliness simply indicating the dark face of ignorance. After the Rites have been successfully negotiated, however, he emerges as Taliesin the Bard, who is called 'Radiant Front'.

Hu is one and the same as the old British god Bilé, or the Welsh Gwydion, who is referred to by the Bard Aneurin as 'Lion of the Greatest Course', the Bull/Lion/Serpent appellations being frequently conferred upon Initiates in ancient magical cults. Keridwen's daughter, Creiwy, is identified with Arianrod of the Silver Wheel and with Iris, Goddess of the Rainbow, although the Rainbow is also referred to in the old triads as one of the attributes of Gwydion, the British Hermes, who is spoken of as being synonymous with Hu Gadarn. In fact, there are many names for the one principle as we have already established. Keridwen cast her Coracle containing the infant Taliesin into the sea on 29 April, which probably meant that it was conveniently discovered by Elphin in time for the Beltaine celebrations. In other words, old feast days were utilizied in Initiation Rites.

The following poem, entitled 'Chair of Taliesin', furnishes a long list of apparatus requisite for the celebration of the Feast of Keridwen, including several of the ingredients of the mystical Cauldron. These celebrations probably coincided with the completion of the Rite and the welcoming of the Initiated to Adepthood:

Kadeir Taliesin

I am he who animates the fire, to the honour of the god *Dovydd*, in behalf of the assembly of associates, qualified to treat of mysteries — a Bard, with the knowledge of a *Sywedydd*, when he deliberately recites the inspired song of the Western *Cudd*, on a serene night amongst the stones.

As to loquacious, glittering bards, their encomium (sic) attracts me not, when moving in the course: admiration is their great object.

And I am a silent proficient, who address the Bards of the land: it is mine to animate the hero; to persuade the unadvised; to awaken the silent beholder — the bold illuminator of kings!

I an no shallow artist, greeting the Bards of a household, like a subtle parasite — THE OCEAN HAS A DUE PROFUNDITY!

The man of complete discipline has obtained the meed of honour, in every nightly celebration, when *Dien* is propitiated with an offering of wheat, and the suavity of bees, and incense and myrrh, and aloes, *from beyond the seas*, and the gold pipes of *Lleu*, and cheerful, precious, silver, and the ruddy gem, and the berries, and the foam of the ocean, and cresses of a purifying quality, laved in the fountain, and a joint contribution of wort, the founder of liquor, supplied by the assembly, and a raised load secluded from the moon, of placid, cheerful Vervain.

With priests of intelligence, to officiate in behalf of the *moon*, and the concourse of associated men, under the open breeze of the sky, with the *maceration* and *sprinkling*, and the portion after the sprinkling, and the *boat of glass* in the hand of the stranger, and the stout youth with pitch, and the honoured Segyrffyg, and medical plants, from an exorcised spot.

And Bards with *flowers*, and perfect convolutions, and primroses, and leaves of the *Briw*, with the points of the trees of purposes, and solution of doubts, and frequent mutual pledges; and with wine which flows to the brim, from Rome to Rosedd, and deep standing water, a flood which has the *gift of Dovydd*, or the tree of *pure gold*, which becomes of a fructifying quality, when that *Brewer* gives it a boiling, who presided over the cauldron of the five plants.

Hence the stream of *Gwion*, and the *reign of serenity*, and *honey and trefoil*, and horns *flowing with mead* — Meet for a sovereign is the lore of the Druids.[3]

The main feature of the Taliesin/Keridwen story is undoubtedly the form changing, or 'shape-shifting' as it is sometimes called. This is a phenomenon commonly expressed in all Celtic writings, part of the Initiation into the Rites involving the ability to effect changes of form at will. Stewart comments: 'Celtic deities, for example, merge into one another with the ease of the shape-changing of Keridwen, while we childishly demand that they stand still to be counted!' So ephemeral are the old British deities, in fact, that it is difficult to fit them into a classical mould in the way that one can with the Greek, Roman or Babylonian immortals. But this, surely, is after the Celtic nature itself. Like water, it flows around objects and principles, always finding its own level but never being contained except in the Cauldron of Initiation. Stewart continues: 'Why should a goddess be the same today as she was yesterday, and who are we to demand that she stays the same tomorrow? The nature of a dream or magical power is constant, but its FORM changes. Madness lies in fixity of thought and not fluidity'.[4] How very true, and one up for the Celtic character!

And yet there is more to form changing than the names and shapes assumed at certain times by gods, goddesses, or old archetypal forces. There is that which must be learned and understood by the Initiate concerning other life forms which inhabit not only our own planet, but other parts of the universe. Metaphysically speaking, the universe is a cohesive whole which can be likened to a giant tree with many branches. Although we represent one small, albeit fundamental twig on that tree, we are of no more importance than any other extension, leaf or branch. But issuing from the same roots makes us part of the cosmic family the tree represents, and it therefore behoves us to acquire an awareness of our cosmic relations in adjoining branches. This the Initiate achieves through the process of form changing.

In order to relate to other evolutionary streams, and in so doing understand them, we need as part of our magical training to become as they are. In other words, we mentally assume the roles of the dog, cat, boar, flower, hen, grain of corn, etc. and in thus learning, adjust our consciousness to sensations alien to the normal modes of living as expressed in the experiences of everyday life. This teaches us speedy and effective mobilization of the mind, so that it will react instantaneously to any given stimuli and so lessen the impact of unforeseen and unanticipated stresses and traumas. All these things need to be accomplished within a disciplined framework, however, or the psyche will fragment and mental illness will result. Hence the old Rites in which the Initiate was faced with a series of sudden and unexpected situations, the speed of his or her reaction and ability to cope being one of the deciding factors as to the outcome of the test.

I am wondering how many of my readers will have experienced this form changing. It is something I have been familiar with for years, in fact since childhood, so I must have learned it in another time zone (I don't like the term 'former life' as I do not subscribe to the linear time concept.) I recall an instance during a dream when I became aware that around a corner, just ahead of me, a malevolent enemy in the guise of someone I knew at the time lay in ambush. Recalling the old axiom that offence is the best method of defence, I promptly changed myself into a full grown male tiger and stalked through the undergrowth, gradually closing in on my would-be opponent in ever-decreasing circles. She came into my view before she had chance to see me and I sprang... out of the darkness ... This time it was not me who was frightened as is sometimes the case when the Law of Equalities balances the other way, but my enemy, who doubtless awoke in a sweat after dreaming that a huge tiger had leapt out of the undergrowth and given her a scare!

I have, in fact, effected many form changes during my long occult career and have taught my pupils to do likewise. It is always advisable to form-change when retreating or when under attack, and the wider the comprehension of the universe the more forms there are available into which one can change. As a wise instructor said to me recently, 'If you can imagine it, then it is'. One should always choose the form appropriate to the circumstances. For example, if you dream of a difficult situation in, say, an aeroplane, where someone is trying to throw you out against your will, change into a bird, or better yet, a sylph and you won't fall! This principle is well illustrated in the Keridwen/Gwion tale.

When working the Celtic ray the best way of recording what happens to you, the aspirant, during your journey along the path is to write it as a poem in the Celtic style, adding to the narrative in the symbolic language of the Bards as you proceed. My own initiatory poem was started years ago, so it is far too lengthy to include in this work. Also, it is written mostly in Greek allegory which would not be of much help to anyone who wishes to stay exclusively on the Celtic path. However, I will include a few sample verses to give the student an idea as to how this is done:

Ahead shines straight the face of the archetype,
The soul moves forth to grasp the mirage
Which it does not recognise ...
Movement generates momentum.

The dark harshness of the spiritual autumn descends.
Its surface is beautiful, hued in golden rust
But beneath lie the rotting fragments
Of the sloughed skin, as yet unclaimed by vultures.

The first door gives entry to the chamber beyond.
Hope blinds the eye of the beholder
So that the dark corners are unobserved
And the lurking destroyers lie at vantage.

Too late the soul's retreat to the closing portal
After the final lamp is extinguished.
Only the grappling darkness yields up its denizens
Solid to the touch, yet lifeless where light rules.

Nor do the harsh winds of spiritual winter
Lessen their physical sting to pleas of friendship.
Nothing is inviolate, neither man, love nor reason,
Only the distant whisper from the voice of Time.

The fumbling hand feels through the icy air
Seeking for the next door ... The latch is heavy,
Heavy with the weight of tears. Beneath its burden
The body drops and is prostrate.

Kind hands remove the pain with forgetfulness.

The recuperative touch is lit by the lantern of the past.
The swelling seas conceal its message and yield forth
The sandals, so that the feet shall bleed no more.

Ahead lies a road, thickly populated by sounds
Confusing and promising. But the path slopes
Downwards. The wilderness is empty yet full, and ahead
Stand the Gates of No Return.

I will stop at that point as I think it is sufficient for the
aspirant to grasp the general idea.

In another long and descriptive poem Keridwen herself (or
her priestess) speaks of her adventures during the episode
leading up to and following the birth of Taliesin. In the
following stanzas she draws particular attention to the
privileges to which her position entitles her:

> When the merit of the presidencies shall be adjudged, mine will
> be found the superior amongst them — my *chair*, my *cauldron*,
> and my *laws* and my pervading *eloquence*, meet for the
> presidency. I am accounted skilful in the Court of Dŏn, and with
> me Euronwy and Euron.[5]

It was the word 'laws' which caught my eye, reminding me
that the Nine Occult Laws were spoken by the Nine Muses or
Nine Priestesses who warmed and guarded the sacred
Cauldron. Since I have found it necessary to make frequent
reference to these codes I will insert them in full.

THE NINE METAPHYSICAL OR OCCULT LAWS

The Law of Rebound

Which designates that a superior force will always rebound a
lesser power. In other words, should you, the aspirant, come
up against another practitioner, or a disembodied energy, that
is more adept or stronger than you, whatever you project in
his, her or its direction will return to you PLUS the force of
the Rebounder.

The Law of Three Requests

All requests from the subtle dimensions are repeated in
triplicate. At the first utterance the conscious mind is alerted,
the repeat engages the reasoning faculties while the third

statement makes direct contact with the psyche or soul force. (As in the Biblical story of Peter's denial). This particular Law is very strictly observed in Celtic magic, representing an aspect of the mystique of the sacred '3'.

The Law of Challenge
All visions, dreams, sources of inspiration, suspicions, anything, in fact, that would appear to issue from beyond the bounds of rational, logical thinking, should be challenged. The lesson here is one of absolute honesty, as the aspirant should be aware of the subtle line that divides the present reality from interpenetrative alien frequencies, and inspiration from delusion.

The Law of Equalities
When two equal forces meet, one will eventually give way to the other who then rises in status as a result. This Law is re-echoed in the natural laws of science and may be clearly evidenced in particle physics.

The Law of Balance or Equipoise
According the the Law of Balance, everything should function according to its own frequency or at its correct level. For example, sitting for hours concentrating on drumming up sufficient psychokinetic energy to move a table six inches, when the same effect can be produced by giving it a slight push, is a fruitless task and a waste of power that could be better spent in more constructive avenues of expression. The Law of Balance is also concerned with the state of equipoise necessary for the satisfactory functioning and correct expression of energy at any level, which relates it particularly to the field of disease and healing. It denounces excesses of any kind, and demands, for example, that the physical body be treated with courtesy because it is host to many other life forms including the four Elements, without whose kind offices there would be no molecular structure and therefore no physical body in the first place.

The Law of Summons
This Law designates how things do or do not work for one, which will, of course, be according to one's degree of adeptship. If, upon issuing an occult summons, the student

finds that the response is not correct, then the right to so do has not yet been earned. This will frequently occur with aspirants whose workings tend to sterility, or who 'command' intelligences from the Elemental Kingdoms only to find that they are being led a merry dance by those they would supposedly control. Should this be the case, it is a 'back to the drawing board' situation.

The Law of Polarities
Positive and negative, anima and animus, masculine and feminine, the process of individuation both spiritual and rational — all these are expressions of this Law. The Initiate must be well polarized within him or herself before he or she can pass a certain point along the path. This Law, although eschewed by some people, is strictly adhered to by the Elemental Kingdoms who will not pay due deference to those who refuse to abide by it. The further up the planes — or to use a term which I prefer — the finer the frequencies, the more the polarity distinctions become blurred and therein lies the danger. The ideal stage, we are told, is the anima and animus in perfect balance within the individual, neither obtruding or breaking cosmic law.

The Law of Cause and Effect
Commonly referred to as The Law of Karma. But Karma is strictly an eastern term, although it is loosely used by many people to express the 'as ye sow so shall ye reap' principle. A generally unheeded aspect of this Law involves the exchange of energies, meaning that we should never expect anything for nothing, although the exchange need not always be in 'kind'. For example, a poor person receiving a gift of money need not repay in cash, but could render a service to the giver which is appropriate to their means and talents. Likewise the rich person who inherits money that he or she has not laboured to obtain. A simple healing prayer said in deep sincerity is often, by cosmic law, equal in energy output to the rich man's gift of a thousand pounds!

The Law of Abundance (sometimes referred to as The Law of Opulence)
This Law expresses the attraction of like for like, e.g. money makes money, a fear is an unrequited wish, etc. My old nanny

used to have an appropriate saying, 'Show me your friends and I'll tell you what you are'. As it is associated with non-conservation, in the olden days it was referred to as 'The Miser's Dread'. The occultist who is down to his or her last pound is advised to go out and spend it, for an energy spent attracts a similar energy. I have frequently given away something I valued to a friend whose need I have deemed to be greater than mine, only to find an article of similar type or value is presented to me shortly afterwards, usually within a 'three'! I'm sure that many of my readers will have experienced likewise.

Those are the Nine Laws with which the student will need to thoroughly acquaint him or herself before proceding along the path. Any problems that are likely to be encountered, and one wouldn't be here in the first place if there were not, will be traceable to the breaking of one or other of these, so it will be up to the pupil to stop, think carefully, and make the necessary peace with whoever or whatever has suffered as a result of their mistake.

Please note that membership in, or affiliation with, a major religion in no way exempts one from the consequences of breaking these laws. Adherents to established credos are just as likely to suffer from physical or mental disorders resulting from a disregard for these statutes as are students of the occult; fanaticism, for example, under any guise contravenes cosmic law.

To conclude this chapter I have selected some passages from a very famous piece of Celtic writing, the *Cad Goddeu*, or 'Battle of the Trees', attributed to Taliesin or Gwion. The complete work, which I do not have the space to feature here, is something of an enigma. It may be viewed as a comment on the mythic path along which the Initiate must pass in pursuit of wisdom — note the allusion to the nature of time — or the experiences of one's other soul fragments which, together with the form changing technique, must be understood and negotiated. Another school of thought, however, sees it as a record of the past history of the world and the old gods in their various manifestations since the beginning of time, written in the secret Tree code. As it would certainly appear to contain both these elements, it must surely consititute a powerful indicator as to the sheer antiquity of the hidden Celtic tradition. The translation I have chosen is by Edward

Davies, but the fuller version by Graves is featured in his book *The White Goddess*.

I will therefore leave you, the aspirant, to find your own answer to the riddle.

CAD GODDEU

1.

Existing of yore, in the great seas, from the time when the shout was heard, we were put forth, decomposed and simplified, by the tops of the birch. The tops of the oak connected us together, by the incantation of Mael Derw; whilst smiling at the side of the rock Nêr remained in calm tranquillity.

2.

When my formation was accomplished, not of mother and father was I produced; but of nine elementary forms — of the fruit of fruits; of the fruit of the primordial god; of primroses; the blossom of the mount; of the flowers of trees and shrubs; of earth in its terrene state was I modelled; of the flower of nettles, and the water of the ninth wave.

3.

I was exorcised by Mãth, before I became immortal. I was exorcised by Gwydion, the great purifier of the Brython, of Eurwys, of Euron and Medron, of the multitude of scientific teachers, children of Mãth.

When the removal took place, I was exorcised by the sovereign, when he was half consumed. By the sage of sages was I exorcised in the primitive world, at which time I had a being: when the host of the world was in dignity, frequent was the benefit of the Bard. I am he who influences the song of praise, which the tongue recites.

4.

I sported in the gloom; I slept in purple; I truly was in the ship with Dylan, son of the sea, embraced in the centre, between the royal knees, when, like the rushing of hostile spears, the floods came forth, from heaven to the great deep. On the perforated surface, fourscore hundred assemble, attendant on their will. They are neither older nor younger than myself in their divisions.

5.

'Tis the animated singer who chaunts. The complete number of nine hundred pertained to me, with my blood-stained sword. To me was dignity alloted by Dovydd; and where he was there was protection.

If I come to the green plain of the boar, he will compose, he will decompose, he will form languages. The strong-handed darter of light is he styled: with a gleam he sets in order his numbers, who will cause the flame to spread when I ascend on high.

6.

I have been a spotted adder on the mount — I have been a viper in the lake — I have been stars among the supreme chiefs; I have been the weigher of the falling drops, drest in my priest's cloke, and furnished with my bowl.

Not unskilfully do I presage, at fourscore smoking altars, the fate which will befal every man. To my knife, a multitude of thighs have submitted.

Six steeds there are of yellow hue: than these, a hundred times better is *Melyngan*, my steed, swift as the sea-mew, which will not pass by me, between the sea and the shore.

With the circle of ruddy gems on my golden shield, do I not preside over the area of blood, which is guarded by a hundred chiefs? The man has not been born, who can compare with me in the gap, excepting it be Goronwy, from the dales of Edrywy.

7.

Long and white are my fingers. It is long since I have been a herdsman. I wandered in the earth, before I became a proficient in learning. I wandered, I went the circuit, I slept in a hundred islands; through a hundred Caers I toiled.

With my precious golden device upon my piece of gold, Lo, I am that splendid one, who sportively come from the invading host of the Feryll.[6]

Endnotes

1. Davies, Edward. *The Mythology and Rites of the British Druids*, p. 188.
2. Ibid. Davies, pp. 108, 109.
3. Ibid. Davies, pp. 271–279.
4. Steward, Bob. *Where is Saint George?*, pp. 44–5.
5. Op. cit. Davies, p. 265.
6. Op. cit. Davies, pp. 538–46.

27. DRUIDIC LORE

I have no intention of constructing a Druidic ceremony.
There are Orders of Bards and Ovates operating in parts of
this country already who make a fairly good job of this. What
I would like to do, however, is to supply a few magical
connections for those whose interest in Druidism is more
concerned with matters occult than religious. I also intend to
leave the Bards of old to do a lot of the talking, so let us
commence in the words of the immortal Taliesin in his poem
Buarth Beirdd, 'The Ox-Pen of the Bards'.

1.

Gliding with rapidity were my thoughts,
Over the vain poetic art of the Bards of Britain,
Who labouring to make an excessive shew at the solemn
   meeting,
With sufficient care hammer out a song.
I require a *staff*, at unity with the Bardic lore.
As for him who knows not the *ox-pen* of the Bards,
May fifteen thousand overpower and afflict him at once!

I am a skilful composer: I am a clear singer:
I am a tower: I am a Druid:
I am an architect: I am a prophet:
I am a serpent: I am love:
In the social banquet will I indulge.

A Bard am I, not doting upon superfluous trifles.
When a master sings his song will be close to the subject.
He will not be searching for those remote wonders.
Shall I then admit *these*, like men suing for garments,
Without a hand to receive them —
Like men toiling in the lake, without a ship!

2.

Boldly swells the stream to its high limit.
Let the thigh be pierced in blood.
Let the rock beyond the billow be set in order at the dawn,
Displaying the countenance of Him
Who receives the exile into his sanctuary.
The rock of the Supreme proprietor,
The chief place of tranquillity.

Then let the giver of the mead feast cause to be proclaimed.
'I am the cell; I am the opening chasm; I am the bull *Becr Llêd*;
I am the repository of the mystery; I am the place of
    reanimation.
I love the tops of trees, with the points well connected,
And the Bard who composes without meriting a repulse;
But him I love not, who delights in contention.
He who traduces the adept shall not enjoy the mead.
It is time to hasten to the banquet
Where the skilful ones are employed in their mysteries,
With the hundred *knots* — the custom of our countrymen.'

The shepherds of the plains, the supporters of gates,
Are like persons marching to battle without their clan.
I am the Bard of the hall; I am the stock that supports the chair:
I shall succeed in impeding the progress of the loquacious
    Bards.[1]

Particularly haunting is the song of Amergin, son of Miled
who, legend tells us, sang this strange lay when his foot first
touched Irish soil.

I am the Wind that blows over the sea,
I am the Wave of the Ocean;
I am the Murmur of the billows;
I am the Ox of the Seven Combats;
I am the Vulture upon the rock;
I am a Ray of the Sun;
I am the fairest of Plants;

I am the Wild Boar in valour;
I am a Salmon in the Water;
I am a Lake in the plain;
I am the Craft of the artificer;
I am a Word of Science;
I am the Spear-point that gives battle;
I am the god that creates in the head of man the fire of thought.
Who is it that enlightens the assembly upon the mountain, if not I?
Who telleth the ages of the moon, if not I?
Who showeth the place where the sun goes to rest, if not I?[2]

What a wonderful illustration of the true Adept's grasp and understanding of the breadth of the cosmos!

There are several references to augury in many Bardic poems, which leads us into our next subject. The aspirant to Celtic Adepthood will naturally wish to employ, for divination and other magical uses, the system appropriate to the Celtic ray: this being the secret *coelbrens*. The reader will recall the description of these given in Chapter 16, which indicates that they were originally pieces of wood described as 'finger length', but we have no idea as to what the basic length of the adult finger was in those days, which of the five digits was involved, or whether this alluded to the male or female finger. Working according to the numbers designated as sacred by the Celts, however, it would be safe to assume that *coelbrens* could be either three or five inches in length and not break any sacred laws. The notches referred to would appear to be Ogham, which would account for the reference to the arrangement of *coelbrens* in a certain order forming words and phrases.

These should not be difficult to make and could be easily carved. It would be prudent, however, to choose the wood carefully in accordance with the Beth-Luis-Nion, oak probably being the best as this tree was especially beloved by the Druids of old. Should the aspirant wish to work privately, then the Ogham notches would be best inscribed on the *coelbrens*, but for general use, and divination in particular, the Tree Alphabet is more suitable. From the descriptions rendered of the symbolism of each letter, it should be easy to put together a fairly simple divinatory system, the accurate use of which would naturally depend upon the perception of the user.

Coelbrens should be fairly substantial and not simply twigs or slivers of wood while, on the other hand, they would be easier to handle if they are not too bulky. The sacred Druidic letters can also be written on stones, rather like runes, in which case they are called *coelvains*. The choice is up to each individual, but it is well to remember that with the Tree Alphabet in particular, the accent is on the nature and energies of the trees, which would render wood the most appropriate material for their composition.

The Druids of old also employed a complex system of hand or finger signals which gave birth to several terms in common use in our language today: 'forefinger', 'fool's finger', 'leech' or psychic finger, 'auricular' or ear finger. This system survives in modern palmistry where the index finger is referred to as the 'Finger of Jupiter', representing ambition, independence and the ego; the middle finger is Saturn's standing for the philosophy, precision and the serious or rigid aspects of one's nature; the third or ring finger belongs to Apollo and denotes the arts, theatricality and self-expression; and the fourth, or little finger, is Mercury's denoting the intellect, diplomacy and eloquence. The thumb stands for will-power and logic.

With this hand symbology goes a multitude of customs, many of which have found their way through to this present day: the placing of the wedding ring on the third finger, for example. The wearing of magical rings on different fingers is also highly meaningful. By examining the ancient Druidic finger allocations it is easy to see why the Heirophantic ring was always worn on the first finger during overt ceremonial occasions, and on the centre finger when working privately.

I am inserting the diagram of the hand with the appropriate alphabetical letters printed on each finger. This whole study, and the gestures in particular, involves a sound knowledge of both palmistry and Druidic lore and constitutes a section unto itself. Those interested are referred to Robert Graves' commentary on pp. 195–199 of *The White Goddess*, and any good book on palmistry from Cheiro to Beryl Hutchinson.

For the remainder of this chapter I am relying upon the messages conveyed at 'inner plane' level by the following two Bardic poems. The first of these, entitled *Marwnad Uthyr Pendragon* ('The Elegy of Uther Pendragon'), includes the many names assigned to the character of Beli/Gwydion/Hu,

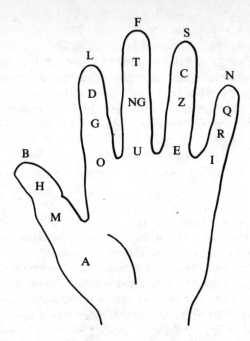

thus vouching for the antiquity of the beliefs and ceremonies
of the pre-Christian Druids.

1.

Behold me, who am powerful in the tumultuous din; who would
not pause between two hosts, without blood. Am I not called
Gorlassar, the *aetherial*? My belt has been a rainbow,
enveloping my foe. Am not I a protecting prince in darkness, to
him who presents my form at both ends of the *hive*? Am not I a
plower, like *Kawyl*? Between two hosts I would not pause,
without blood. Have not I protected my sanctuary, and, with the
aid of my friends, caused the wrathful ones to vanish? Have not
I shed the blood of the indignant, in bold warfare against the
sons of the giant *Nûr*? Have not I imparted, of my guardian
power, a ninth portion, in the prowess of Arthur? Have not I
destroyed a hundred forts? Have not I slain a hundred
governors? Have not I given a hundred veils? Have not I
slaughtered a hundred chieftains?

Did not I give to Henpen, the tremendous sword of the
enchanter? Did not I perform the rites of purification, when
Haearndor moved with toil to the top of the hill?

I was subjected to the yoke for my affliction; but

commensurate was my confidence: the world had not existence, were it not for my progeny.

I am the Bard — as for the unskilful encomiast, may his lot be amongst ravens, and eagles, and birds of wrath! May utter darkness overwhelm him, when he supports the square band of men, between two fields!

It was my will to ascend into heaven from the eagle, to avoid the homage of the unskilful. I am a Bard: I am a master of the harp, the pipe, and the *crooth*. Of seven score musicians, I am the mighty enchanter.

2.

Privileged on the covered mount, O *Hu* with the expanded wings, has been thy son, thy Bardic proclaimer, thy deputy, O father Dëon: my voice has recited the death song, where the mound, representing the world, is constructed of stone work. Let the countenance of Prydain, let the glancing HU attend to me! O sovereign of heaven, let not my message be rejected!

With solemn festivity round the two lakes; with the lake next my side; with my side moving round the sanctuary; whilst the sanctuary is earnestly invoking the gliding king, before whom the fair one retreats, upon the veil that covers the huge stones; whilst the dragon moves round, over the places which contain vessels of drink offering; whilst the drink offering is in the golden horns; whilst the golden horns are in the hand; whilst the hand is upon the knife; whilst the knife is upon the chief victim; sincerely I implore thee, O victorious Beli, son of the sovereign Man-Hogan, that thou wouldst preserve the honours of the HONEY island of Beli![3]

And for the final Bardic poem, I should never be forgiven by followers of the Celtic tradition if I failed to include *Preiddeu Annwn*, the 'Spoils of the Deep'. I have chosen this particular translation in preference to the more popular versions as I feel instinctively that it presents a more occultly accurate picture.

1.

I will adore the sovereign, the supreme ruler of the land. If he extended his dominion over the shores of the world, yet in good order was the prison of *Gwair*, in the inclosure of *Sidi*. Through the mission of *Pwyll* and *Pryderi*, no one before him entered into it.

The heavy blue chain didst thou, O just man, endure: and for the spoils of the deep, woeful is thy song; and till the doom shall it remain in the Bardic prayer — *Thrice the number that would have filled Prydwen, we entered into the deep; excepting seven, none have returned from Caer Sidi.*

2.

Am I not contending for the praise of that lore, if it were regarded, which was four times reviewed in the quadrangular inclosure! As the first sentence was it uttered from the cauldron, which began to be warmed by the breath of the nine damsels. Is not this the cauldron of the ruler of the deep! What is its quality? With the ridge of pearls round its border, it will not boil the food of a coward, who is not bound by his sacred oath. Against him will be lifted the bright gleaming sword: and in the hand of the sword-bearer shall he be left: and before the entrance of the gate of hell, shall the horns of light be burning — *And when we went with Arthur in his splendid labours, excepting seven, none returned from Caer Vediwid.*

3

Am I not contending for the honour of a lore that deserves attention!

In the quadrangular inclosure, in the island with the strong door, the twilight and the pitchy darkness were mixed together, whilst bright wine was the beverage, placed before the narrow circle —

Thrice the number that would have filled Prydwen, we embarked upon the sea; excepting seven, none returned from Caer Rigor.

4.

I will not redeem the multitudes with the ensign of the governor. Beyond the inclosure of *glass*, they beheld not the prowess of Arthur.

Thrice twenty hundred men stood on its wall; it was difficult to converse with its centinel.

Thrice the number that would have filled Prydwen went forth with Arthur; excepting seven, none returned from Caer Golur.

5.

I will not redeem the multitudes with trailing shields. They knew not on what day the stroke would be given, nor what hour in the serene day, Cwy (the agitated person) would be born, or who prevented his going into the dales of Devwy (the possession of the water). They know not the brindled ox with the thick head-band, having seven score knobs in his collar. — *And when we went with Arthur, of mournful memory; excepting seven, none returned from Caer Vandwy.*

6.

I will not redeem the multitudes with unguarded mouths. They know not on what day the chief was appointed: on what hour in the serene day, the proprietor was born; or what animal it is, which the silver-headed ones protect —
When we went with Arthur into the mournful conflict; excepting seven, none returned from Caer Ochren.

7.

Monks congregate, like dogs in their kennel, wrangling with their instructors. —
Is there but one course to the wind — but one to the water of the sea! Is there but one spark in the fire of boundless energy.

8.

Monks congregate like wolves, wrangling with their instructors. They know not when the darkness and the dawn divide; nor what is the course of the wind, or the cause of its agitation; in what place it dies away, or on what region it expands.
The grave of the saint is vanishing from the foot of the altar: I will adore the SOVEREIGN, the GREAT SUPREME![4]

Many attempts have been made to interpret this poem which appears to embrace three different considerations. The first refers to records of ancient knowledge brought over from the Old Country; the second to the early pre-Christian Druidic Initiation Rites; while the third embodies an epic account of the exploits of the Celtic warrior Arthur. Note how the Arthurian allusions inevitably fall at the end of each stanza as though added at a later date. To me this poem is typically representative of a very early oral tradition collecting a series of overlays prior to (and probably during) the time it finally became the written word.

Endnotes
1. Davies, Edward. *The Mythology and Rites of the British Druids*, pp. 535–8.
2. Rolleston, T.W. *Myths and Legends of the Celtic Race*, p. 134.
3. Op. cit. Davies, pp. 559–60.
4. Op. cit. Davies, pp. 515–26.

28. RITUAL PRAYERS AND INVOCATIONS

According to Celtic tradition, prayers or invocations to the deities can be offered in either a specially prepared setting such as a sanctuary or altar, or in open places such as old sites, groves of antiquity or by streams, sacred stones, holy trees etc. One can equally well recite them before retiring at night, on rising in the morning or whenever the necessity dictates. The effectiveness of any request or submission will, however, be governed by the sincerity with which the words are uttered and the amount of emotional or mental energy transmitted by the suppliant.

Prayers and invocations can be by way of a request for help or bounty, an exchange of energies, a search for knowledge, wisdom and understanding, a plea for healing or specialized guidance, or a purely devotional matter. As it has always been my policy to feature both traditional and modern texts I will commence with the former and lead in with a prayer to the Earth Goddess and the deity of healing found in Latin in a twelfth century English herbal *(Brit. Mus. MS. Harley, 1585, ff 12v–13r)*:

Earth, divine goddess, Mother Nature, who dost generate all things and bringest forth ever anew the sun which thou hast given to the nations; Guardian of sky and sea and of all Gods and powers; through thy influence all nature is hushed and sinks to sleep.... Again, when it pleases thee, thou sendest forth the

glad daylight and nurturest life with thine eternal surety; and
when the spirit of man passes, to thee it returns. Thou indeed art
rightly named Great Mother of the Gods; Victory is in thy divine
name. Thou art the source of the strength of peoples and gods;
without thee nothing can either be born or made perfect; thou
art mighty, Queen of the Gods. Goddess, I adore thee as divine,
I invoke thy name; vouchsafe to grant that which I ask of thee,
so shall I return thanks to thy godhead, with the faith that is thy
due....

Now also I make intercession to you, all ye powers and herbs,
and to your majesty: I beseech you, whom Earth the universal
parent hath borne and given as a medicine of health to all
peoples and hath put majesty upon, be now of the most benefit
to humankind. This I pray and beseech you: be present here with
your virtues, for she who created you hath herself undertaken
that I may call you with the good will of him on whom the art of
medicine was bestowed; therefore grant for health's sake good
medicine by grace of these powers aforesaid....[1]

All prayers need not be so lengthy, however. Here are two
examples of short but equally effective verses from Scotland.
The first is these comes from the west of that land, where
Carrot Sunday was celebrated on 28 September. The women
and girls would sing this fertility song while gathering certain
types of wild carrots:

Cleft fruitful, fruitful, fruitful,
Joy of Carrots surpassing upon me,
Michael the brave endowing me,
Bride the Fair be aiding me;
Progeny pre-eminent over every progeny,
Progeny on my womb, progeny on my progeny,
Progeny pre-eminent over every progeny.[2]

The seaweed rituals of the Scottish coast featured the
following verses to the sea god:

O God of the Sea,
Put weed in the drawing wave,
To enrich the ground,
To shower on us food.[3]

The words of these simple verses can easily be adjusted to
accommodate the suppliant's particular request. And lastly,

an old fertility prayer to the Earth Goddess from Saxon times:

> Erce, Erce, Erce, Earth Mother,
> may the Almighty Eternal Lord
> grant you fields to increase and flourish,
> fields fruitful and healthy,
> shining harvests of shafts of millet,
> broad harvests of barley. . .
> Hail to thee, Earth, Mother of Men;
> Bring forth now in God's embrace,
> filled with good for the use of man.[4]

The Christian overlays in these verses are obvious, so it will be up to those who would like to use them whether or not they accept the insertions.

Here now are four prayers of my own composition which can be used either ritually or on their own and I hope they will serve as examples to any would-be poets. The first is to Brigid or Brigantia, and comes in the form of a request for protection, pariularly during the hours of sleep:

> Noble Brigid, who dids't by Dana's Laws
> Stand by the 'steads of those who sought thine aid in days of
>   old.
> Subtly stretch thine arms, oh Goddess bright
> Across this humble place wherein I rest my head
> That I may seek my slumber, knowing all full well
> That they who wish me harm may not approach, being warded
>   by thy Shield.

Next we have an invocation to Midir in his capacity as a Fairy Sovereign, to aid contact with the Middle Kingdoms. I have used the Danaan reference here as Ireland would appear to be one of the final strongholds of the Lordly Ones.

> Why hidest thou, Oh Radiant One —
> Help! I cannot see thee, or thy breed. Why not?
> Are they afeared of all my kind? And yet
> I come in nought but love, and bearing gifts
> As would be deemed acceptable unto thy Lordly lot.
> Guide me in safety through the misty sentinels
> That lead into the portals of thy realms,

That I may so behold those bright and lovely
Planes, and so beholding, know!
If love but be the key here is my entrance
Guaranteed, enclosed in this small gift.

Great Midir, who is beautiful and wise,
Show me how, by nature's Law I may
Be part of thee and those whom thou dost rule.
And thus becoming, spread the good and welcome news
To others of my kind. The Universe is One.
The branch that knows not of its trunk must
Surely die. Remind us here, oh great One,
Of the sap that rises from that Tree.
That we may draw our sustinence therefrom.
And in that feast, have knowledge of the Whole.

Here is a plea to the goddess Rhiannon that justice be done
in whatever situation it may be needed:

Hail, Rhiannon, Consort of the Divine Charger
Who is also Lord of The Sea.
Straight is the path of thy steeds
That step the starlit paving stones
Of firmaments forgotten. Yes, but
Only in the blinkered sight of those
Whose eyes are blinded to thy kingdom.
Count not me amongst these, noble Queen,
For I would know and love thee,
And in doing thus would seek thy counsel
And thine aid. Thou too wert wronged
In eons past, when thy fair Cult was
Judgèd by false evidence to be of
Bloody kind. Yet as the young Pryderi did
By Tiernyons's kind touch deliver thee
From penances unjust, in manner like
Deliver me, Oh Queen, from that which
Thus afflicts me without cause, and see
My bold accusers put to right.
For which great mercy I will hence thy
Praises sing to all of men, and honour thee,
Oh Goddess of the Horse.

Here, now, are a few short verses to Sinend, Goddess of the
Well of Inspiration, for any aspiring poets:

What was it that thou dids't behold
Within those sacred waters, Sinend Fair?
That so transported thee to realms beyond
The stars, beyond the limits set by
Minds of men who see not these dimensions
Wherein are the sacred fires, and those of
Power and might yet unconceived by mortals.

How can I record that which I cannot
Yet behold, as thou dids't by thy well?
But shoulds't thou, in thy kindness
Open up for me one tiny ray of Light
That could inspire me to such words
As Bards themselves might see fit to
Perform. Then in my gratitude would I   .
Forever know thy name and write my stamp
In thy fair hand, across the Page of Time.

And finally, here is a general prayer of homage and acknowledgement to the Old Celtic gods.

Hear my voice, as thrice I knock upon thy doors.
I call thee, from the depths that is this Earth
In knowledge that thou sleepest not, but wait
In calm alertness for the Lord of Time to make
Return the known appointed hour wherein the
Serpent's tail doth meet its head.

Ever watchful, ever patient of our wayward minds
You wait. You whom we in blindness have rejected,
Yet by other names to some are known. Children play
Unkindly with the toys of heaven, dashing and dismemb'ring
Them with boredom in their vain pursuit of all
That new and shiny is at glance. But slowly as
The gloss wears off they move to newer fields,
And brighter gods become their playthings till they, too
Lack lustre, nor amuse.

But, Oh Great Ones, surely Time has deemed
That all must leave the ways of childhood,
Or be moved to other cosmic nurseries.
Fledglings all must fly the nest and flexing thus
Their wings, join in that great migration to the stars
That comes when Cosmic winter spells the lines of
Future frosts.

Carry me with thee, if my youthful wing will bear the
Journey's strain, to fairer parts. And if my tears
For thy rejection bear one portion of the guilt
Of Earth, then let it be. The child who breaks
The toy is but a child, forgive it well, and know
The love and adoration of this thy servant who has
Left his (her) worldly nursery for the Truth
Of thy Estate.

Come, come, come, Oh Old Ones of the Stars who were
Before the time of man.
Whose names have graced the noble strains of life
And borne disgrace through those who have in cosmic
Youth misunderstood thy Principles.
Come, come again, and give us one more chance.

Endnotes
1. Graves, Robert. *The White Goddess*, p. 73.
2. Bord, Janet and Colin. *Earth Rites*, p. 42.
3. Ibid. Bord, p. 119.
4. Ibid. Bord, p. 3.

29. MAGICAL QUATRAINS

In Chapter 3 we recounted the story of Corpry, who employed his Bardic skills to compose a satirical quatrain which proved the undoing of Bres, his churlish host:

Without food quickly served,
Without cow's milk, whereon a calf can grow,
Without a dwelling fit for a man under the gloomy night,
Without means to entertain a bardic company, —
Let such be the condition of Bres.[1]

Verses of this kind, if assembled according to the correct magical formula, can be used for a variety of purposes, much after the style of a runescript. The only difference lies in the employment of the verbiage, the user needing more than a rudimentary knowledge of language. I can only set out the right magical construction; the wording and layout must come from the writer, and therein lies the real magical skill.

Let us analyse the above verse. The writer first takes stock of his grievance. He was left without food, drink or sustenance of any kind in a cold room on a chill night, and deprived of company as would befit a man of his standing. He therefore lists these deprivations in four stanzas, and on the fifth, invokes the Law of Rebound. Simple, if you think about it!

Let us take a few hypothetical examples and compose some

appropriate quatrains to see how it is done. You have loaned
a much-treasured and valued book to a friend who has failed
to return it to you. Many months pass and eventually you feel
the need to remind him that he still has your property. Instead
of rendering an appropriate apology and returning the tome
he becomes offensive, declaring that you actually gave him
the book and he has since seen fit to sell it as he needed the
money. There is no legal way in which you can prove your
case although you know in truth that he is lying. Just the
situation for the following quatrain:

> No book to pass the sleepless hours;
> No friend to witness for the accused;
> No way of retrieving what has been stolen;
> No let up in the time of waiting...
> May such be the lot of _____.

This must be repeated a minimum of three times,
preferably in the morning and upon retiring. And if you have
other close friends and family who share your indignation
over the injustice, then ask them to repeat it with you. It may
not get your book back but it will, by cosmic law, ensure that
retribution is effected in some way. The energy that has been
unjustly stolen from you (as represented by the book) will be
drawn from the offender to provide what the gods feel to be
an adequate substitute for your loss. A *warning*, however,
these quatrains must only be used in cases of genuine
grievance or real injustice, and not out of spite or because you
have fallen out with someone and therefore deliberately
contributed to the situation. If you do break this rule in Celtic
magic beware the Law of Rebound for what you have willed
onto another, should they be stronger than you, will return to
you multiplied by the psychic energies of your opponent!

Assuming, however, that the intentions of the user are
thoroughly honourable, let us take three more hypothetical
examples, to clarify the system even further if we can.

For our next situation, let us suppose you are an elderly and
rather frail lady who has been invited to stay the weekend
with the daughter of a very close friend of yours who is now
deceased. This pleases you and you arrive at your destination
full of anticipation only to find that the lady in question has
forgotten all about your visit and is rather embarrassed to see

you on the doorstep. To make matters worse, she has a house full of noisy teenagers who set about making you feel as uncomfortable as possible. They play loud rock music all night and your discomfort at their language and habits affords them much amusement. You protest to your host who immediately takes the young people's side suggesting that you leave if you don't like it. You have no alternative but to go, but as it is a weekend, there are few trains and buses running so when you do finally reach your own house you are tired, ill and exhausted. What about this little quatrain for the occasion?

> Where the old are welcomed but not the young,
> Where silence is the rule, and no sound permitted,
> Where sleep is denied, and friendship rejected,
> Where no destination is reached without pain and tears —
> There let _____ dwell with her own!

Here is a tale we hear so much about today, probably because the media has brought it to our notice. A young women with a small child is ill-used by her husband who finally abandons her for another who has money and position:

> Where there's nought a caring hand to bathe the wounds,
> Where there's no warm greeting on a friendless night,
> Where there's no one to belong to, or who cares,
> Where there's poverty and need and times are hard —
> Let _____ through these lines a lesson learn.

And finally, a subject dear to the heart of all those who are truly on the Path of Light: animals and their welfare. Cruelty to these, our brothers, is ever a thorn in the side of the Green-minded. There may be times when you see a dog, cat or horse mistreated, and although there is the RSPCA, you are unable to provide the evidence to warrant a prosecution and the animal suffers on. Try a good old Celtic quatrain:

> As the hungry hound bays in the cold night, chaffed by his evil fetter;
> As the abandoned kitten dies in the still of the stream, its cries unheard;

As the overburdened mule drags its painful load along the
dustbaked streets;
As the gentle pheasant drops to earth to please the laughing gun;
So shall these things be visited upon the perpetrators.

That, dear reader, is how it is done.

Endnotes
1.   Rolleston, T.W. *Myths and Legends of the Celtic Race*, p. 108.

30. THE OCCULT POWER OF MUSIC

Music is an extremely powerful magical agent, being evocative of its higher frequencies in more sublime dimensions. Therefore, the type of music used either in ritual magic or purely for meditative or devotional purposes is very important. The one thing that music used in the magical context must *not* do is to effect any form of fragmentation of the psyche. By this I mean that one should always be in control when effecting magical links and not 'spaced out', so while relaxation is a good thing if controlled by one's own mind, it should not be induced by false methods or 'externals' that are guaranteed to put one off balance or out of control. Drumbeats, for example, that are just slightly faster than the average human heart beat can induce self-hypnosis or abreaction. While these states might be welcomed by the psychiatrist or psychotherapist, or appear convincing to the observer, they are hardly conducive to successful magical operations. Any music which stimulates the lower chakras should also be avoided or the energies attracted will tend to settle in those parts and adversely accentuate the physical desire nature with disastrous results as far as health is concerned.

The many levels at which magic may operate could be likened to musical octaves, each re-echoing the former at a higher or lower frequency. Musical sounds also correspond with colours and in the following chart I have outlined the keynote, colour and corresponding chakra which should help the pupil to note and assess the effects of certain keys. I have already touched on four of these in Chapter 20, so those correspondences will now become more distinct in the light of the whole setting.

Colour	Note	Chakra
Red	C	Muladhara
Orange	D	Svadisthana
Yellow	E	Manipura
Green	F	Anahata
Blue	G	Vishuddu
Indigo	A	Ajna
Violet	B	Sahasrara

Just as musical notes correspond with colours, sound can paint graphic tonal pictures. The sombre cadences of browns, greys and dull reds contrast sharply with the light airy tones of the pastels, while the bright celebratory sounds of exultation loudly proclaim the primaries. Martial music blares the brighter shades of energy-inducing red, while peaceful, blue-green tones are conducive to meditation, relaxation and tranquility. As certain colours blend, so are some note combinations harmonious (or otherwise as the case may be).

The modern modes in European usage consist of the major scale and the harmonic and melodic minors. It is interesting to note that the ancient Egyptians, who were adept at colour healing, used a scale which went: C, D, E, F#, G, A, B. On the colour chart I have just given this would mean that their greens tended to partake of a turquoise hue, which in fact they did.

If the octave is split into semitones one can accommodate the twelve formula and all associated therewith. (Apostles, Olympians, Knights, zodiacal signs, etc.) Add the upper octave and we come back to our rhombic dodecahedron or 'thirteen' code.

Music, like medicine, is divided into four classes: Tonic, Stimulant, Sedative and Narcotic which should be borne in mind when employing it in any magical workings. The nature of the forces or deities being invoked should be taken into consideration, and the musical contributions adjusted accordingly. For example, bright, joyful music obviously belongs with the solar deities, intellectual pieces with immortals such as Gwydion or Merlin, who symbolize the mind rather than the emotions, and more sombre tones for those gods or goddesses of the underworld who are representative of the deep subconscious. There is a certain kind of music that is evocative of the Middle Kingdoms and if the pupil is unsure of his or her ground here, safe bets include Mendelssohn's incidental music *A Midsummer Night's Dream*, or Stravinski's *The Fire Bird* and *The Rite of Spring*. There is also a goodly selection of appropriate folk music with fairy emphasis.

Some instruments feature more than others in sacred rituals:

The Flute — representing the element of Air.
The Harp — representing the element of Water.
The Sistrum — representing the element of Earth.
The Lyre — representing the element of Fire.

In later years the flute gave way to the organ, the sistrum to the bells and the lyre to the human voice. These Elemental principles can also operate through other instruments according to the stage of spiritual development of the user or group in question. For example, the drum or percussion instrument is considered by some to represent a more primitive aspect of the sistrum — notice how a small child likes to bang things about in order to gain attention or effect a deal of sound.

The music of the Gnostics has come down to us, albeit in a somewhat religiously mutilated form as plainchant, although there is still a degree of the old sound to be found in its resonances. Gustav Holst incorporated some of the old Gnostic Dance Rituals in his 'Hymn to Jesus'. These were said to have originated in the Eleusinia from which they were borrowed firstly by the Therapeutic Order of the Essenes and then by the early Christian Gnostics. In this excerpt there were two sets of participants representing the Celestial Ogdoad or Company of Eight and the Celestial Dodecad of Twelve. The symbolic instruments employed were the Lyre, Harp and Pipes and this translation is by G.R.S. Mead (referring to the dance or perpetual movement of evolution):

I would pipe — dance ye all
I would play a dirge — lament ye all
The eight harps with us as one harp.
The twelve above doth dance with us,
The whole on high is a dance.[1]

From the 'Acts of John' Gnostic Gospels (pseudepi-
grapha): Rituals of the Dance: Apocrypha Anecdota 11; we
find: 'The disciples make a ring around Jesus who stands in
the centre.' There are some lost pages but the ritual is picked
up with:

I would be saved
And I would save thee.
(Grace) Sophia dances . . . I would dance,
I would pipe, oh dance ye all.
The Ogdoad plays to our dancing.
The Dodecad dances above us.
(Dance) observe what I do, for it is for thee to follow.[2]

The Sophia or female aspect of the Christos dances or sings
while the Christos or male aspect of its polarity plays and
composes.

Taliesin re-echoes the substance of these verses in the
following stanzas:

Eminent is the virtue of the free course, when this *dance* is
performed. Loud is the horn of the lustrator, when the kine
move in the evening. Manifest is truth when it shines; more
manifest when it speaks; and loud it spoke, when it came forth
from the cauldron of Awen, the ardent goddess.[3]

The Masons employ the key of E^b for their ritual work and
famous composers who were also prominent masons
frequently featured this key in their works. Mozart's *Die
Zauberflöte* ('The Magic Flute') contains a wealth of magical
symbolism in the masonic idiom, much of which can be
traced back to Gnostic and pre-Christian sources. The
famous 'Song of the Armed Men' from the finale of this
opera combines vocal acknowledgement of the goddess with
the appropriate magical music. I do not have space to
produce the full score, but anyone with a real interest is at
liberty to check the highly significant intervals Mozart

employs and note how they accord with those of earlier pieces from folksong and plainchant that I mentioned in Chapter 20. The words, however, occupy little space and could, if the aspirant so desired, be altered to accommodate the appropriate Celtic deity (for Isis — Keridwen).

Man wandering on his road must bear the tribulation
Of fire and water, earth and air's probation.
If he prevails against the lures of evil's might
He soon will know the joys of heaven's delight.
Enlightened, he will himself now prepare,
The holy mysteries of Isis all to share.[4]

Here are the first few bars of the tenor line from the 'Song of the Armed Men' which serve to demonstrate the relevant intervals:

Even within the musical context there are many ways in which the aspirant can relate to the Celtic ray and its attendant mysteries. In reviewing a recent work of Bob Stewart's entitled *The Underworld Initiation*, Michael Howard, whose occult judgement I trust implicitly, comments:

Here he uses his knowledge of oral folk tradition to provide the basis of an initiatory process within the Western Mystery Tradition based on Celtic and pre-Celtic mythological patterns. He has called this process *The Underworld Initiation* because it involves contact with other worlds through a symbolic journey. He argues that these inner worlds are not the product of the human imagination but have a real existence in time and space. They can be entered and experienced by the use of a set of magical keys — which are revealed in this book. Stewart believes that these are to be found concealed in folk ballads which preserved esoteric knowledge despite tremendous outside pressures which sought to repress the ancient wisdom.[5]

Exactly what I have been saying in previous chapters, and although I have never had the pleasure of making Mr Stewart's acquaintance, if this new book is an interesting and informative as his previous one *(Who Was Saint George?)*, it might well merit consultation by any aspirant to the Celtic magic arts who is particularly drawn to the folk music idiom.

Equally, the musical approach can be made via the classics, in which case the relevant composers would be those whose works are particularly associated with either the British or Elemental rays. But as far as Celtic magic is concerned there is one piece of music which for many people, myself included, is totally evocative of the British or Celtic ethos, the Vaughan Williams *Fantasia on a Theme by Tallis*. The magical modes or musical sequences in this piece move in an undulating fashion so that the rhythms rise and fall like the waves on a misty and mystical British sea-shore at that time of day when the Bright Llew hands over his solar timesheet to Gwyn ap Nudd for the period of the Dark Hours.

Much of the heavier and harsher beat music popular today, referred to by the Master with whom I studied as 'disharmonious, unbeautiful, the sounds of the formless ones who are of the lower planes' is known to produce ill effects on the lower chakras. Personally, I will refrain from making judgements as I feel that truth and light, which are their own advertisements, reside in the mind of the individual who will translate these cosmic principles in accordance with his or her own individual stage of spiritual development.

Some people are spiritually or emotionally affected by the music of one composer while the work of another leaves them cold. This is because each kind of music produces an undertone or overtone that is either jarring or harmonious to the personal keynote or evolutionary level of the individual. Those who favour the romantic idiom tend to eschew the more disciplined, severe or intellectual type of music, although one cannot generalize, and a real musician will see good in many modes of musical expression.

Some believe that the music of the flute can raise the Kundalini or Serpent Fire that normally lies coiled at the base of the spine, but personally I have not found this to be the case. Flute music can induce certain altered states of consciousness, but these are not necessarily synonymous with spiritual attainment, as any occultist knows. The ancient

Egyptians had a secret initiatory musical summons that was known as 'The Call of the Ibis', and although there are no records of this, it was probably not dissimilar to the Pan Call in Greek magic.[6] Any piece of music in which this occurs in its inverted state, either by accident or design, is likely to have adverse effects on the mood of the listener. This cannot be attributed to any particular type of music, however and, as far as the keynote of the individual is concerned, adverse note formations are likely to turn up in the best and worst of music although, strangely enough, the great masters like Mozart, Handel and Bach somehow managed to avoid them. Or is there such a thing as coincidence?

It is a mistake to think of all sacred music as being of intellectual content and therefore lacking in emotion. Much of it appeals to the heart and solar plexus chakras and many of the well-known hymns which help to give the Fundamentalists emotional sway over their congregations fall into this category.

Different types of music are associated with different countries, which is as it should be, and if the student finds solace in Chinese music or West Indian rhythms, then fair enough, as neither is better nor worse than the other. But excellent as these may sound during periods of relaxation or leisure, they may not all be correct for magical purposes, which should be borne in mind when the aspirant is making his or her musical choice. If in doubt, look to the old folk tunes, or to the type of classical sequences I have already outlined.

The true power of music lies in harmony rather than unison. Unison implies a singleness of line or thought and the fact that large numbers of people think alike or follow a certain path is no guarantee of it being right. Is there not an old saying to the effect, 'When the world adopts the fool's beliefs, he is no longer the fool.'?

Each of us represents a cosmic note which, blended with all others, goes to create the Symphony of Life. In contributing our own unique sound we help to enrich the overall harmonies, but if our notes are discordant we do not blend, and the whole musical picture is adversely affected. If harmonious music is good for us why do so many people seek disharmony and noise, and why can they not see the beauty in gentleness and melodious symmetry? They strive for the irregular, the jarring and the unbeautiful. Neither animals nor plants share this quirk with man which prompts one to question as to who is or who is not the most spiritually advanced? But perhaps these irregularities constitute part of our initiation through the dark regions of the mind, from which we ultimately emerge into the spheres of light, with all that this implies.

Let music and poetry feature strongly in your magical work, you who would aspire to the Celtic arts. Take your musical lead from the peoples in whose veins the blood of the old Celts still surges strongly. Listen to the magnificent voices of the Welsh; heed the call of the pipes as the blithe and bonny steps of the Scottish dancers acknowledge their rhythms, and hum the broody dirges from the Irish past. From across the channel there are the wisdom lays of the troubadours and the chants from those secret orders that have carefully preserved the old sounds and rhythms from the mists of antiquity.

This has been a book of history, magic, mystery and folklore, but most of all it has been a book of memories; memories that many of you will share as your genes dance to the strains of the old sounds of word and song that they knew in generations past. Let the song be heard by many, and may its lyrics loudly proclaim that the Age of the Future is the Age of Harmony and Symmetry, when the velvet strains of poetry and song will once again herald the return of the Old Ones.

Endnotes
1. Mead, G.R.S. *Quests Old and New*, p. 173.
2. Ibid. Mead, p. 174.
3. Davies, Edward. *Mythology and Rites of the British Druids*, p. 530.
4. Mozart, W.A. *The Magic Flute*. Translation by Ruth and Thomas Martin, G. Shirmer, New York/London.
5. *Prediction* magazine, December 1986, p. 67.
6. Hope, Murry. *Practical Greek Magic*, p. 116.

BIBLIOGRAPHY

Baigent, Leigh, Lincoln. *The Holy Blood and the Holy Grail*, Jonathan Cape, London 1982.

Bergamar, Kate. *Discovering Hill Figures*, Shire Publications, Tring, Herts.

Bord, Janet and Colin. *Earth Rites*, Granada, London 1983.

Cirlot, C.E. *A Dictionary of Symbols*, Routledge & Kegan Paul, London 1962.

Davies, Edward. *The Mythology and Rites of the British Druids*, London 1809.

Elder, Isabel Hill. *Celt, Druid and Culdee*, Covenant Publishing Co., London 1973.

Gantz, Jeffrey. *The Mabinogion*, Penguin Books, London 1984.

Graves, Robert. *The White Goddess*, Faber & Faber, London 1984.

Green, Michael. *Unicornis*, Running Press, Philadelphia, PA. USA 1983.

Harper, Peter S. and Sunderland, Eric. *Genetic and Population Studies in Wales*, University of Wales Press, Cardiff 1986.

Hope, Murry. *Practical Egyptian Magic*, Aquarian Press, Wellingborough 1984.

Hope, Murry. *Practical Greek Magic*, Aquarian Press, Wellingborough 1985.

Hope, Murry. *Practical Techniques of Psychic Self-Defence*,

Aquarian Press, Wellingborough 1983.

Lethbridge, T.C. *Gogmagog*, Routledge & Kegan Paul, London 1957.

Matthias, Michael and Hector, Derek. *Glastonbury*, David & Charles, London 1979.

Mead, G.R.S. *Fragments of a Faith Forgotten*, John M. Watkins, London 1931.

Mead, G.R.S. *Quests Old and New*, John M. Watkins, London 1929

Murray, Margaret A. *The God of the Witches*, Oxford University Press, London 1979.

Pepper, Elizabeth and Wilcock, John. *Magical and Mystical Sites in Europe and the British Isles*, Abacus (Sphere Books), London 1978.

Rolleston, T.W. *Myths and Legends of the Celtic Race*, George G. Harrap & Co., London 1919.

Ross, Anne. *Everyday Life of the Pagan Celts*, Carousel Books, Ealing, London 1972.

Rhys, John. *Celtic Folklore, Welsh and Manx*, Vols I & II, Wildwood House, London 1980.

Spence, Lewis. *The Magic Arts in Celtic Britain*, Aquarian Press, Wellingborough 1970.

Spence, Lewis. *The Mysteries of Britain*, Rider & Co., London 1932.

Stone, Merlin. *The Paradise Papers*, Virago, London 1976.

Stewart, Bob. *Where is Saint George?*, Moonraker Press, Bradford-on-Avon 1977.

Thorsson, Edred. *Futhark*, Aquarian Press, Wellingborough 1984.

Waddell, L.A. *The British Edda*, Chapman & Hall, London 1930.

Waite, A.E. *The Occult Sciences*, Kegan Paul Trench Trubner & Co. Ltd., London 1891.

Wood, David. *Genisis*, The Baton Press, Tunbridge Wells 1985.

Witt, R.E. *Isis in the Graeco-Roman World*, Thames & Hudson, London 1971.

The Distribution of the Human Blood Groups and Other Polymorphisms, Oxford University Press 1974.

Larousse Encyclopedia of Mythology, Paul Hamlyn, London 1959.

INDEX